Recipient of the 1984
C.L. SONNICHSEN BOOK AWARD
of The University of Texas at El Paso

WAR, REVOLUTION, AND THE KU KLUX KLAN
A Study of Intolerance in a Border City

War, Revolution and the Ku Klux Klan

A Study of Intolerance in a Border City

by

Shawn Lay

TEXAS WESTERN PRESS

The University of Texas at El Paso
1985

Library of Congress Catalog Card No. 85-090937
ISBN 0-87404-094-9

For Imelda, Alexander, and my
grandmother, Pauline Lay.

With deepest thanks to my mentors, Dr. Kenneth K. Bailey,
Dr. Wayne E. Fuller, and Dr. Oscar J. Martinez.

TABLE OF CONTENTS

[v]

LIST OF FIGURES

Introduction

During the late summer of 1921, Frontier Klan No. 100, Knights of the Ku Klux Klan, was established in El Paso, Texas. In subsequent months, hundreds of local citizens joined the organization and it became an important factor in the city's political, social, and religious life. By the end of 1922, El Paso Klansmen had forged an imposing alliance with the city's moral reformers, including several leading Protestant clergymen, and had gained numerous successes in local elections. The Klan's rise to prominence, however, had left the community severely divided, as was noted by a local newspaper editor:

> The 11 months since the Klan announced its existence cover the worst period in all El Paso's history. They have been marked by bitterness and strife. Friends of a lifetime have become estranged. Families have been divided. Every man has become suspicious of his neighbor. Bigotry and intolerance have thrived as never before. Poison pens and serpent tongues have been busy spreading scandal. . . . The old El Paso spirit of enterprise, co-operation and neighborly goodwill, the spirit that built on the sun-baked desert a mighty city, has been well nigh strangled. Religious intolerance, hate, suspicion, and anger have entered into every civic activity from the deliberations of the Chamber of Commerce to the political primary.
>
> The secret machinations of the Klan, like the foul breath of a plague-spreading monster, have blighted every effort of decent self-respecting citizens to restore to the community its old spirit of tolerance and forbearance.[1]

[vii]

As the city Democratic primary of 1923 approached, El Pasoans found themselves in two hostile camps and facing the very real prospect of city-wide violence if the Klan succeeded in taking over the municipal government. "Those were very, very frightening times," recalls one long-time city resident. "It's hard to make people understand how scared we were back then."[2]

Since this saga is among the more revealing episodes in the city's history, one might suppose that it would have received considerable scholarly attention heretofore. But such is not the case. To a certain extent this is typical; as Charles C. Alexander has noted, the sum of Klan scholarship can best be characterized as "a hiatus in the historiography of the twenties."[3] In regard to El Paso, however, the near total absence of serious historical work in this sphere appears to be more than an uncalculated "hiatus." Rather, a conspiracy of silence can be reasonably inferred.

The first mention of the El Paso Klan in a historical treatment was in Owen P. White, *Out of the Desert: The Historical Romance of El Paso* (El Paso, 1924), which was released shortly after the order had declined as an influence in city affairs. The page and a half in which the author discusses the local Klan's involvements offer few details and almost no analysis, but White's comments about the mood of the community during this time are interesting.

The next mention of the Klan in a local history came almost a quarter of a century later, in Robert N. Blake, "A History of the Catholic Church in El Paso" (M.A. thesis, Texas Western College, 1948). Here one finds just one sentence on the subject, a hasty reference to "Ku Klux Klan trouble" that hampered the pastorate of Father Malachi O'Leary.[4]

An equally obscure Klan reference appears in Sister M. Lilliana Owens, *The Life of Bishop Anthony J. Schuler, S.J., D.D.* (El Paso, 1953), in which the author asserts without elaboration that the local Klan proved to be "somewhat violent" during early 1922.[5] John M. Denny, *A Century of Freemasonry at El Paso* (El Paso, 1956), also contains passing mention of the Klan, noting that El Paso Masons passed an anti-Klan resolution during the time of the local KKK controversy. In his "Past and Present Life of William H. Fryer, Attorney at Law" (History seminar paper, Texas Western College, 1958), Ralph W. Scoggins made a four-sentence reference to former county attorney Will Fryer's court case against local Klan candidates.

Also appearing in 1958 were two relatively extensive accounts of the

El Paso Klan. The first consists of twenty pages in John J. Middagh, *Frontier Newspaper: The El Paso Times* (El Paso, 1958), which discusses the *Times'* fight against the local Klan and gives a general outline of the order's activities. Though *Frontier Newspaper* lacks footnotes, it is evident that most of the information on the Klan was culled from *Times* articles. Middagh attempts no serious historical analysis of the El Paso Klan, nor was this in anyway his purpose — he was simply telling the story of a newspaper. He does, however, provide interesting insights into the characters of the members of the board of directors and of the editor of the *El Paso Times* during the early 1920s.

A more detailed history of the El Paso Klan appears in Edward F. Sherman, "The Ku Klux Klan and El Paso Politics Following World War I" (History seminar paper, Texas Western College, 1958). Though Sherman's paper went beyond anything that had previously appeared, it was inadequate in many respects. Its major shortcoming was its failure to consider *particular reasons* for the Klan's appearance in El Paso. The overall situation circa 1921 was never appropriately considered, thereby indicating that the author did not properly understand local history. Moreover, the work suffers from confusion as to names, places crucial elections involving the Klan in the wrong year, and fails to mention several important elections. The lack of in-depth research is most blatantly revealed by Sherman's assertion that the "Klan is rarely mentioned in the El Paso papers in 1921 and even in 1922, even after they [the Klan] won control of the school board, the papers never crusaded against them, or really considered them much of a threat."[6] These statements signify that the author did not properly utilize the best sources for studying the local Klan, namely, the El Paso newspapers.

The El Paso Klan received almost no attention from local scholars during the 1960s. Charles E. Hershberger, "The El Paso Labor Advocate and Its Editors From 1909 to 1939: A Study of Labor Journalism In the Southwest" (M.A. thesis, Texas Western College, 1962), makes passing mention (two pages) of the Klan and the local-labor-press opinion of it. Unfortunately, Hershberger fails to note the close cooperation between the Klan and union members within the El Paso Good Government League, a civic group that was very influential during local elections in 1922.

In 1969 the El Paso Historical Society's publication, *Password*, made note in its Fall edition of valuable sources that could be used in researching the local Klan.[7] These consisted of four scrapbooks and assorted memorabilia that former Mayor Richard M. Dudley had bequeathed to the El Paso Public Library. Included among the memorabilia were old El Paso Klan newspapers which provide an interesting view of the Klan from its own members' perspective. In his *Dr. Lawrence A. Nixon and the White Primary* (El Paso, 1974), Conrey Bryson utilized these sources for a short (three page) discussion of the local Klan, which also drew heavily from Middagh's *Frontier Newspaper*. El Paso's Klan was likewise mentioned in a two-page segment of William J. Hooten's memoirs, *Fifty-Two Years a Newsman* (El Paso, 1974).

A more extensive examination of the El Paso Klan is presented in the first chapter of the second volume of C. L. Sonnichsen's *Pass of the North* (El Paso, 1980), which is essentially a reprint of his article, "El Paso — From War to Depression," *Southwestern Historical Quarterly*, LXXIV (January 1971), pp. 357-384. The portion of Sonnichsen's article which pertains to the Klan (four pages) relies heavily on Middagh and Sherman; and, though providing valuable insights, it is flawed by certain inaccuracies. Most important of these is the author's assertion that the Klan was established in El Paso by an outsider, "a man named C. L. Sirmans, a professional organizer who came to El Paso in the summer of 1921"[8] City directories indicate that C. L. Sirmans had lived in El Paso at least since 1909, and a careful reading of newspapers during the 1920s reveals that Sirmans was a respected local businessman, a Mason of high degree, and the past potentate of the El Maida Shrine. Clearly, if the Klan was the creation of an outside organizer, Sirmans was not the one.

Among the most recently published material on the Klan in El Paso is a paragraph in Leon C. Metz, *City at the Pass: An Illustrated History of El Paso* (Woodland Hills, California, 1980). After presenting six sentences concerning the local KKK, Metz makes the assertion that the Klan was "finally beaten in the municipal elections of 1922 and 1924."[9] In fact, no municipal elections were held in those years. A more satisfactory presentation can be found in J. F. Hulse, *Texas Lawyer: The Life of William H. Burges* (El Paso, 1982). In a short chapter (six pages), Hulse discusses the local school board election of 1922, but he attempts no serious examination of the local branch of the Invisible Empire. The book is useful, however, in providing new information concerning the school board election.

In sum, existing historical literature concerning the El Paso Klan is woefully inaccurate and otherwise inadequate. The following study is submitted in the hope of filling this serious gap and also of establishing the groundwork upon which future research in related topics can be based. Because the El Paso Klan episode was an extremely complex phenomenon involving the intricate interplay of a wide variety of social forces and personalities, an almost limitless number of relevant questions can be raised. In an effort to maintain some degree of coherence, this work will focus upon these specific queries:

1. How and why did the Ku Klux Klan become an influential factor in El Paso during the early 1920s?

2. To what extent did the Klan succeed or fail in achieving its goals in El Paso?

3. Why did the El Paso community ultimately reject the Ku Klux Klan?

4. How was El Paso's experience with the Ku Klux Klan different or similar to the Klan experiences of other Texas communities?

While addressing myself to these questions, I have found it necessary, often to my chagrin, to examine a considerable amount of material which at first appears to be only remotely related to my topic. Accordingly, an extensive chapter describing the unique social heritage of El Paso will be presented, as well as chapters that assess the local impact of both the Mexican Revolution and World War I. In retrospect, I can confidently state that a failure to include a discussion of these topics would have left the study severely flawed.

CHAPTER 1

The Social Heritage of El Paso 1846-1910

On a sunny Christmas afternoon in 1846, the future destiny of the Mexican community at El Paso del Norte was profoundly altered. Inspired by a message from Chihuahua governor Angel Trías that said they were "led by the God of battles," more than 1,200 troops had issued forth from defensive breastworks at the Pass to do open battle with the "sacrilegious invaders of Mexico."[1] Presenting a cavalier appearance in their colorful uniforms of green, blue, and scarlet, the sun reflecting brilliantly off the brass plates of their plumed hats, the Mexican soldiers marched northward for some twenty-five miles to confront the advance forces of Colonel Alexander Doniphan.

The ensuing Battle of Brazito was over in thirty minutes. Though taken by surprise, and with their mounts grazing unbridled nearby, five hundred Missouri Mounted Volunteers greeted the initial Mexican charge with a deadly display of marksmanship that cut down more than two hundred. Realizing that their situation was hopeless, the Mexican troops hastily retreated, leaving the settlements at the Pass open to invasion and occupation by North American forces. Later that evening, a private in the First Regiment of the Volunteers recorded in his diary that the battle had been but "a Christmas frolic."[2]

The Battle of Brazito determined that the first Americans to arrive *en masse* at the Pass would come as conquerors, and this fact has done much to shape bicultural relations in El Paso ever since. However, if the first major contact between Americans and Mexicans at this isolated outpost was tainted by wartime anger, resentment, and mistrust, there was also a surprising degree of accommodation and generosity. Long isolated from and neglected by the Mexican federal government, their military force inadequate to cope with the dangers posed by the frontier, the *paseños* did not seem to share the patriotic ardor of their fellow countrymen to the south. Famine, disease, and continual Indian warfare had afflicted the Pass communities throughout 1846, and the American invasion seemed only the climax to a dismal year.[3] Indeed, as was noted by a German visitor, "the people of Paso seemed very indifferent to who should be the conqueror."[4]

When the conquerors did arrive, the *paseño* tradition of openhandedness asserted itself, no matter what misgivings the populace may have felt inside. Soon after their entry into El Paso del Norte, the Missouri Volunteers were shoulder to shoulder with Mexican natives, engaged in an orgy of "perpetual gambling, monte-dealing, chuck-luck etc. — Spaniards & American soldiers block[ing] up the streets at monte-dealing." Private John Taylor Hughes found the townspeople extremely cordial, and spent the night with "an old Castilian" who gladly shared the contents of his wine cellar. Other invaders mingled closely with the local inhabitants, consuming native *mescal* and *pulque*, cavorting at *fandangos*, and acquainting themselves "with the fair Señoritas of the place, whose charms and unpurchased kindness almost induced some of the men to wish not to return home. . . ."[5]

After several weeks of rest and relaxation, Colonel Doniphan's troops departed Paso del Norte in February 1847, carrying few bitter memories with them and evidently leaving few among their hosts. The Americans had been very well-treated during the occupation of the Pass, and at least two Missourians preferred desertion to separation from their El Paso sweethearts. However, not all of the soldiers had enjoyed such rapport with the local females, and Colonel Doniphan had felt it necessary to court-martial three of them "for ravishing a Mexican woman."

Yet, no incidents of significant violence had occurred between the two races, the most spectacular brawl having been a knife-fight between two American officers.⁶ A situation which at the outset had seemed to hold every potential for trouble had been defused by a spirit of accommodation nutured by both the conquerors and the conquered. In this first large-scale encounter between Anglos and Mexicans at the Pass, racial and cultural relations had been characterized by remarkable toleration.

The Treaty of Guadalupe Hidalgo transformed Paso del Norte into a border town, the north side of the river being ceded to the United States. Mexican settlements on the north bank, such as San Elizario, Ysleta, and Socorro, were quickly declared to be under American jurisdiction, as were certain north-of-the-river communal lands belonging to towns on the Mexican side.⁷ Despite this, a clash between the conquerors' belief in private property and the ancient Mexican system of communal land-ownership was averted by one of the foremost geographical facts concerning the Pass — its isolation. Americans in distant places might take out deeds and issue proclamations, but life in the El Paso valley continued much as it had been during the Spanish and Mexican periods.

El Paso's isolation was lessened somewhat after the Mexican War when the first tentative transportation link was established between the Pass and east Texas, it being reported in a June 1849 edition of the *Texas Democrat* that "By this time there is an excellent wagon road opened from this place [Austin] to El Paso. . . ."⁸ During the early 1850s the tiny American communities at the Pass — Concordia, Franklin, Magoffinsville, and Hart's Mill — were more securely tied to the outside world by mail and stage service, as well as by the establishment of a nearby military post.⁹ However, remoteness and a paucity of non-Hispanic settlers hindered the transplantation of Anglo institutions. Though Major Robert S. Neighbors claimed success in organizing El Paso County in March 1850, following elections that went off in "fine style," for several years thereafter the Pass remained in a state of political confusion as officials from New Mexico, Texas, and Mexico variously exercised control. Not until 1853 was El Paso represented in the Texas legislature.¹⁰

Once American political and judicial institutions had been established, the region's isolation and the presence of an overwhelmingly Mexican population called for considerable cultural accommodation. Political campaigns and court proceedings in county and justice-of-the-peace courts were frequently conducted in Spanish.[11] *Alcaldes* were still appointed in Lower Valley towns, and *varas, fanegas,* and *almuds* were accepted as standard units of measurement.[12] Local Anglo society evinced great adaptation to the Pass's unusual conditions. Isolated from American population centers, surrounded by a Mexican majority, and presented with a dearth of women of their own kind, the male Anglos in El Paso had no hope of recreating a typical American city. This had been recognized by the first Americans who settled at the Pass during the 1830s and 1840s. For example, traders such as Hugh Stephenson and James Wiley Magoffin married into the prominent Ascárate and Valdéz families, took the titles "Don Hugo" and "Don Santiago," and contentedly adopted the lifestyles of "avaricious Anglo-American *gachupines.*"[13] After the Mexican War, Simeon Hart continued this pattern with his marriage to Jesusita Siqueiros, deftly parlaying his new family connections into a fortune based on the milling of grain.[14] Though Anglo men who arrived in El Paso during the 1850s did not always make such successful matches as had Stephenson, Magoffin, and Hart, they, too, often married Mexican women or kept them as mistresses.[15]

In addition to amorous and physical involvements, most El Paso Anglos developed financial ties with local Mexicans. The American retail trade in items such as bread, sugar, lard, and clothing was mostly dependent upon the patronage of *paseño* farmers, while Anglo importing concerns were maintained by a steady supply of Mexican saddles, cigars, wine, and agricultural products.[16] Economic interdependence contributed to harmonious social relations and also helped to perpetuate the spirit of toleration that prevailed after the Battle of Brazito. W. W. Mills, a resident of El Paso in the late 1850s, commented on this spirit when he wrote: "Common trials and dangers united the two races as one family, and the fact that one man was a Mexican and another an American was seldom mentioned, and I believe as seldom thought about."[17]

However, some minimal racial and cultural tensions were experienced. Not all Anglos were disposed to respect the rights of the native populace, one such person being Esler Hendree, formerly of De Soto County, Mississippi. While serving as district attorney, he led an Anglo mob across the river in an abortive attempt to free an American from the Paso del Norte jail. Other incidents and situations which similarly disrupted the peaceful relations at the Pass included confusion over the Gadsden Purchase in 1853; James Magoffin's attempt to exert control over communal salt deposits in Doña Ana County in 1854; and armed incursions across the border by soldiers from both the regular American and Mexican armies.[18] Still, instances like these were relatively rare. Never did intolerance develop at the Pass on a level comparable with that in east Texas, where Mexicans were evicted from entire counties by old-line Americans who feared that such "peons" might interfere with slavery.[19] By 1860, race relations in El Paso differed significantly from those in other parts of the Lone Star State.

As historian C. L. Sonnichsen has noted: "For all practical purposes, El Paso was wiped out by the Civil War."[20] Almost all Americans residing at the Pass were fervent supporters of the Confederate cause, and in 1861 El Paso County voted overwhelmingly for secession, the vote being unnaturally swollen by the importation of Mexican voters.[21] Among the most ardent of the southern sympathizers were local notables Simeon Hart, Josiah F. Crosby, and James Magoffin. One might be tempted to assume that these men shared the bigoted racist mentality of their compatriots in the deep South, but this was by no means the case. As has been seen, both Hart and Magoffin had Mexican wives and were practically indistinguishable from the local Hispanic aristocracy. Josiah Crosby had also adapted well to life in the Southwest and maintained an avid interest in Mexican customs and culture throughout his lifetime.[22]

Nevertheless, as Confederate forces arrived at the Pass in preparation for their ill-fated expedition into New Mexico, a tense situation faced the El Paso community. Confederate Colonel John R. Baylor reported that the Mexican *paseños* were "decidedly Northern in sentiment, and will avail themselves of the first opportunity to rob us or join the enemy."[23] The behavior of the rebels did little to convince local Mexicans to support the Stars and Bars. Despite official assurance by General H. H. Sibley that such "forage and supplies as my army shall require will be purchased in open market and paid for at fair prices," it was soon noted by Union spies that Confederate troops were stealing blankets, horses, and food stores, and acting "in such a manner as to enrage the whole community against them."[24]

By the summer of 1862, *paseños* no longer had to contend with the unruly Confederates, as Union forces under General James H. Carleton arrived, sending the defeated rebels and their sympathizers fleeing eastward.[25] General Carleton observed that the residents of the valley were happy to be under Union control again, noting that "The abhorrence they expressed for the Confederate troops and of the rebellion

convinced me that their loyalty to the United States is now beyond
question."²⁶ In following months, relations between the local population and the United States troops remained good; the blue coats paid
for their supplies in reliable scrip, and in 1864 a grand *baile* was held in
Paso del Norte in honor of General Carleton. The only sour note during
the Union occupation resulted from an unauthorized American expedition into Mexico in search of Confederates, but the resentment produced by this incident soon subsided.²⁷

Thus though the American Civil War had at first strained ethnic relations at the Pass, an amicable situation was restored by 1862, and no
lasting damage occurred. The fact that Mexican *paseños* had been persuaded to vote in favor of secession stands in stark contrast to the Civil
War experience of Zapata County, Texas, where abolitionist Mexicans
raised a small army and marched on the town of Carrizo in 1861. Indeed, Mexicans in Texas were the object of great distrust wherever slavery existed on a significant scale; but in areas where the number of
bondsmen was only nominal, as in El Paso, there was little cause for
such apprehensions.²⁸ The toleration that had characterized life at the
Pass during the 1840s and 1850s emerged intact from the turmoil of the
Civil War.

With the departure of the southern sympathizers and the subsequent
confiscation of their property, a political and economic vacuum was
created within the El Paso community. During Reconstruction, new
arrivals took advantage of this situation to establish themselves in positions of prominence. Included in this group were former Union officers
such as Albert H. French, James A. Zabriskie, and Albert J. Fountain.²⁹
As had been the case before the Civil War, economic opportunities in
El Paso remained minimal and the few public offices were vigorously
contested for. The only viable industry in El Paso, the milling enterprise of Simeon Hart, had fallen victim to the fortunes of war, and during Reconstruction, New Mexican communities established a monopoly
over the grain trade and other forms of commerce that had once sustained the Pass economy. Throughout the post-Civil War years, El
Paso suffered from a lack of cash and currency; most of the money that
did become available was quickly invested in political campaigns or
other speculative ventures.³⁰

Because governmental positions were more precious than ever, El
Paso's Reconstruction politics came to be characterized by vicious personal feuding and scandalous electioneering. Much turmoil revolved
around W. W. Mills, who held the coveted appointment as customs

collector at El Paso and who was accused by his enemies of maintaining a corrupt "customhouse ring."[31] Mills was a good example of how El Paso politicians adapted to life at the Pass. He spoke fluent Spanish; he had lived with a Mexican mistress; and he dominated local affairs through a lucrative political alliance with local Mexicans. Office-seekers who alienated the native *paseños* simply had no chance of political success in El Paso. In an election in 1868, Mills was chosen as delegate to a state constitutional convention because Mexican voters resented his opponent's disparaging remarks about "niggers."[32] When Mills himself was defeated for state senator the next year, in a highly irregular election, the victor was Albert J. Fountain, a man who had married a Mexican and who viewed himself as best representing the interests of El Paso's Latin population.[33]

Throughout the 1870s, El Paso remained an isolated community. Stage and mail service were unreliable, and a trip to Austin required eight exhausting days of travel. Far removed from Anglo population centers, El Paso's political institutions continued their tradition of accommodating the Spanish-speaking majority. Court reports were still written in Spanish, and Mexicans frequently held office as justices of the peace, county commissioners, and county judge. Ninety-five percent of El Paso County's voters were Mexican, and the county seat was located either in San Elizario or Ysleta, communities that were almost exclusively Hispanic.[34] Social arrangements were equally accommodating, and violence was related to racial differences only infrequently, unlike the situation in other parts of Texas where belief in a "dehumanized stereotype" of Mexicans and the tensions of the Cattle War of the 1870s produced widespread bloodshed.[35] Probably the most spectacular violence at the Pass before 1877 was a gun battle in which an El Paso lawyer wounded a state senator and killed a district judge before being gunned down by a former county judge. All individuals involved in the *mêlée* were Anglos.[36]

In 1877 a political and personal feud did evolve into a crisis that temporarily undermined the amicable state of race relations. The two principals involved were Charles Howard, an ex-Confederate officer and Democrat, and his onetime ally who later became an enemy, Louis Cardis. Cardis was an Italian immigrant who controlled the local Mexican vote. A fruitful political alliance between the two ended in 1875, at which time Howard found his future in El Paso politics ruined. The burly ex-Confederate thereupon took the reckless action of seeking title to certain salt lakes near Guadalupe Peak that native *paseños* regarded as communal property. After attempting to prevent Mexicans from procuring salt from these deposits, Howard was seized by a mob in Ysleta and forced to sign a bond wherein he promised to leave the county. He did leave, but soon returned, and in a fit of rage, cold-bloodedly murdered Cardis. Attempting again to enforce the claims to the salt lakes, Howard and a small party of Texas Rangers were attacked in San Elizario and forced to take refuge in one of the town's buildings. After holding out for three days, the besieged Americans surrendered, whereupon a Mexican mob executed three of them, including Howard.[37] By this time, rampaging Mexicans had looted the stores of the few Anglo merchants in San Elizario, killing one of the owners in the process.[38]

In response to the trouble in San Elizario, a hastily organized force of Texas Rangers arrived and proceeded to commit what a United States army officer described as "deeds of violence and outrage matched only by the mob itself." The Rangers' accomplishments included the murder of two helplessly bound Mexicans in Ysleta, and the wanton shooting of an innocent Mexican in his home.[39]

On first appraisal, the violence of 1877 would appear to have been the result of racial tensions at the Pass, a clear clash between cultures with differing concepts of justice and property rights. Other factors, however, were probably more significant. Times had been bad for the people in the Lower Valley: The federal board that investigated the "Salt War" in 1878 found the valley's inhabitants united in "a community of suffering through poverty and privation," a people who in preceeding years had endured economic depression, Indian raids, and devastating floods.[40] During such a bleak period, the hauling and selling of salt was one of the few reliably profitable enterprises, thus making Howard's attempt to restrict access to the Guadalupe deposits seem especially outrageous.

In addition to depressed economic conditions, border communities in the area of the Pass were greatly affected by the political turmoil in Mexico following the death of President Benito Juárez, in 1872. Throughout much of the 1870s the Mexican press was vehemently anti-American, and towns such as San Elizario were not immune to its influence.[41] However, many, if not most, of those in the mob that murdered Howard were not San Elizario residents but rather Mexican nationals who crossed over the river to participate in the riot. Only a few days before the Salt War, a fair in El Paso had attracted strangers from throughout the Southwest. When local Mexicans, understandably outraged at the slaying of Cardis, besieged Howard, they "brought in their train a mongrel following of thieves and robbers," who used the occasion to loot San Elizario stores. It is significant to note that only one man from the El Paso precinct, the precinct where most of the region's Anglos resided, was a member of the San Elizario mob.[42]

Other evidence also undermines the contention that the Salt War was the result of underlying racial and cultural tension in El Paso. Throughout the entire affair, Mexican officials at Paso del Norte did everything in their power to prevent their nationals from crossing over to San Elizario, an indication of good relations with local American authorities which probably would not have existed if there had been any considerable racial problems. It is also noteworthy that the rioting in San Elizario did not divide discretely along racial lines; the mob threatened several Mexican-Americans during its rampage. Nor were all Anglo-Americans in danger during the rioting. When United States troops arrived in San Elizario, they encountered no trouble whatsoever; the anger of the Mexicans had focused upon Howard and the Texas Rangers.[43] The most convincing evidence that the El Paso Salt War was not caused by enduring social problems was its aftermath. Soon after the rioting of 1877, valley *paseños* quietly ceded their communal property rights and agreed to pay for salt taken from the Guadalupe deposits. By 1879, Mexicans from towns across the river were fighting side by side with the Texas Rangers against marauding Apaches. As one El Pasoan later recalled, after the Salt War the "good feeling which has usually existed between the two races in the valley was soon restored. . . ."[44]

During the three decades between 1880 and 1910, the dusty desert hamlet of El Paso was transformed into a small, rapidly growing city. By the time of the United States' entry into World War I, over 60,000 residents would work and live in the same area where a visitor in 1876 had found mostly deserted buildings and an Anglo population that numbered no more than one hundred.[45] The key elements that sparked this remarkable growth were four railroad lines that by 1884 linked El Paso with commercial, industrial, and population centers in the distant north, east, south, and west. The extraordinary isolation that had so greatly shaped the Pass's earlier economic and social relationships was breached.[46]

The ensuing influx of Anglos drastically changed local society. White Americans were no longer a tiny enclave in an isolated community; now they had the numbers, financial backing, and rail connections with which to assert themselves. Being recent arrivals, they still carried the cultural "baggage" acquired during their lives in Anglo population centers, and they naturally wanted Anglo culture, values, and institutions to prevail in El Paso. This was soon manifest in a physical transformation of the city, as brick homes and buildings replaced the adobe *jacales* which had served the *paseños* for over two hundred years. By the end of 1884, Anglo El Pasoans could take additional pride in their electric, gas, water, and telephone service. The establishment of newspapers, churches, and a school system further confirmed the arrival of American civilization.[47]

After railroads linked El Paso with other American cities, the need for local Anglos to accommodate to the Mexican population lessened. Anglo men now generally mated with women of their own race; they could live in typical American homes, eat traditional American foods, and feel relatively secure that their children were being brought up in an American community. Soon, Protestant churches and other Anglo organizations afforded a social life that did not entail substantial mingling with Mexicans. Increasingly, many Anglos did not see a need to speak Spanish or feel motivated to understand Mexican culture. Of course, this is not to say that El Paso became a bastion of racial intolerance. Despite its rail connections, the city was more than six hundred miles from any large American population center, and the local economy continued to mandate a symbiotic relationship between Mexicans and Anglos at the Pass.

Due to its ideal geographic location and the fact that it was now the nexus for four railroad lines, El Paso became an important supply and transportation center for the expanding mining interests of northern Mexico and the southwestern United States. By 1885 El Paso had become a smelting center, and in addition, was attracting thousands of dollars and pesos as a recreational and entertainment mecca for the region's miners and ranchers. However, if prosperity had come to the Pass (and it certainly had, compared to the dismal situation of the 1870s), it was a prosperity based upon extractive industries such as mining, ranching, and agriculture. These industries, in turn, depended on an ample supply of cheap, unskilled manpower, which in the Southwest meant Mexican labor. Thus the local economy was in many respects "colonial" in that it produced raw materials and depended upon distant industrial centers for manufactured products, capitalization, and markets.[48] Because the economy was ultimately related to cheap labor, per capita income was low, a condition that was made even more acute by the community's border location.[49] Despite its great growth in population, El Paso was commercially inferior to Ciudad Juárez (formerly Paso del Norte), while that Mexican city benefited from an unrestricted free trade zone. The Pass's economic backwardness was perhaps best evidenced by the fact that El Paso County had to issue its own ad hoc scrip during the 1880s and 1890s, due to a continuing dearth of currency.[50]

Economic developments after the arrival of the railroads drastically affected the city's social makeup. Due to cheap Mexican labor, a substantial Anglo proletariat did not develop. The men in the nearby mines, the workers in nearby cotton fields, the laborers on the railroad, were alike overwhelmingly Mexican. Inside the city, domestic servants, construction workers, laundresses, streetpavers, and workers in the sanitation department were almost exclusively Hispanic, working longer hours and for lower wages than most Anglos.[51]

Fully aware of the region's dependence upon Mexican workers, local financial interests exerted themselves to maintain amicable race relations. It simply made no sense to agitate the labor force that the city thrived upon. Moreover, El Paso's status as a growing export-import center would surely suffer if the city developed a racist reputation. Many small businessmen had an additional interest in avoiding racial friction; if Mexicans were reluctant to come to El Paso, this would curtail the local retail trade.[52]

But the need and desire for racial tolerance did not in themselves perpetuate the region's heritage of extensively accommodating Mexicans within the political system. As more Americans arrived in the city after 1880, the Anglo grip on local politics intensified. The first step in exerting control was the removal of the county seat from Ysleta (where the justice of the peace could not speak English) to El Paso in an 1883 election that was exceptionally suspect. In tribute to their triumph, El Paso Anglos provided for the construction of a grand new courthouse, an impressive edifice topped by a statue of the Goddess of Justice.[53] Despite this, not all Anglos were satisfied and soon the county grand jury was accusing Mexican-American officials of incompetence and corruption, stating:

> We find the justices-of-peace at Ysleta, Concordia, Cuadrilla, and Socorro incompetent and their dockets are found in unsatisfactory condition. In most cases, we find them kept in the Spanish language, and not in proper form, as required by Law. The constables in most precincts do not speak English. We also find

great dissatisfaction regarding water rights in the lower valley. The Alcaldes are showing favoritism in allowing water rights.[54]

The days of cultural accommodation in politics were over.

Though they might decry the "un-American" characteristics of local Mexican officials, El Paso politicians did not hesitate to use Mexican votes. By the late 1880s, El Paso's stalwart Democrats had assumed control of the city's affairs, forming a "Ring" that stayed in power with the support of the Spanish-surnamed citizenry. The Ring included influential bankers, lawyers, and members of the "entertainment" industry. Corrupt elections, long an El Paso tradition, continued well into the second decade of the twentieth century as the Ring resorted to the importation of Mexican voters who were provided with liquor and female companionship before going to the polls.[55]

Control of the important Mexican vote usually depended upon an alliance with a local Latin *político*. *Políticos* who delivered the vote were awarded elective political offices such as district clerk, or patronage privileges within the sanitation department.[56] But even with political success depending in large part on Mexican voters, Mexican *políticos* rarely held important county-wide offices after 1883. While during the period 1866-1875 Mexicans had served as county tax assessor and collector, county clerk, and even county judge, the only county office held by a Mexican in the late 1880s was that of county commissioner.[57] Thus a pattern of reduced Mexican power within the political system was well-established by the turn of the century. With the great influx of Mexican immigrants into El Paso during the early twentieth century, Hispanic political influence declined even further, primarily owing to the immigrants' general lack of interest in American politics.[58]

Throughout the early 1900s, increasing resentment was focused upon El Paso's political Ring, which not only was sustained by illegal Mexican votes and kickbacks from municipal employees, but was also closely tied to local saloonkeepers and gamblers.[59] As Anglo newcomers continued to arrive in El Paso, many of them were disgusted by the unsavory practices of the Ring, especially on election days. Such open defiance of democratic principles was particularly outrageous during a period when the spirit of progressive reform swept the nation. Equally upsetting to reform-minded El Pasoans was the presence of a local vice industry which seemed to pose the final obstacle to "civilizing" El Paso. It was an issue that would persist for decades.

Though vice, in various forms, had always existed at the Pass, it became particularly evident after the American invasion. As has been seen, it did not take long for Colonel Doniphan's men to turn Paso del Norte into a giant casino. Gambling remained popular in later years, it being reported by a visitor to El Paso during the 1860s that games of chance ranged from "the boy's game of pitching *quartillas* (three-cent coins)," to serious wagering in "great saloons where huge piles of silver dollars were staked at monte."[60] After the arrival of the railroads, El Pasoans continued to delight in such diversions; a local grand jury reported in 1902 that the city's population included six hundred professional gamblers.[61]

Being the only American city of any consequence for miles and miles around, El Paso was an ideal entertainment center for a vast hinterland. As El Paso's first historian delicately explains: "There was not a thing in the way of commercial accommodation or of excitement and lurid entertainment that El Paso was not ready, as a kind hostess, to furnish to her guests."[62] As early as 1883 the city sported a line of bordellos on Utah Street that, by the early 1900s, included lavish establishments endowed with private bars, liveried servants, small orchestras, and elegant women imported from Paris. Less sumptuous were the sordid "cribs" that flourished between larger houses of ill-repute, where lonely miners and cowboys could acquire a partner for the low price of a dollar.[63]

An examination of El Paso's vice industry reveals much about local society in the early twentieth century. Though the city was rapidly growing, the region's depressed economy provided only a limited variety of investment opportunities. With an increasing number of miners, cattlemen, soldiers, and railroad workers arriving in the Southwest, the "entertainment" industry was one of the surest routes to financial success. Local interests were cognizant of this and invested accordingly. Almost all businesses in El Paso were linked to some extent with the vice industry: hotels, restaurants, laundries, and retail stores all derived revenue from the proprietors, employees, and customers of entertainment concerns. City government also reaped financial reward in the form of license fees and *sub rosa* kickbacks.[64] Thus it was not surprising to find powerful business and political interests allied with the "sporting crowd" during El Paso's first decades as a city.

Naturally, not all El Pasoans condoned open gambling and prostitution. Desiring a decent place for themselves and their families, many citizens banded together in such reform groups as the Law and Order

League and the Citizens' League.[65] When the clamor for reform had become irresistible, El Paso began a slow and reluctant cleanup process. In the early 1900s many dance halls, houses of prostitution, and gambling parlors closed and relocated in Ciudad Juárez, whose economy was becoming increasingly dedicated to tourism.[66] However, rampant vice continued in El Paso also, and as late as 1917 an authorized red-light district was an irritating reminder of the city's tainted past and present.[67]

The obstacles to reform were considerable. Not only did important politicians and businessmen maintain close connections with the entertainment industry; many other citizens who were in no way connected with that industry also objected to moral zealotry. Due to its isolated location, El Paso still retained the vestiges of a frontier town, including a code of rugged individualism that rejected interference in other people's affairs. But as more residents arrived with expectations of making the Pass their permanent home, Protestant values demanded an end to shameless, officially condoned vice. Thus, by 1910, the stage was set for increased conflict between "enlightened" newcomers who wished to "clean up" El Paso, and older residents who desired to perpetuate the Pass's tradition of tolerance in moral matters.

Conclusion: El Paso's social heritage was drastically different from that of most other Texas communities. Although Americans had taken the Pass by force of arms, events neither during nor after the Mexican War had generated much racial animosity. This contrasts with a legacy of bitter resentment found in east Texas after the Texas Revolution.

For thirty-five years after it became a part of the United States, El Paso was a small isolated community. The few Anglos at the Pass were forced by circumstances to accommodate the native Mexican population in their legal and political institutions, and they also mingled closely with them on a social level. Dehumanized stereotypes of the Mexican people such as existed in other parts of Texas were not maintained by American residents in El Paso due to the close and intimate relations between the two races. Certainly prejudice did exist, but not of the variety found in eastern and southern counties of the state. The only major incident involving racial conflict in nineteenth-century El Paso was the Salt War of 1877, but this episode was primarily related to other factors and probably cannot be properly classified as a "race war." In fact, the rioting at San Elizario pales in comparison to the East Texas Cattle War of the same period, during which more than a dozen whites and one hundred Mexicans were killed within a four-month span in 1877.[68]

After 1881 and the arrival of railroads, El Paso changed dramatically, with the number of Anglos vastly increasing. As a result, social and political accommodation of Mexican residents decreased, and El Paso became more like a typical Texas city. Increased racial exclusion, however, was mitigated by the nature of El Paso's economy. Dependent on Mexican labor, Mexican consumers, and Mexican trade, Anglo businessmen strove to avert racial tension. Local financial interests were supported in this policy by the city's political Ring, which also had an interest in amicable race relations: Open animosity between Anglos and Mexicans might disturb the basis of the Ring's political power — the Mexican vote.

Because El Paso was a remote, southwestern border city, the local economy was typically depressed, and the range of profitable investments remained limited. Due to this, and also because of the city's location, a thriving vice industry arose. Although, by 1910, many of the entertainment establishments had been removed to Juárez, vice remained a serious problem. The fact that the community stayed "open" longer than most other Texas cities was reflective of the region's economic backwardness, the locality's remoteness from major institutional control and opinion centers, and a frontier mentality that was repelled by restraints and curtailments. However, during the decade prior to 1920 the Pass experienced profound strains and pressures that threatened to eradicate forever the region's tradition of social tolerance.

CHAPTER 2

The Mexican Revolution and the Growth of Intolerance in El Paso, 1910-1920

The corpses arrived at the Juárez train depot during the cold hours of early morning, crated in crude wooden coffins that were draped with simple black cloth. The eighteen bodies were not a pretty sight, most of them having been mutilated by repeated gunshots to the head and face. The head of one had been "blown completely off." A solemn group of Americans took charge of the grisly cargo and escorted it across the border, on guard against any last minute trickery by the Mexican customs officials. The border crossing was effected without incident, but, in the city of El Paso, tensions began to rise toward the breaking point.[1]

Throughout the next day, January 13, 1916, the mood grew increasingly ugly. For the two previous days the community had been seething over reports that a group of American mining men, nine of them El Pasoans, had been cold-bloodedly gunned down near the Mexican town of Santa Ysabel, by soldiers in the employ of Pancho Villa. Reportedly, the victims had been stripped and physically abused prior to their murder, and the savagery was said to have extended even to the clubbing and shooting of the victims' pet dogs.[2] Now that the corpses provided bitter confirmation of these dispatches, an enraged citizenry flailed about in an attempt to vent its fury. In the lobby of a downtown hotel, a hostile crowd taunted the United States Consul to Ciudad Juárez for being "Villa's consul, not ours," forcing him to flee for his safety. Equally displeased, the editor of the *El Paso Times* blamed the murders on President Wilson's "wishy-washy" policy toward Mexico, noting that the incident clearly showed that local Anglo complaints did not derive merely from a "borderland prejudice toward the Mexican." Even a visiting man of the cloth protested that "We are advised to keep our heads, but I say, for God's sake, let the men of America keep their honor and courage, too." As evening approached and fresh earth was shoveled over those first interred, irate Anglos took to the streets.[3]

Violence commenced with sporadic fist fights between American soldiers and Mexicans in saloons. By nine o'clock, a thousand or more Anglo civilians had joined the fray and were headed south into the Mexican district, waylaying and assaulting anyone who appeared to be of Méxican descent. By the time the police arrived, the mob's route was marked by a trail of bruised and bleeding Hispanics, some of them possibly the victims of stab wounds.[4]

Only by the greatest exertion on the part of local authorities were the enraged Anglos restrained. Police were forced to draw their revolvers to halt the mob's advance, and eventually the entire sixty-five-man police force had to be called out. Further reinforcement was provided by a company of soldiers from the nearby 16th Infantry Division which double-timed into the heart of the city to form a human cordon between the Mexican residential area and the Anglo business district; five more companies arrived later in the night. Chihuahuita was thus sealed off and quiet was restored. El Paso's first race riot was over.[5]

As was demonstrated by the violence following the Santa Ysabel massacre, El Paso's tradition of peaceful race relations was severely tested by the chaos and turmoil resulting from the Mexican Revolution of 1910. By the time the United States declared war on Germany in 1917, the Pass was experiencing the seventh year of tension that was more acute than any it had theretofore experienced since the American invasion of 1846. Whereas newcomers to the city before 1910 had arrived in a community remarkable for its relatively tolerant racial and cultural arrangements, the great influx of new Anglo and Mexican residents during the revolutionary period found an El Paso seething with resentments over wounded national pride, and with attitudes so volatile that thousands of armed troops frequently patrolled the streets. As had been the case for so much of its history, El Paso's experiences during the decade prior to 1920 were not those of the typical American city. In order to understand the emotions and prejudices that prevailed during the years after World War I, it is necessary to examine the previous decade of unprecedentedly vexing borderland problems.

From the beginning, El Paso seemed destined for an important role in the Mexican Revolution. A convenient location for purchasing arms and ammunition, the city had often served as a base for plotters against the dictatorial regime of Porfirio Díaz. When Francisco Madero issued his *Plan de San Luis Potosí* in 1910 and declared himself the provisional president of Mexico, it was not surprising that his sponsoring junta was headquartered in the Caples building, in downtown El Paso.[6]

Far from being alarmed by a revolution in their "backyard," most El Pasoans seemed enthusiastic about the Madero revolt, some even to the extent of enlisting in the *insurrecto* army.[7] Although the important Mexican import-export trade was frequently interrupted, local boosters and businessmen included themselves in the excitement, elated by the prospect that the first important battle of the revolution would take place in Ciudad Juárez. This would attract national and international attention to the Pass. Local merchants also stood to profit from the sale of supplies to the contending Mexican armies, and El Paso's banks would prosper as Juárez institutions transferred their cash holdings to the United States, pending the outcome of the conflict.[8] With their pocketbooks so attuned to the Madero revolution, a group of prominent El Pasoans was quick to petition Congress and President Taft to forego any steps "which would in any manner or in any degree interfere with the revolutionists and insurrectos."[9]

Aside from financial considerations and publicity, El Pasoans were thrilled by the suspense and drama of a real revolution. Since there were so few diversions in the middle of the desert, it was exciting to have the pageantry of an actual war so close at hand. Pascual Orozco's encamped rebel army on the outskirts of Juárez sometimes attracted as many as 15,000 "Kodak fiends" in a single day, who flocked across the river to photograph the "fierce looking insurrecto warriors." More ad-

venturous gringos motored into the Mexican desert to witness preliminary skirmishing between the opposing armies; one such group visited
the scene of a waylaid train, where they pilfered souvenir saddles and
bridles amidst decaying corpses.[10]

The three-day battle for Juárez, from May 8 to May 10, 1911, was a
show of shows. Despite Mayor Charles E. Kelly's earlier warning that
combat would cause Mauser bullets to "rain on the banks of the Rio
Grande," downtown streets had to be roped off to avert a veritable
stampede of sightseers to the river front; others perched on rooftops to
view the action.[11] Once the fighting had subsided, the souvenir hunters
moved out in strength again, crossing over to Juárez to haul off "everything movable," even the ritual vessels of a church.[12]

After the *insurrecto* victory at the Battle of Juárez, El Paso was quick
to embrace Francisco Madero as the new leader of Mexico. Surrounded
by Mexican and American flags, local leaders feted the short *científico*
at a banquet at the Sheldon Hotel, apparently unmindful that only a
few weeks before, city businessmen had been moved to praise the
"hearty assistance and co-operation of Mexico's President, General Porfirio Díaz."[13] However, El Paso had little to fear from the moderate
Madero, who acknowledged the "friendship shown our cause by the
Americans," and whose *Plan de San Luis Potosí* claimed that it was "the
duty of every Mexican to respect the persons and property of foreigners."[14] With such a man controlling Mexico, El Paso could anticipate a
prosperous resumption of Mexican import orders and ore shipments,
with expectation that the arrival of backlogged shipments would create
a business boom.[15]

But the Mexican Revolution proved to be less tidy than the El Paso
business community had expected. After assuming the presidency, Madero failed to initiate comprehensive economic reforms and was thereby alienated from the lower classes at the same time that reactionary
interests were plotting his downfall. As the months of the Madero presidency went by, it became increasingly evident that another rebellion of
some kind would soon break out. Accompanying the resentment
toward Madero was a release of great pent-up anger towards foreigners,
especially the Americans, who were seen as the plunderers of the Mexican nation. Even prior to the Battle of Juárez, anti-American riots and
demonstrations erupted in Mexico City, the streets ringing with cries of
"Down with the Gringos" and "Death to the Yankees."[16] In April 1911,
an investigator for an El Paso business concern found Torreón and
Monterrey to be "hot-beds of 'gringo hating'" and noted that Ameri-

cans frequently were the victims of staged incidents in which crowds of hate-filled Mexicans extorted money from them.[17] Such reports and rumors inevitably fueled the fears at the Pass.

North-of-the-border hopes that Madero would restore order proved to be ill founded. By February 1912 the United States Consul in Chihuahua City was reporting that "The State is a unit against the Federal Government, and open war will follow [the] entrance [of] any Federal troops into the State."[18] By then Ciudad Juárez had already fallen to anti-Madero forces, the municipal government being taken over by revolutionaries who variously gathered under the banners of Emiliano Zapata, Emilio Vásquez Gómez, and Pascual Orozco.[19] Confusion of this magnitude was disconcerting to Anglos across the river, who were already concerned about the rise of anti-American sentiment. Gone were the exciting days of 1911, the El Paso Herald lamenting the "drab colored revolution that is now in progress. There is no enthusiasm and everyone is sick and tired of war as it has been bared to the bone in the old border town."[20]

Moreover, El Pasoans began to fear that the violence might spill across the international boundary and threaten the safety of their city. Military reports brought notice that armed Mexicans were riding about in New Mexico thirty miles west of the Pass, and from the nearby hamlet of Anthony came rumors of a Mexican threat to capture the Upper Valley in the event of United States intervention in their homeland.[21] Anti-Yankee sentiment was also rampant in Juárez, where an incident involving American soldiers brought day-long street demonstrations, the United States Consul there reporting that "much feeling against the Americans is in evidence."[22] By late February, local apprehensions were such that a five-hundred-man sheriff's posse was formed to react against "any possible trouble," and Mayor Kelly formally requested the Secretary of War to send troops into Juárez due to "nightly robberies, holdups, and assaults . . . in which Americans were victims."[23] Fortunately the federal government did not follow this rash course of action, and in a matter of days local hysteria subsided.

By the end of the summer, Mexican federal troops once again controlled Ciudad Juárez, the "red-flaggers" of Pascual Orozco departing amidst "general rejoicing."[24] However, local Anglos' nerves had been rubbed raw, and resentment toward Mexicans in general was increasing. The continuing turmoil in Mexico seemed to confirm Texan stereotypes of Mexicans as a mercurial, undisciplined people who were inherently given to cruelty and bloodthirstiness.[25] Early in 1912 the Herald had noted that "None but a Latin mind can comprehend and keep abreast of the lightning changes [in Mexico]," and a native El Pasoan would later write that the chaos of 1912 was due to the Mexicans' "following out a legitimately inherited instinct for combat which had come down to them from a line of ancestors who, only a short four hundred years before, had been in the habit of eating one another."[26] Believing that Mexicans had a peculiar penchant for violence, many El Pasoans were considerably relieved that three thousand United States troops were stationed in or near their city by September 1912.[27]

Events in 1913 devolved from bad to worse. During "ten tragic days" in February, President Madero was deposed and executed by General Victoriano Huerta. To the El Paso press it was now evident that only United States intervention could restore order in Mexico, that the Mexican character would never permit that nation to return to a peaceful condition through its own efforts. One local editor concluded that "Mexicans dote on chaos. They love it so, they would like all the human brotherhood to share in their enjoyment."[28] The *El Paso Times* urged a change in United States policy toward Mexico that would be supported "by real Americanism . . . a change . . . backed up by the bone and sinew of this great American republic."[29] Clearly the dissolute Latins to the South had proven their inability to run their own affairs and needed the forceful guidance of their more civilized northern neighbors. Nor was this opinion altogether confined to the Anglo community; one Mexican-American El Pasoan declared that intervention "would be a Godsend [because] Uncle Sam would take these poor, ignorant peons, earning 25 cents per day, and educate them, teach them to be progressive and broadminded."[30]

The revolution continued throughout 1913, with Acting President Huerta's federal troops contending with the Constitutionalist forces gathered under the banner of Venustiano Carranza, a former governor of Coahuila who had promptly denounced Huerta's "villanous coup-d-etat."[31] During the early hours of November 15th, El Paso was suddenly awakened by the "bark of the Mauser, the rattle of the machine gun, and the deep booming of cannon at intervals" as Constitutionalist forces under Pancho Villa took Ciudad Juárez. United States soldiers rushed into El Paso to stand guard at the river, but Villa quickly restored order on the opposite side by ruthlessly shooting looters, and he pledged that, in the event of further combat, "no battle will be fought within range of El Paso."[32] El Pasoans were generally pleased with Villa, the *Times* speculating that it might be best for local business if

Pancho captured all of Chihuahua.[33] This amicable relationship with the *villistas* in Juárez would serve El Paso well during the tense months of the following year.

Mexican-United States relations worsened in early 1914, culminating in the American occupation of the port city of Veracruz. Woodrow Wilson's democratic sensibilities were greatly offended by the manner in which Huerta had come to power, and he accordingly made the general's resignation an essential prerequisite for United States diplomatic recognition. When Huerta refused to leave office, Wilson seized upon a minor incident in Tampico — involving the arrest of American sailors — to justify the military occupation of Veracruz, a move whose real intent was to topple the Mexican dictator. But Wilson had not adequately appraised the extent of Mexican nationalism, and the American incursion was denounced even by Huerta's Constitutionalist enemies.[34]

Reverberations from the intervention naturally reached El Paso, where the situation appeared especially dangerous because of the presence of some 15,000 Mexican refugees and *federalista* prisoners.[35] As American marines were battling their way into Veracruz, army troops in El Paso patrolled the streets of Chihuahuita, and all suspicious residents of Mexican descent were placed under surveillance. To prepare for the eventuality of anti-American demonstrations, additional troops were placed on highest alert, and the local police force was enlarged.[36] Because of the suspicion directed at them, six hundred local Mexican-Americans felt it was best publicly to pledge their loyalty to the United States, announcing their readiness to "march in the ranks with the American soldier who is of Anglo-Saxon or Celtic origin."[37]

The greatest local danger stemmed from the hysteria of Anglos. Buffeted by three years of border turmoil and feeling victimized by what the *Times* characterized as "spineless Washington diplomacy," certain El Pasoans were perhaps *hoping* for trouble to erupt in the city. On April 23, 1914, at the height of the crisis, Federal Customs Collector Zach L. Cobb warned his superiors of the "grave danger of race conflict and bloody riots being started by irresponsible people," who he later explained were involved in a movement "to have [Texas] Governor Colquitt [a persistent critic of federal policy towards Mexico] pull off a horse play here."[38]

Whatever such plans for "horse play" there may have been, they were never actuated. On the 24th of April the Pass remained calm, it being reported that "Juárez is quiet. No anti-American feeling [is] noticeable."[39] That same day Pancho Villa took pains to squelch rumors that he intended to attack El Paso in reprisal for the Veracruz invasion, declaring that "It's that little drunkard Huerta's fight; let him fight it."[40] Clearly, the crisis had passed.

The next year and a half provided no spectacular incidents in El Paso. The resignation of Huerta in July 1914 gave some basis for hope, a local editor musing that "Doubtless there will be an end to revolutionary activity now, and [Mexico] will settle down in the paths of peace and the enjoyment of prosperous tranquility."[41] However, the victorious Constitutionalist coalition divided into two opposing factions, one supporting Villa, the other Carranza, and the bloodletting worsened. From the autumn of 1914 and throughout 1915, Mexico was ravaged as never before, with perhaps as many as 200,000 dying in battle and millions of others suffering from starvation and disease.[42] In response to such monumental violence, the number of American soldiers stationed near El Paso continued to grow until, by the fall of 1915, the Pass was home to "perhaps the largest body of troops in the nation."[43]

The massing of troops near El Paso in 1915 was partly a specific response to rumors of new revolutionary plots by Mexican refugees. In May, nine Mexicans, including a former *huertista* general, were arrested in the city for planning to invade Mexico, the papers reporting that "not less than 4,000 men are living in El Paso and drawing pay as officers and soldiers in the [proposed invasion army],"[44] Though the suspects were soon released, fears of a possible *huertista* uprising persisted, an official report in June mentioning "the recruitment of a force in El Paso for a new revolution" and a plan by "filibusters" to invade Mexico via the Zaragosa crossing in nearby Ysleta.[45] Existence of a pro-Huerta plot seemed to be confirmed that same month when Victoriano Huerta himself, along with Pascual Orozco, was arrested close to El Paso and charged with violating United States neutrality laws. At the same time, stories were circulating that bands of heavily armed Huerta sympathizers were on the move in Chihuahua.[46]

El Pasoans were not pleased by the prospect of yet another revolution, realizing that it would very probably unsettle the city's large Mexican population. In late August, after federal officials received word of an imminent "uprising" among El Paso's Mexican refugees, troops were moved into the city to man the international bridge and patrol southside neighborhoods. The *Times* noted that the unrest in Chihuahuita could result in the "horrors of a race riot."[47] Racial animosities were fueled even further a few days later when it became known that Pascual Orozco, who had recently escaped from prison, had been slain by

a party of ranchers near Sierra Blanca, Texas. Fearing reprisals by Orozco supporters, El Paso County ranchers began arming themselves, and
city officials took the precaution of dispersing Mexican crowds that
awaited the train that carried Orozco's body back to El Paso. In order
to prevent demonstrations, the slain general's corpse was removed from
the train prior to its arrival at the downtown station.[48]

The apprehensions of El Paso Anglos during 1915 cannot be appreci-
ated without realizing that, by the late summer of that year, south
Texas had exploded into general border warfare involving Mexican
bandit raids and savage Texan reprisals.[49] Throughout August, El Pasoans read of violence in the southern part of their state, bannered by
headlines such as "RACE HATRED FLAMES ALONG LOWER RIO
GRANDE BOUNDARY" and "WIDESPREAD CONSPIRACY
AGAINST AMERICAN RULE IN TEXAS," and no doubt wondered if
these troubles might not reach their own locality.[50] Anglo concerns certainly were not eased by the revelation of the *Plan de San Diego*, an incredible Mexican scheme that called for the "liberation" of Texas, New
Mexico, Arizona, California, and Colorado and the subsequent exter-
mination of all Anglo males over age sixteen in these regions.[51] Partially
in response to this plot, El Pasoans requested that even more troops be
stationed at the Pass.[52]

Eventually the south Texas violence subsided, especially after United
States *de facto* recognition of the Carranza government on October 19,
1915. By that time, Texas' southern counties had amply demonstrated
what a vicious tradition of racial hatred and discrimination could lead
to; for example hundreds had lost their lives, and there had been
millions of dollars in economic loss. Much of the violence was caused
by Anglo protective societies which engaged in lynchings and forced a
large percentage of rural Mexican families to flee south across the river.
Even the commander of the United States troops in the area was moved
to condemn the "malicious deviltry" of the lower Rio Grande American
"scoundrels."[53]

In El Paso, where discrimination against Mexicans was traditionally
less severe than in the lower Rio Grande valley, and where there was
no appreciable tradition of racial violence, 1915 proved to be a relatively quiet year, Anglo anxieties notwithstanding. The *El Paso Times*
summed up the situation accurately in September when, in reference to
south Texas problems, it stated: "Fortunately we have no serious trouble of this kind along the border in the El Paso section, due largely to
the fact that there is more harmony between the two nations in this ter-

ritory."[54] However, events in 1916 were to prove that borderland violence could extend even to the area of the Pass.

During the final days of 1915, Ciudad Juárez underwent yet another change in city governments, *carrancista* authorities replacing *villistas* under a negotiated settlement that provided for a peaceful transition of power. The transfer took place under tense circumstances, an American official wiring the State Department that "There was rioting and looting in Juárez today incident to [the] change in government. . . ." Another official noted that almost all Americans were avoiding the Mexican side and reported: "Conditions menacing, with probable further rioting tonight." By the next day, however, the *carrancistas* were firmly in control.[55]

Pancho Villa's abandonment of Juárez aptly demonstrated the decline in his fortunes, his once proud Army of the North having been drastically diminished by the effective generalship of *carrancista* commander Alvaro Obregón. Now little more than the leader of a large group of bandits, Villa blamed his decline on the United States' support of Carranza. In retaliation, his forces began attacking Americans in Chihuahua, killing sixteen of them near Santa Ysabel in January 1916.[56]

As was noted above, the Santa Ysabel massacre ignited El Paso, producing the city's first genuine race riot. However, local authorities acted quickly, preventing a chain of events which might have produced violence on a scale with that recently experienced in south Texas. Mayor Tom Lea pleaded for calmness, stating: "We have been patient and shown a fine wisdom through all these distressing and harrowing experiences and I hope that we shall not lose our heads at this late hour."[57] The *Herald* used terms such as "disgraceful," "cowardly," and "despicable" in commenting on the riot, and the *Times* proclaimed that "it is folly for us to engage in street brawls with Mexicans, and [this paper] urges El Pasoans to curb their feelings. Rioting can accomplish nothing."[58] Local boosters were apprehensive that any press dispatches about the mob violence would give El Paso a bad reputation, one Chamber of Commerce member warning that "exaggerated stories must not get out from El Paso." It certainly did not enhance the city's image to have a headline such as "AMERICANS FIGHTING MEXICANS IN EL PASO" on the front page of the *New York Times*.[59]

Most El Pasoans probably agreed with local leaders that open racial conflicts could bring nothing but harm. In order to avoid further violence, an "indignation meeting" to protest the Santa Ysabel massacre was cancelled. Although a crowd gathered anyway, it dispersed quietly.[60] No further attacks on Mexicans occurred in the days following the riot, but the city had been put on edge, and the atmosphere remained tense. This mood was best described in a military report from Fort Bliss that noted:

> The excitement of last week, due to the murders at Santa Ysabel, has apparently subsided. But there exists an undercurrent of bitter resentment that might easily lead to personal acts of violance [sic] against individual Mexicans on either side of the line. . . . There exists here along the border the elements of a situation similar to that which has recently prevailed along the lower Rio Grande.[61]

If further trouble occurred, El Paso could be expected to explode again.

And trouble did occur. On March 9, 1916, the United States Secretary of State was wired from El Paso: "Columbus [New Mexico] attacked this morning, four thirty o'clock. Citizens murdered."[62] Pancho Villa had struck again, this time invading United States territory and leaving dead Americans in his wake for the second time.

The Columbus raid, only seventy-five miles from the Pass, naturally enraged El Pasoans; yet there was no repetition of the rioting that had taken place in January. Though there was probably small-scale scuffling, most El Paso and Juárez residents appear to have heeded the advice of the *Herald* to "keep the peace, and to see that no unfortunate outbreaks by irresponsible individuals or others shall disturb the friendly relations that exist."[63]

After Villa's surprise attack, the Wilson administration realized the need for military action against the renegade general, especially in light of approaching national elections in the United States. Accordingly, troops were massed at Columbus, and the well-known Punitive Expedition began its march into Chihuahua on March 15.[64] As the invasion commenced, anxiety ran high in El Paso, prompting city authorities to shut down several Spanish-language newspapers that had been running anti-American articles.[65] At one point, anxious Anglos asked officials what protection their families would get in the event the city's men were summoned downtown in response to a Mexican uprising or invasion.[66] The local Chamber of Commerce, understandably sharing such fears, requested the government to arm a select group of four hundred El Paso citizens. However, a local federal official warned his superiors in Washington that "There is [a] danger private parties lacking full Government control might start something that could otherwise be prevented."67

As things turned out, El Paso never required the services of local vigilantes. As the Punitive Expedition entered Mexico, Juárez remained calm, the American consul there reporting that "nothing unusual has occurred."68 The next day, Collector of Customs Cobb noted that the "Situation in Juárez and El Paso since American troops entered at Columbus [is] quiet and without incident of consequence."69 Mexican officials were especially cautious and made no move to strengthen the small Juárez garrison, the *carrancista* commander there promising full cooperation in "running down the worst enemy Mexico has ever had."70 But Mexicans were still the object of suspicion, as was reflected in a federal agent's report that:

> A large proportion [of the] Mexican population of El Paso have arms and ammunition in their houses which will create [a] dangerous situation here in the event of complications with [the] Juárez garrison. They should be disarmed. The possibility exists of their resenting it and starting something serious . . . . The deeper our troops penetrate Mexico the [greater] resentment becomes.71

The Mexicans of Fabens, Texas, were also the object of concern, the American military commander there reporting that they had recently been conferring with a Mexican army officer.72

Events involving the Punitive Expedition kept El Paso on edge throughout the spring of 1916. In April, troops from the American force clashed with Mexican soldiers and civilians near Parral, Chihuahua, resulting in two Americans and over forty Mexicans being killed.73 Nevertheless, the Pass remained undisturbed, as local officials on both sides of the river tried to minimize the incident.74 The *Herald* cautioned against magnifying the encounter into "something really important."75 It is revealing of local Anglo attitudes that the killing of sixteen Americans constituted a "massacre," while the deaths of dozens of Mexicans at the hands of invading foreign troops were considered nothing to get excited about.

With the summer of 1916 there came the very real prospect of war between the United States and Mexico, as First Chief Carranza became increasingly strident in his demand that the Punitive Expedition be removed. President Wilson refused to comply with Carranza's wishes until he was satisfied that the Mexican government could restore order along the border. As the impasse daily became more likely to result in open hostilities, Wilson placed the National Guard in Texas, New Mexico, and Arizona on border duty and increased the number of regular troops along the Rio Grande. First Chief Carranza also increased his forces along the border, ordering thousands of additional troops to duty in Chihuahua and Coahuila.[76]

Throughout the summer of 1916 the Pass was the scene of a huge military buildup, especially after President Wilson mobilized the entire National Guard on June 18.[77] By August, 70,000 regular troops and guardsmen were stationed in or near the city, almost doubling the local population.[78] The presence of such a large number of troops brought a wartime atmosphere to the Pass which generated great excitement but also raised racial tensions. Local fears increased in May when two Mexicans were arrested for arson at Fort Bliss. And in early June two Latin railroad workers were given ten days in jail after they were caught counting the number of American troops in a Flag Day parade.[79] Mindful that thousands of El Paso residents were possibly hostile to the American government, the local commander of federal troops warned on June 19 that "all Mexicans who misbehave and cause troubles for the United States authorities will be severely dealt with."[80] At the same time, the *Herald* noted that "it is doubtful . . . there has ever been so disquieting an undercurrent of ill feeling and distrust [locally]," citing the "unquestionable development [in El Paso] of new and bitter race hostilities, whose blight we have escaped in the past."[81]

On June 21, 1916, a detachment of troops from the Punitive Expedition clashed with Mexican forces stationed at Carrizal, Chihuahua, an incident which set off unprecedented saber-rattling along both sides of the border.[82] In Ciudad Juárez, where the populace had already been urged to take up voluntary military training, citizens were issued rifles by the mayor, and militiamen began wearing ribbons identifying themselves as "Volunteers to Defend the Nation."[83] With activities such as these going on across the river, fears began to grow of an impending Mexican attack on El Paso; Collector of Customs Cobb reporting on June 25 that he had received information:

> . . .from Mexican sources which impress me as most probably true of an intended attack on El Paso in force by the Mexicans and of heavy troop movements from the South into Chihuahua. . . . I believe the situation here, the danger here, their freely discussed plan to attack El Paso, most serious.[84]

Another federal official warned at the same time that, though El Paso's Mexican residents had been "behaving admirably," they could "be expected to take [an] active part if the city were attacked."[85] Equally mindful of such suspicions, Cobb later urged that the National Guard:

> . . .go through the Mexican district of El Paso with a fine tooth comb and take possession of all guns, ammunition and explosives and thereby eliminate the danger that we continuously face of racial riots and consequent destruction of life and property in this city.[86]

Anglo fears of a Mexican uprising proved to be unfounded, it being reported during the most tense days of June that "El Paso continues to maintain its self-control and the city is as calm as a summer night."[87] Juárez was equally tranquil, the *carrancista* garrison there practically evacuating the city after the Carrizal incident. In the weeks that followed, the local border remained calm, and it was clear that once again a crisis had come and gone.[88]

For the city of El Paso, the summer of 1916 would prove to be a turning point in the tension resulting from the Mexican Revolution. By July of that year, overall opinion in the United States seemed to be shifting overwhelmingly toward ending the crisis with Mexico, especially after the Carranza government released American soldiers captured at Carrizal. Subsequently, both the United States and Mexican governments retreated from their belligerent posturing and agreed to refer differences to a Joint High Commission. Though the commission accomplished little, it allowed a cooling-off period during which President Wilson decided to withdraw the Punitive Expedition. This was fully accomplished on February 5, 1917, when the last American soldier left Mexican soil.[89]

Though ill-feelings between Mexicans and Anglos in El Paso subsided during the years after 1916, the tradition of cultural and racial accommodation that prevailed prior to 1910 was irreparably damaged. The revolution in Mexico had activated previously controlled racial attitudes and had reinforced prejudices. This sharpening of racial divisions blended with the atmosphere of domestic intolerance generated by American participation in World War I and played an important role in shaping El Paso society as the city entered the 1920s.

It should be realized that the turmoil caused by the Mexican Revolution did not suddenly go away in 1916. Bandit raids and other troubles continued to plague the boundary throughout the remainder of the decade, as was reflected (for example) by an issue of the *El Paso Times* in 1918 which proclaimed in headlines: "Mexicans Open Fire Upon Americans During Parley and Pay Penalty Promptly," "Mexican Snipers Fire on Officers of U. S. Patrol," and "Mexicans Hold Americans Under Death Sentence."[90] In that same year, the *Times* lamented the continuing "bitter resentment" that resulted from "frequent raids across the border, accompanied by robbery and destruction of property, and often by murder."[91] Much of the violence was due to unsettled economic conditions and chronic food shortages in Mexico. In June 1918, Ciudad Juárez was completely without meat, and throughout that entire year all of Mexico suffered from shortages of corn and beans.[92] The industrial situation was equally bleak, but in the following months the Mexican economy started to improve slowly. In the interim, however, the border was fated to be an area of general poverty and unrest.

In 1919, Ciudad Juárez was the scene of a final spasm of the Mexican Revolution, as forces of Pancho Villa captured much of the city. The resulting gunfire was deemed a hazard to El Paso residents, and a detachment of American cavalry troops was sent across the river to chase off the *villistas*.[93] The incident revived bitter memories, and, in a speech to Congress, local representative Claude B. Hudspeth summed up the anger and frustration that had accumulated in El Paso during the revolutionary period:

> For eight years the town of Juarez, having a population of 20,000 across the river from the city of El Paso, has been in the hands of first one band and then another of Mexican revolutionists. We go to bed in El Paso with Juarez under one government and awake in the morning to find it under another one, and in almost every instance the taking of Juarez has been accompanied by loss of life in my home city of El Paso. . . . We have stood this for eight long years. I ask you, gentlemen, as Americans, as Representatives of a red-blooded, self-reliant, self-respecting people, how long must [we] continue to suffer?[94]

The answer to Representative Hudspeth's query was, "Not much longer." After a quiet revolution dislodged President Carranza in 1920, Alvaro Obregón took over the reins of government and restored at least the semblance of order in Mexico. The bloody battles and dramatic changes in government were over for the moment, and El Pasoans could rest much easier.

Conclusion: In 1975 an El Pasoan who had lived at the Pass during the years of the Mexican Revolution made this observation:

> Certainly the fact of the revolution being right next door had an impact on El Paso that was different from that on any city in the United States because we were the only large border city. We were the only people that were directly involved in revolutionary affairs. This makes a hell of a difference.[95]

Indeed, El Paso's experiences during the Mexican Revolution were unique, and an understanding of them is fundamental to an accurate appraisal of the growth of intolerance in the city prior to 1920. As has been shown, the years following the Madero revolt of 1910 brought racial tensions that greatly undermined the city's tradition of cultural and racial accommodation. Frightened by the bloodshed, confusion, and anti-American sentiment in Mexico, many local Anglos became more prejudiced against Mexicans, seeing them as a "disturbing element" that had no place in a progressive American city. This attitude was probably most frequently held by the thousands of new Anglo residents who arrived during the decade between 1910 and 1920 and were not socialized into the older, more tolerant tradition. Arriving during a period of unprecedented tension between Mexicans and Anglos, these newcomers — many of them natives of the racially intolerant South — experienced only limited contacts with local Hispanics and thus became increasingly isolated from the economic and social realities of their city. This ominous trend was noted in 1916 by the *El Paso Herald* when it stated:

> Many El Pasoans, especially those who have come here in more recent years, do not seem to realize that this city's prosperity, growth, economic power, financial and commercial prestige, and social welfare most largely depend on our retaining reasonable, just, and friendly relations with the Spanish speaking population within our own borders, and with the neighbors of the southern republic. It is folly, that will be terribly costly, for any group of El Pasoans or other American border citizens to permit race hostilities to warp and poison the spirit of our place.[96]

And many El Pasoans worked to perpetuate the old traditions. A local resident who was a teenager during this period later recalled the "great contrast between the frontier pioneer nature of half the society and the cultural interests of the people who were newcomers."[97] Those who had lived in the Southwest for a number of years realized the feasibility and necessity of peaceful racial coexistence. Though Anglos in this group were surely prejudiced against Mexicans, most of them had had friendly experiences with Hispanics prior to the revolution and their racism was not blatant. Allied with El Paso's "oldtimers" were businessmen who realized that harmonious race relations were essential to the region's biculturally based economy. These interests recognized El Paso's dependence on a steady supply of cheap Mexican labor and the great profits to be reaped from economic exchanges with Mexico. "Our destiny — and by our destiny I mean the destiny of the people of the southwest —," declared a local Chamber of Commerce member in 1917, "is so largely bound up with the destiny of the republic to the southward, that to place a ban upon free intercourse which we have enjoyed in the past would have a tendency to postpone the development of ourselves and our Mexican neighbors along all lines."[98] In this case it was the literacy act that was under attack; but the same could be said of hostile race relations — that open animosity between Anglos and Mexicans could do nothing but hurt the local economy.

Thus the Mexican Revolution had helped set the stage for a struggle between two Anglo factions over the future direction of El Paso. Though both groups were racially prejudiced, the newcomer faction was strident; and it was gaining influence as more and more residents arrived. The conflict would become particularly evident during the months of American participation in World War I.

CHAPTER 3

The Heyday of the Vigilante: El Paso During the Great War

E ven as El Pasoans braced themselves for the possibility of a war with Mexico during the traumatic summer of 1916, it was becoming increasingly apparent that the United States might become involved in the Great War that ravaged Europe. By then, "preparedness" was the national watchword, and patriotic demonstrations were frequently being held across the country. As United States relations with both Mexico and Germany soured, El Pasoans turned out by the thousands to affirm their patriotism in a giant "El Paso Preparedness" parade on June 14. Among the more than 9,000 participants was a vast assortment of local politicians, businessmen, members of civic organizations, and working people. Marchers included Macabees, Woodmen, Knights of Pythias, streetcar employees, and twenty-six female employees of the S. H. Kress Company, who were neatly attired in white uniforms. Both senior citizens and the youth of the city were represented, Civil War veterans parading alongside Campfire Girls costumed as Indians. Additional thousands turned out as spectators, clogging city streets and sidewalks to cheer and wave American flags. Reactions were such that the marchers had difficulty in hearing the band music with which they were supposed to keep step.[1]

Although the procession was primarily intended as a warning to Mexico, by early 1917 the tension between the United States and its southern neighbor had greatly eased, especially after the withdrawal of the Punitive Expedition. It was symbolic of the improvement in the border situation that by March the commander of the Juárez garrison was reviewing United States troops at nearby Camp Stewart at the side of his American counterpart, while junior officers from both nations chatted pleasantly with each other.[2] German-American relations did not fare as well, however, and war appeared increasingly inevitable. Fully realizing this, the Chamber of Commerce gave a dinner dance for a company of Texas national guardsmen in March 1917, at which it was ostentatiously acknowledged that the soldiers might soon fight at "the side of English and French soldiers for the peace of the world."[3]

The transition from anti-Mexican hysteria to anti-German hysteria came with remarkable ease. After the Zimmermann telegram revealed German plotting in Mexico, the Times' editor directed little comment towards the neighboring republic, opting instead to declare that "the film of deception is ruthlessly torn away and Germany, hissing in desperation, writhes before us in the slime of intrigue." Soon the same editor was stressing the un-Americanism of persons of German ancestry in the United States, making the rather incredible comment that "the Germans contributed so little to the upgrowth of [our] country that they are a negligible quantity in our history."[4]

Evidently many El Pasoans agreed with the Times' assessment, including the six thousand who attended a patriotic rally in late March, at which the Hohenzollerns were vehemently denounced. When war was declared a few days later, city residents again displayed their patriotism by driving their Hupmobiles, Oaklands, and Franklins in a massive auto parade that included over two thousand motor vehicles.[5] The preparedness campaign now became a matter of utmost national urgency, and El Pasoans were anxious to do their part. In early April, plans were laid for a woman's rifle club, whereby El Paso's female population could "band themselves together under arms to defend the homes in this city, if need be, against a foreign enemy."[6] At the same time, the local Chamber of Commerce proclaimed its readiness to "stand unreservedly behind the President of the United States in his determination to maintain the dignity and honor of the nation." In the following months the Chamber did its utmost to turn El Paso's business conventions into orgies of patriotism.[7] The young men of the city were also quick to rally, as plans for volunteer units were hastily formulated. By May the Popular Department Store alone had contributed twelve employees to the armed services, and had honored the new recruits at a farewell banquet beneath a "liberty shield of red, white, and blue electric light bulbs."[8]

Although few American communities were more remotely located from the European battlefields than El Paso, the city, nevertheless, experienced its full share of war hysteria. The tense racial situation of the past six years had spawned widespread doubts that the local Mexican population was trustworthy, especially now that the military forces at the Pass would presumably dwindle temporarily, as soldiers were transferred to Europe. The national spokesman for those harboring such fears was the rabid interventionist, Senator Albert B. Fall, who called for increasing troops along the border because "For 800 miles from the border back into the states the railroads are entirely in the hands of Mexicans of Old Mexico." Fall went on to claim that the majority of such Mexicans were "ex-bandits" who might easily "put out of commission every coal mine, every copper mine and every railroad by concert of action."[9] Perhaps because they shared similar fears, city authorities decreed in May that all firearms, weapons, explosives, and ammunition in El Paso were to be registered, with each owner's nationality being recorded.[10] Earlier, the Chamber of Commerce held a meeting at which the disarming of local Mexicans was discussed, but one participant wisely pointed out that "disarmament along racial lines would be a joke and a serious joke at that."[11] Federal officials remained wary of Mexicans, nonetheless, and ordered the censorship of all telegraph and telephone lines to Mexico. It is significant that by the end of 1917, El Paso was home for a new army cavalry regiment, an outfit best suited for tight patrolling of the border.[12]

Though Mexicans were a source of concern during American participation in World War I, the lion's share of El Paso's war propaganda and hysteria was reserved for the German enemy. Only three days after the declaration of war, local fears intensified when two Germans in the city's southside were apprehended with "important papers" and were arrested on conspiracy charges.[13] In subsequent months continuous anti-German propaganda constructed the frightful apparition of a blood-lusting Teutonic beast that made the earlier stereotypes of Mexican cruelty pale in comparison. By late summer the *Herald* would display a grotesque cartoon featuring the Kaiser gorging himself on ox-horns full of blood.[14] "It's not the fault of the Kaiser, nor of Zimmermann," thundered Zach L. Cobb at a patriotic rally, "that El Paso is not in flames today, and her women carried off into shame and dishonor."[15] In an atmosphere such as this, it was not surprising that the German language instructor at the local high school soon found that his contract had been cancelled.[16]

World War I produced unprecendented interference in the daily and private affairs of American citizens in El Paso and elsewhere, as the government and various patriotic organizations utilized all facets of society in channeling public opinion in the proper direction. In El Paso this included the public schools, where even before the war a daily flag ritual was instituted that consisted of students saluting the flag, pledging their loyalty to the United States, and singing "America." Ritual questions and answers were then exchanged:

Q. Who are enemies to our flag?

A. Every person who strikes at our flag by force of arms or breaking the laws that have been made to preserve our liberties.[17]

The Pass's adult population was also encouraged to demonstrate its patriotism, especially during the Liberty Bond drives of the next two years. "If you buy a bond you will be worthy of the great name, 'American,'" stated the *Times*, "[However,] if you refuse, you will be unworthy. In which class do you propose to place yourself?"[18]

Increasingly, the government sought to coerce reluctant Americans into performing their patriotic duty. In early June thousands of El Paso's young men registered for a military draft, and those who were found eligible for duty emerged from the selective service stations with badges reading, "I Am Registered and Ready." As it turned out, however, many more were registered than were ready — out of over 9,000 signing up for the draft, only 1,877 would admit that they were qualified for military service. Part of the problem was that many of the registrants were Mexican aliens and therefore could not be drafted. Due to the fact that the federal government had established a set quota of draftees from the El Paso district without considering the high percentage of ineligible aliens, Mayor Charles Davis was concerned that the city might not provide its share of men and thus would appear unpatriotic. "The city must do something," he warned, "to combat any impression that the white population is slacking."[19]

In order to insure that every El Pasoan gave total support to the war effort, various government-sanctioned organizations sprang up. Chief among these was a Home Defense League, which was intended to constitute a "second line of police force" to work for law and order, and to "protect the populace against criminals and traitors."[20] At first the Defense League was basically a paramilitary group to function during civil emergencies, but as time went by it took on more of a vigilante-like nature. By November 1917, League members were being urged to report to appropriate officials "any information they might acquire as to suspicious characters." That same month, it was recommended that the League form a local vigilance committee which would "classify all residents under the following terms: First, loyal; second, disloyal; third, doubtful; fourth, unknown." After such a list had been compiled, it was to be handed over to the police department and federal officials. It was reported that, although a local vigilance committee had not yet been formed, the League had already gathered "much valuable information," which it had turned over to the Department of Justice.[21]

In El Paso, with a tradition of frontier individualism and distaste for uninvited intervention in private matters, certain wartime programs found rough going. Although El Pasoans were exceedingly generous in supporting Liberty Bond drives, the edicts of the Food Administration were widely resented. In one case, an El Paso merchant advised his customers to refuse to sign food conservation pledge cards, and when a concerted campaign for the signing of such pledges was made, El Paso produced a very poor showing. "The indifference and lassitude of the thousands [of El Pasoans] who failed to sign the cards is intensely disappointing," lamented the state food administrator.[22] The spirit of the times did not allow for such laxness, and government officials relayed word "that those who have displayed pro-German sentiment [by refusing to sign the pledges] will be dealt with severely." Local grocers were later admonished to keep careful track of their patrons' purchases: "If your customers are unpatriotic and attempt to hoard food, you will pay the penalty."[23] Thus, whatever their misgivings, El Pasoans had no choice but to settle down to a regular schedule of Meatless Tuesdays and Wheatless Wednesdays.

If the World War brought increased governmental interference into the lives of El Pasoans, it also held out the prospect of great profits for the local economy. The Pass had long had a close relationship with the military, and the city eagerly anticipated a large increase in the number of troops in the area. The unprecedented prosperity resulting from the presence of the thousands of soldiers in 1916 was fondly remembered, and expectations ran high that the city would receive a divisional cantonment of thirty thousand men.[24]

Just as their hopes were soaring, city residents received the unwelcome news in June 1917 that El Paso might not be awarded an army cantonment after all. Local leaders were bewildered and examined a variety of explanations: Perhaps the government did not need as many military camps as was originally thought; maybe the El Paso climate was not a desirable one in which to train troops who would fight in humid France; possibly the Pass was too windy.[25] On June 2, Secretary of War Newton D. Baker put an end to the speculation when he announced: "El Paso must clean up. I am in receipt of daily reports showing social conditions to which our soldiers are subjected which can no longer be tolerated." Citing illegal sales of alcohol to soldiers and unrestricted prostitution around army camps, Secretary Baker went on to warn that if conditions in El Paso did not improve, the city might find itself without *any* troops.[26] The Pass's tradition of being a wide-open recreation center had run afoul of Wilsonian morality, and amid rampant super-patriotism this could not help but appear disloyal.

In response to the Secretary of War's accusations, city officials soon began a crackdown on vice. Mayor Davis promised to end the local red light zone, though he admitted he did not "want to pose as a reformer and did not want to assume he could regulate a vice which had been in existence for thousands of years."[27] Accordingly, the police force was sent into the restricted zone to evict the prostitutes, and it was soon reported that half of El Paso's seven hundred fallen women had departed, the remainder being scattered throughout the city and Juárez. Left destitute and homeless, two unfortunate prostitutes attempted suicide by poison.[28]

The new cleanup campaign was welcomed by many "respectable" El Pasoans who had long deplored the vice within their community. Protestant evangelical churches were especially enthusiastic. "In this moral clean-up," declared the congregation of the First Presbyterian Church, "we proffer our hearty co-operation to the city and county authorities."[29] This sudden display of reformist zeal was not enough to sway federal officials, however, for they announced on June 15 that there would be no divisional cantonment for El Paso. To add insult to injury, the widely sought cantonment went to the small town of Deming, New Mexico.[30]

For El Paso, always concerned about whether it was doing enough to support the war effort, the failure to secure a catonment was a severe blow. Not only would this hurt the city economically, but it left the impression that El Paso was letting down the country and the brave boys who would be fighting and dying in Europe. By the summer of 1917 many local men had entered the service, and an all-El Pasoan company had been raised for the Texas National Guard. On July 3 the first soldier from El Paso arrived in France with the 16th Infantry Division, and by the end of the year American soldiers were dying in battle.[31] The war had become a reality, and it became more and more imperative that El Paso clean up to help the war effort.

At the same time that reform sentiment was thus asserting itself, certain other war-related manifestations likewise intensified. The spectre of an ubiquitous network of German spies continued to haunt the Southwest: When two thousand sheep mysteriously died in Arizona, German agents were blamed, and in December guards were dispatched to Elephant Butte Dam to "guard that waterway from possible damage at alien enemy hands."[32] In El Paso the Home Defense League maintained its careful vigil, assisted by the Boy Scouts, who were under orders to report all violators of the city's sanitation laws.[33] As during the previous months, patriotic speeches, Liberty Bond drives, and campaigns to sell War Savings Stamps and Red Cross Christmas seals combined to generate an intolerant climate of superpatriotism and blind loyalty.

Patriotic pressure was such by the end of the year that many influential El Pasoans were convinced that a new cleanup campaign was necessary to redeem the city in the eyes of the federal government. Despite the closing of the red light district, vice had persisted, forcing the local military commander to place the entire southside of the city off limits to troops. Local prostitutes had proven to be persistent, however, as was demonstrated by a raid in early December that netted nine "lewd women" ensconced in the immediate vicinity of Fort Bliss.[34] It was increasingly apparent that much of the vice problem was due to corrupt local officials with ties to bootleggers and prostitutes. A series of raids on suspect liquor clubs later in the month uncovered six deputy sheriffs who ran illegal establishments. A few days later, federal investigators reported that there was no record in police dockets of the arrest of soldiers and prostitutes nabbed in one local raid.[35] The *Times* complained

that the police had "shamefully neglected" their duty in the past to
crack down on vice, and an officer in the United States Sanitary Corps
stated that "the efforts to keep [El Paso] clean are weak and half-heart-
ed; the officials charged with enforcing the law either do not believe in
their job or are incapable of performing it."[36] Corruption in local
government, long a serious problem in El Paso, became a factor in the
debate over a moral cleanup.

By the end of December, State Senator Claude B. Hudspeth had returned from Washington, D.C., with an important message from federal officials. If a wholehearted moral cleanup were undertaken, and if
El Paso succeeded in purging itself of bootleggers and immoral women,
the Pass would receive a divisional cantonment of 30,000 or more men.
As things stood now, however, local conditions were totally unacceptable. Hudspeth revealed secret Sanitary Corps reports on El Paso that
stated: "Prostitution widespread; no police suppression," and "Bootlegging universal, mainly by jitne [sic] drivers and Mexicans." Both the
senator and Mayor Davis had been personally informed by the federal
director of training camp activities that reports on El Paso were "the
worst of any in the United States."[37] The choice was now clear: El Paso
could do the patriotic thing and clean up, or the city could continue its
sinful ways and abandon any hope for a large military cantonment.

Senator Hudspeth's report set off a serious new effort against vice.
The city council passed an ordinance forbidding sale of liquor to soldiers; county officials launched an intensive drive to close down suspect
roadhouses; and the city police force formed two special "purity
squads" to search for prostitutes in hotels and rooming houses. Civic
groups heartily endorsed the crackdown, and even the city's saloonkeepers promised to assist by requiring customers to leave their names,
addresses, and auto numbers when purchasing liquor for takeout.
Army officials cooperated by providing soldiers for undercover operations against bootleggers.[38]

Yet, some El Pasoans felt that more should be done. Accordingly, local Protestant pastors and businessmen circulated a petition requesting
a local option election on the prohibition of alcohol.[39] On January 8,
1918, Samuel J. Isaacks, legal advisor for the "dry" forces, presented the
petition to county commissioners, who approved it by a vote of three to
two.[40] Isaacks had cleverly managed to schedule a date for the election
(January 30, 1918) which would exclude all voters except those who
had paid their 1917 poll tax. Because many of the city's Hispanics had
not paid the tax due to fear of becoming eligible for the draft, prohibi-

tion advocates were confident that "the Mexican vote will [not] hold the balance of power, as has been the case in years gone by." Determined that the election would not be marred by corruption, drys warned Mexican voters that they had lists of local residents who had claimed draft exemptions as aliens, and that if such aliens tried to vote they would "be severely dealt with. . . ."[41] Thus, even from the beginning, the local option election was associated with the issues of race, culture, and political reform.

The prohibition election of 1918 would prove to be one of the most revealing episodes in El Paso's history. After the election was scheduled, the city divided into two discrete camps — one "dry" and one "wet." On the dry side were arrayed the self-proclaimed forces of morality and patriotism, including the two daily newspapers. The *El Paso Times* said that the enactment of prohibition was a matter of patriotic duty; that the community must protect nearby soldiers from the "machinations of the bootleggers and the 'harpies' that prey upon them whenever they come to the city."[42] As the campaign heated up, the *Herald* also came out in favor of prohibition, claiming that alcohol "turned men into beasts, women into prostitutes, children into orphans, [and] happy homes into hovels."[43] As was to be expected, the Protestant churches strongly supported the dry crusade. The Reverend Charles L. Overstreet of the First Presbyterian Church rejoiced that at last El Pasoans could redeem themselves and abandon "the old squatter's claim [that] 'this is Satan's preserve: no trespassing!'" Other Protestant ministers were equally outspoken, notably the Reverend Percy Knickerbocker of Trinity Methodist Church.[44]

During the three-week campaign, the drys pulled out all stops. Large advertisements were placed in the local papers; outside professional prohibition workers and Chautauqua lecturers were brought in to give speeches; and a seemingly nonstop series of meetings and assemblies was held.[45] Virtually every conceivable argument in favor of prohibition was adduced. Zach L. Cobb asserted that the liquor interests were "the kaiser's ally in this country" and that the "man who shoots a leaden bullet at our boys in the trenches is no greater enemy of ours than the man who stands behind the bar and shoots booze into the manhood of the country."[46] From the economic standpoint, the drys held out the possibility of a nearby military cantonment, it being noted that the director of training camp activities had stated that the enactment of local prohibition would be greeted by federal officials "with satisfaction and approval."[47] In addition, it was asserted that better moral conditions resulting from prohibition would attract industry to El Paso and drive up real estate prices, and that local Mexicans would also benefit because they would have more "opportunity for clean, wholesome social life" rather than clustering around saloons. Evidently in the expectation that many Mexican residents would agree with them, the drys launched a concerted drive to win their votes, holding rallies at which the teetotaling virtues of Francisco Madero, Venustiano Carranza, and Pancho Villa were extolled.[48]

Who was there to oppose the formidable campaign of the drys? Naturally the wets included local saloon owners, brewers, and restaurateurs, whose businesses would be hurt by prohibition. Other businessmen were likewise concerned that prohibition might bring economic decline. When a resolution to support prohibition was submitted to the El Paso Chamber of Commerce's board of directors, it was promptly tabled with only one dissenting vote.[49] Having been at the forefront in establishing railroad and motorcar links with the military camp at Deming, the Chamber no doubt realized that a dry El Paso would attract few soldiers.[50] There was also the possibility that the loss of liquor revenues would depreciate property values (the exact opposite of what the drys claimed), increase unemployment, and raise taxes.[51] In a border community where economic opportunities were limited, such reasoning could prove exceedingly persuasive.

In addition to businessmen who wished to perpetuate El Paso's traditional role as a recreational center, other important groups eventually sided with the wets. Many Mexican voters felt no compulsion to give up their tequila and beer, and they emphatically signified this on election day. From the beginning, the dry campaign had been tinged with elements of anti-Hispanic racism, and most likely this was a factor in influencing the Mexican vote. Also backing the wets were many of the Anglos who resided in the older parts of the city.[52] El Paso had always been a drinking town and, war or no war, many longtime residents viewed prohibition as an unwarranted incursion into their private lives. Reform movements had always had an uphill struggle at the Pass, and prohibition was no exception.

One group of naysayers was especially conspicuous — local politicians. "I decline to make any statement about the [prohibition] question," announced State Senator Claude B. Hudspeth. "It is," asserted County Attorney William H. Fryer, "a new question that I haven't had time to give much thought [to]." "I do not wish to be quoted on the question," stated State Representative Richard M. Dudley. Clearly, lo-

cal politicians were hedging their bets, realizing that the election might
go either way. The few officeholders who took a stand on prohibition
usually opposed it. The judges of the 65th and 41st district courts
proudly declared that they were wets, and County Auditor Joseph
Escajeda vowed that he would do everything possible to defeat prohibition, wisely observing that "our proximity to Mexico would make it a
farce here."[53] The impression that the political establishment was opposing prohibition was given further credence by the fact that former
Mayor Joseph U. Sweeney, a prominent figure in the political "Ring"
that had ruled El Paso for so long, was campaign chairman for the
wets. One ardent local prohibitionist saw a conspiracy between corrupt politicians, saloon owners, and foreign voters, remarking that
"the saloon was the enemy of the purity of the ballot box."[54] Another
dry spokesman decried the failure of so many local officials to take a
positive stand:

> These gumshoe pussyfooters who refuse to be quoted on the local
> option question won't get you anywhere. They're moral cowards
> — bleating calves . . . when you get the ballot put the sharp
> edges across their necks and remove their heads. I don't want you
> to kill any one, but I do want you to bury 'em under other politi-
> cal corpses, where they belong.[55]

Thus, by the day of the local option election, much more was to be
decided than just the issue of prohibition. The election had evolved
into a test to determine where El Paso stood on questions of patriotism,
morality, religion, and culture. Assembled into one faction were the
Protestant clergy, the crusading press, and many local residents who
felt that prohibition had become a matter of civic, moral, and economic necessity. Opposing them were most of the city's Mexican residents,
powerful business interests, a majority of the political establishment,
and an assortment of Anglos who wished to preserve the community's
tradition of avoiding reform. The two groups had campaigned as vigorously as possible, and now the verdict of the public was awaited.

The election returns on the local option issue were a rude shock to
the forces of morality and superpatriotism. The city of El Paso voted
down prohibition 2,421 to 2,207, and El Paso County rendered the
same verdict by a majority of 2,668 to 2,497.[56] It had been a close election, but, even at the height of wartime hysteria, and with the War Department and many prominent citizens clamoring for reform, El Pa-

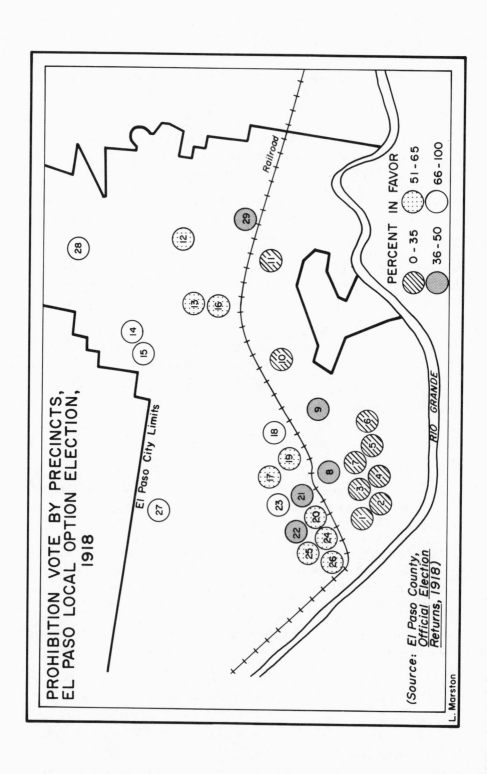

PROHIBITION VOTE BY PRECINCTS,
EL PASO LOCAL OPTION ELECTION,
1918

El Paso City Limits

Railroad

RIO GRANDE

PERCENT IN FAVOR

0 - 35

36 - 50

51 - 65

66 - 100

(Source: El Paso County,
Official Election
Returns, 1918)

L. Marston

soans opted for the profits of the liquor trade and the right of an individual to run his own life as he saw fit. In the end, the Pass's social heritage had asserted itself.

Despite their failure in the local option election, El Paso's reformers remained active. In March a local delegation was personally informed by the Secretary of War that the city's most recent cleanup had been wholly inadequate, a failure the Secretary attributed to local officials. At a subsequent meeting of El Paso businessmen and city and county officeholders, Sheriff Seth B. Orndorff admitted that there was much truth to the charges, and that even some of his own deputies were "on intimate terms with immoral women." To most of those attending the meeting the only answer to the problem seem to lie in community action "under the lead of a vigilance committee [that would] use 'roughshod' tactics to put prostitutes and illegal liquor selling clubs out of business."[57] Accordingly, a special Committee of Twenty-Five was formed to aid in the war on vice. James McNary, president of the First National Bank, was chosen as chairman of the vigilantes; he would be assisted by a "secret executive committee of seven." The anonymity of the executive committee would result in "law violators being hit harder, inasmuch as blows would come from unknown sources."[58]

By the end of September 1918, the Committee of Twenty-Five had assisted in the arrest of over five hundred people on charges varying from prostitution to driving too fast.[59] Other volunteer citizens' groups were also involved. In May 1918 the El Paso Federation of Women called for the formation of a "feminine purity squad" to monitor conditions in the city. By June it was rumored in the Negro part of El Paso that Willie Manwell, a well-known Negro detective from Houston, had been hired by the purity squad to weed out "evildoers."[60] The El Paso County Council of Defense (successor to the Home Defense League) also kept an eye on the city's moral conditions by appointing block captains to scrutinize all residents, and by the formation of neighborhood "vigilance committees" to investigate and report "any irregularities."[61]

Even as such vigilante groups were being organized, word arrived from Austin of a great victory for local reformers. On March 11 the state legislature, under strong pressure from Governor William Hobby, passed a bill providing for ten-mile prohibition zones around all military training camps in Texas, a decree which would in effect make El Paso a dry city. Less than ten days later, the legislature expanded upon this measure by passing a statewide prohibition bill that would go into effect on June 26, 1918. Accompanying the prohibition edict was another law that made it a felony for any diseased woman to have "immoral relations" with a soldier. El Paso now had no choice in the matter of cleaning up. On April 15, in compliance with the legislation concerning training camps, all saloons in the city were closed, and the Pass reluctantly entered the prohibition era.[62]

Although local reform was important in 1918, El Pasoans had their thoughts primarily directed towards faraway Europe, where many of the city's young men were now stationed. By the time of the Armistice, 3,781 El Pasoans would have served in the armed forces, out of which eighty-one died and one hundred and sixteen were wounded. The gallantry of these men was attested by forty-seven meritorious citations and nine distinguished service crosses.[63] As daily headlines bannered the bravery and sacrifice of El Paso's fighting men, patriotic zealotry rose to an unprecedented level, and the new standard of loyal behavior became "100 per cent Americanism." As a symbol of El Paso's dedication to the war, a giant Liberty War Loan Tower was erected in Pioneer Plaza. The garish multitiered edifice was topped by a replica of the Statue of Liberty and appropriately was the headquarters of the El Paso County Council of Defense.[64]

To insure that all El Pasoans were dedicated to pursuing the war to a satisfactory end, anti-German propaganda and hysteria were systematically intensified throughout 1918. "German agents in our midst are not a figment of the imagination, but a very real danger," announced a local member of the American Defense Society, in March.[65] In the event that this did not sufficiently alarm El Pasoans, one of the many large newspaper advertisements paid for by local businessmen ranted:

> THE KAISER SAYS: HE WILL
> — kill you!
> — ravish your daughter!
> — enslave your son!
> — pull down the Stars and Stripes forever![66]

Such superpatriotic activities continued throughout the war, most frequently taking the form of patriotic speeches to civic organizations and to the ten community branches of the County Council of Defense.[67] At the Morehead Community Council, propaganda came in the form not only of speeches but also of movies and the singing of patriotic songs.[68] The public schools similarly extolled the war effort and encouraged teachers to discuss with their classes such topics as "The German spy system" and "Liberty bonds: what and why." In addition, all school employees were ordered to report "every anti-American sentiment or declaration, past or future, expressed by any teacher, employee, or pupil connected with our schools."[69]

As had been the case from the beginning of the war, certain El Pasoans refused to accede to many of the excesses of domestic vigilance. Evidence of this had been demonstrated during the food conservation program and the local option election on prohibition, and such indication would continue throughout 1918. Failure to follow food rationing edicts prompted a number of local cafe managers to organize in February to report the "45 per cent Americans" whose "lower class restaurants" were violating conservation guidelines.[70] The unabashed vigilantism manifested by the Committee of Twenty-Five was a source of concern to some residents, the *Times* commenting that there was "no reason to talk of forming a vigilance committee — no reason for going outside the law or creating any extra legal agencies."[71] In July superpatriot and diehard prohibitionist Zach L. Cobb, now running for the United States House of Representatives on a platform of "100 per cent Americanism," was soundly rejected by local voters in favor of the more relaxed Claude Hudspeth.[72] Moderation in zeal was also shown by resentment over detailed questionnaires distributed by the Council of Defense, and the refusal of local waitresses to be examined for social diseases.[73] Although the war had demanded unprecedented conformity and intervention in private spheres, El Paso's tradition of frontier individualism had survived and would continue to assert itself.

When the war ordeal came to an end, El Paso could afford a degree of relaxation. In anticipation of an armistice, the El Paso County Council of Defense had already planned a victory celebration:

If the news comes between 6 p.m. and 6 a.m. everybody must bring as much wood, tar, or other combustible matter with them, so that on the stadium grounds at the high school can be built the biggest bonfire El Paso has ever seen — a bonfire big enough and hot enough to give the Kaiser, were he here, some idea of what is coming to him hereafter.[74]

When word of peace finally did come on November 11, 1918, a huge rally was held, whistles shrieked, bells clanged, and excited El Pasoans celebrated long into the night.[75] But in the midst of the merriment, at least a few residents probaby pondered the true cost of the war — including a diminution of individual privacy and of the liberty to express oneself unguardedly, and the advent of suffocating pressures to conform. Worst of all was the feeling that the fear, paranoia, and superpatriotism of the war era were here to stay. The fact that *The Birth of a Nation* was featured at the Grecian Theater on Armistice Day was a ghostly portent of what El Paso had yet to experience.[76]

Conclusion: The impact of World War I on El Paso contributed further to the intra-Anglo schism that had appeared during the revolutionary period. Because of the militaristic atmosphere created by the crisis with Mexico in 1916 and the fact that El Paso had close links with the military, wartime pressures arrived earlier and were felt more intensely at the Pass than in most other American communities. As was the case throughout most of the country, El Pasoans became less tolerant as conformity and uniformity of purpose were stressed by the federal government and patriotic organizations. As has been shown, El Paso had more than its fair share of war hysteria and superpatriotic zeal and, by the end of the war, vigilantism for the sake of the public good had been endorsed by the city's most prestigious officials. Yet, there were limits as to how far much of the populace would go. This was most dramatically demonstrated in the prohibition election of 1918 when a coalition of Hispanics, businessmen, local politicians, and longtime city residents fended off a formidable bloc of moral reformers. The local option election had revealed a clear contrast between El Paso's southwestern traditions and the southern progressive moralism of the Wilsonian era.

Therefore by 1920 El Paso's experiences during the Mexican Revolution and World War I had sharply divided the city's Anglo community into two ideological camps. In one camp were the keepers of El Paso's older tolerant tradition; in the other was a determined group of intolerant reformers. Eventually the two groups would clash, culminating in El Paso's experience with the Ku Klux Klan.

CHAPTER 4

The Ku Klux Klan Comes to El Paso

I t was a cold, dark night in late November, 1915, and the wind was so strong that the fifteen men struggling up the mountain found it impossible to keep their hats on their heads. They continued with their climb, nonetheless, and eventually arrived at the summit, breathless and filled with curiosity as to what the sixteenth man, their leader, would ask of them next. Solemnly, the large man ordered the group to gather a number of the large boulders that were scattered about. After this task was completed, the stones were arranged into a crude altar upon which the leader placed a faded American flag, an old sword from the Civil War, and a copy of the Holy Bible. He then struck a match and touched it to the tall wooden construct that he had carried to the top of the mountain earlier in the day. The gasoline-soaked wood quickly burst into flames, producing a giant fiery cross that blazed through the pitch-black Georgia night.

Beneath this burning cross the group of climbers began to intone their dire vows. The Ku Klux Klan lived again.[1]

The Ku Klux Klan that was resurrected in 1915 was a curious organization destined to go through stages of fraternalism, vigilantism, political activism, and slow disintegration. The founder of the new Klan was William Joseph Simmons, a Spanish-American War veteran and former Methodist circuit rider, who had found his true calling in life as a "fraternalist." Besides holding the esteemed rank of "Colonel" in the order of Woodmen of the World, Simmons was also a Mason of high degree and held membership in the Knights Templar and several other fraternal societies. Despite the satisfaction and success that he had encountered during the course of his work with these established orders, it had long been Colonel Simmons' ambition to found an organization of his own. As Simmons envisioned it, his new order would be the grandest of patriotic fraternities, a banding together of true Americans that would "destroy from the hearts of men the Mason and Dixon line and build thereupon a great American solidarity. . . ."[2]

After an accident placed him in the hospital for an extended stay, Colonel Simmons had time to develop more fully his plan for a new fraternal society. Drawing upon the colorful tales his father had told him concerning the activities of the post-Civil War Ku Klux Klan, Simmons decided to create a Klan of his own, albeit an essentially fraternal one. In the days that followed, the Colonel devised an elaborate ritual for his new organization, and designed the eerie masked and robed costume that would become so well known.[3] By the time of his release from the hospital, all that remained for Simmons to do was to persuade others to join the new Klan, a task for which his earlier fraternal work had left him well prepared.

Putting all his energy into finding members for his new order, Simmons had by October 1915 recruited thirty-four Georgians, who successfully petitioned their state to grant an official charter to the new Ku Klux Klan. On the following Thanksgiving night, the organization held its first initiation on Stone Mountain, outside Atlanta, and the Colonel's brainchild became a reality.[4] The rebirth of the Klan could not have been more shrewdly timed. Only a few days after the bizarre initiation on Stone Mountain, David W. Griffith's cinematic masterpiece, *The Birth of a Nation*, was shown for the first time in Atlanta. Griffith's film, with its idealization of the Reconstruction Ku Klux Klan, was part of a widespread revival of interest in the Klan, a mood which was first heralded by the popularity of two fictional works, *The*

Clansman and *The Leopard's Spots*. Although it had been an exceedingly violent and lawless organization, the original Klan was now generally acclaimed for rescuing Southern civilization from sinister carpetbaggers, scalawags, and semisavage Negroes. As the *New York Times* would favorably note in 1916, "This generation is being taught to idealize the Klan."[5]

Recognizing that the public mood was auspicious, Colonel Simmons utilized the vogue of the Ku Klux Klan to full advantage, placing large advertisements for his new order next to those announcing showings of *The Birth of a Nation*. This tactic proved successful, and by the end of December 1915 there were enough new members to enable the formation of Atlanta Klan No. 1, the first full-fledged local chapter of the Klan.[6] The following year, the entire Klan organization acquired a stronger hold on permanence, becoming a Georgia-based corporation under the direction of "Imperial Wizard" Simmons.[7]

During the first months of its existence, the new Ku Klux Klan was a far cry from its namesake. Though founded on the avowed principles of Protestantism, Americanism, and white supremacy, it was not at first identified with nightriding or vigilantism. Rather, it was essentially a highly ritualistic fraternal order that sold insurance among its members. The First World War thrust the Klan into a broader role, however, as the organization became involved with the Citizens' Bureau of Investigation, a volunteer, home-front vigilante group of which Colonel Simmons was a member. Appointed as "secret-service men" by their Imperial Wizard, Klansmen engaged in the wartime harassment of those they perceived to be slackers, enemy aliens, or immoral women. As spirited as these activities were, they nevertheless drew little special attention to the Klan during a period when many of the nation's citizens were participating in vigilante activities of one kind or another. As an El Paso newspaper editor observed in 1918, "In a hundred American communities the Ku Klux Klan is riding again . . ., not by that name, but in that spirit."[8]

Despite its increased activity during the war, the Klan's membership remained small, numbering only a few thousand by the end of 1919, almost all of whom resided in the deep South. The upturn in the Klan's fortunes would not transpire until 1920, following Imperial Wizard Simmons' decision to acquire the services of two public relations specialists, Edward Young Clarke and Elizabeth Tyler. Correctly observing that the postwar mood of the nation was ideal for the expansion of an ultrapatriotic society advocating pure Americanism, Clarke and Tyler invested thousands of dollars in a new membership drive, sending out over 1,100 recruiters (Kleagles) across the South. The response was overwhelming; within a few months tens of thousands of new Klansmen had been added to the ranks of the Invisible Empire.[9]

Much of the Klan's spectacular new growth was in Texas. The Klan first appeared in the state in the fall of 1920, when Colonel Simmons came to Houston on a recruiting junket that coincided with a reunion of Confederate veterans. The Lone Star State proved to be fertile ground for the KKK; by 1922 there were over 200,000 Texas Klansmen.[10] This remarkable appeal of the Klan was primarily related to its shift from a passive fraternal posture toward a more active role in promoting law, order, and social morality. In communities where a postwar crime wave and the upsetting pace of social change had created great tension, the Klan was seized upon as an agency for restoring order and for insuring the continuing ascendency of traditional conservative values.[11] As confidence in public officials drastically ebbed, many earnest citizens felt the need for an extralegal instrumentality. Through the medium of the Klan, frustrated Texans at last had the opportunity to strike back at moral degenerates, bootleggers, radicals, alien enemies, and religious deviates.

With such outlooks prevailing, the Ku Klux Klan quickly spread throughout Texas after 1920, generally moving from east to west. Houston was the first city to be organized, and by the summer of 1921 there were nearly one hundred local Klans in the state. On occasion, a new branch of the Invisible Empire would be dramatically announced to the public. This was the case in Dallas when hundreds of Klansmen marched through the city the night of May 22, 1921, bearing placards reading "Dallas Must Be Clean" and "Parasites Go."[12] In other localities, without public announcements, the presence of the mysterious order was manifest by the appearance of hooded men on various occasions, frequently at the scene of violent incidents. Often it was difficult to prove that the Ku Klux Klan itself was to blame for the violence, Klan members on grand juries and in sheriff and police departments taking care to protect their own.[13] By the summer of 1921, the summer the KKK arived in El Paso, nothing definite had been proved in the courts against the organization. To many it appeared that the Klan was being persecuted for doing what was desperately needed.

At this point, we should consider local conditions that help explain the advent of the Ku Klux Klan in El Paso. First and foremost, as has already been discussed, the arrival of the Klan coincided with the end of one of the most traumatic decades in the long history of the Pass. The unsettling impact of both the Mexican Revolution and World War I was still being strongly felt in El Paso in 1921. Indeed, without the underlying spirit of general intolerance that had been generated by the events of the past ten years, it can be seriously questioned whether the Ku Klux Klan could have met with any degree of success in El Paso. The repercussions of both the Great Rebellion and the Great War were profound and enduring in nature, giving rise to urgent problems that El Pasoans would have to face as their community entered the uncertain decade of the 1920s.

As we have already seen, the Mexican Revolution greatly strained race relations in El Paso, bequeathing to the Pass a decade of unusual resentment, anger, and impulse towards racial violence. Nevertheless, the situation had markedly improved by the early 1920s, as order was restored in Mexico and Mexico-bound exports once again flowed through the Juárez customs house.[14] The re-establishment of the Pass's traditionally close economic ties with its southern neighbor delighted local businessmen, who continued to strive in tandem with El Paso's political leaders to restrain displays of animosity that might damage the local economy. Many rank-and-file Anglos refused to march to this tune, however, and were increasingly defiant as certain long-term ramifications of the Mexican Revolution became manifest. Of special concern was the problem of Mexican immigration.

The official United States census for 1920, taken in a year of growing apprehension over the large number of alien immigrants in the country, revealed that El Paso was the nation's most "foreign" city. Among a population of 77,580, forty-three percent were foreign born. Not even New York City, popularly pictured as being overrun with "huddled masses" of immigrants, could claim as high a percentage of non-natives. And not only was El Paso's foreign born population large; it was monolithic, more than ninety percent having migrated from Mexico. Indeed, American-born and alien taken together, all local residents of Mexican descent probably constituted at least fifty-six percent of El Paso's inhabitants, easily the largest percentage of Mexicans residing in any urban American community.[15] Since United States censuses traditionally undercounted the Mexican population and since, on almost any given day during the 1920s, El Paso accommodated a large number of transient Mexican laborers — together with their families — the percentage of Mexicans in the city was probably significantly higher than that reflected by official figures.[16]

The burgeoning Mexican population resulted from many factors, foremost among which was the devastation of the Mexican Revolution. As famine, disease, and chaos swept across their homeland, thousands of Mexicans fled their country. "Thousands, literally thousands of Mexicans have poured into El Paso in the last two or three months and I don't doubt but there are 30,000 Mexicans in town now," opined one city resident in 1914. He further reported that "Most of these new-comers are practically without funds and it's a wonder to me that cases of death from starvation are not beginning to be discovered."[17] By 1916 the number of Mexican residents had grown even larger, totaling near-ly 40,000 (compared to a local Anglo population of only 27,000).[18] Such an influx of destitute humanity created grave social problems. Due to their poverty, the vast majority crowded into the pestilential southside slum of Chihuahuita, a district that had long lacked adequate water and sewage systems. Here their presence contributed to already serious health problems.[19]

It should be noted that conditions in Chihuahuita had long been abominable. A city health inspection of 1,194 southside homes in 1910 revealed that 526 were "unihabitable" and that over 2,500 persons were "living in homes not fit for animals." Quite properly the El Paso Times dubbed the area the city's "PLAGUE SPOT."[20] But with the ar-rival of so many new migrants and refugees after 1911, Chihuahuita deteriorated even more. An eastern visitor declared in 1914 that "It re-minds me of Hell's Kitchen in New York the way the Mexican people live in the south part of the city and in the smelter settlement."[21] That same year, General John J. Pershing, the commander of Fort Bliss, offered the city the services of an experienced sanitation engineer who was familiar with "such conditions as those met in Panama, Cuba, and the Philippines."[22]

Having become more active in responding to health problems, city officials adopted housing regulations in 1917 that placed new responsi-bilities on southside landlords.[23] Continuing immigration undermined these efforts, however, and living conditions in south El Paso remained appalling throughout the 1920s.[24] The main problem was congestion: in El Paso, in 1920, there were only six dwellings for every ten families. In other rapidly growing Texas cities such as Dallas and San Antonio, there was an average of more than eight dwellings for each ten fami-lies.[25] Mexican immigration was thus presenting unique health and housing problems that challenged the progressive aspirations of the day. Anglo newcomers who arrived in the city during this period, many of whom had never encountered Hispanics before, viewed these problems and drew mostly adverse conclusions. To progressive Americans the squalor of the Mexican district was proof that Mexicans were inherently "unprogressive," that they were "out of step with the ever-forward movement of American civilization," and that they were holding the city back from its goal of becoming a truly progressive community.[26] In the words of one local newspaper editor:

> Our border days are over, and we now prefer to go to our daily labors along well-kept streets, lined on either side with emerald lawns and nodding flowers and spreading trees. . . . [We will work] to the end that no unsightly thing will be left to the view of our citizens or visitors, and our municipal pride will rapidly grow, the while our city will become the model for those other great municipalities which are seeking to be as clean and beautiful as they are progressive and prosperous.[27]

What role could there possibly be for the begrimed and backward Mexican immigrant in this verdant vision of a modern El Paso?

Though some Anglos might view the Mexican immigrant as an obstacle to progress, it was a harsh reality that the much venerated progress was inextricably linked with abundant and cheap Mexican labor. The region's economic establishment was aware of this and was quick to forego racial scruples whenever the labor supply was threatened. Just such a threat arose in May 1917, when, in accordance with a new federal law, all immigrants to the United States were required to pass a literacy test and pay an eight-dollar head tax; these regulations were expected to reduce Mexican immigration by ninety percent.[28] The new requirements were not received favorably by the El Paso business community. The Chamber of Commerce took a stand against the literacy act, and a spokesman for the local smelter warned that "our industries along the border will be seriously crippled." The *El Paso Times* called the law a "monument of legislative stupidity."[29] Influential interest groups throughout the nation held similar views, and the next year, owing to wartime labor demands and effective lobbying by industries that utilized Mexican workers, the federal government suspended the new requirements for laborers in certain industries, including railroad workers, who constituted the bulk of Mexicans passing through El Paso. These exemptions were routinely renewed in following years and continued in effect through early 1921, despite the restrictive immigra-

tion sentiment that was sweeping the nation.[30] When a new danger to
El Paso's source of cheap labor appeared that same year, this time in
the form of the highly restrictive Immigration Act of 1921, local interests once again lobbied vigorously.[31] These efforts, combined with pressures exerted by other interests throughout the country, met with considerable success; neither the Immigration Act of 1921 nor that of 1924
had much effect on immigration through the Pass, due to their specific
exemption of the Western Hemisphere from the newly established
quota system.[32]

As a result of the effective lobbying of Southwestern businessmen
and allied pressure groups elsewhere, El Paso would receive an increasing flow of Mexican immigration throughout the 1920s. Between 1921
and 1930, the push of the impoverished Mexican economy and the pull
of American prosperity would send unprecedented numbers of legal
Mexican immigrants to the United States, many of whom first arrived
at the Pass. In 1923, for example, out of 80,793 Mexicans legally emi-
grating to the United States, more than 40,000 were processed through
El Paso.[33] These immigrants were supplemented by thousands of illegal
aliens who did not bother with the technicalities of documentation.
Only a small percentage resided in El Paso permanently, but, even so,
the influx was sufficient to further Hispanicize the city. By 1930 fully
sixty-seven percent of El Paso's population was comprised of persons of
Mexican ancestry.[34]

Coming as it did during a period of restrictive immigration legislation and general nativist intolerance, the growing Mexican population
was bound to be a source of concern for local Anglos. Events of the past
ten years had often divided the city along racial lines and the Mexican
immigrant had been increasingly deplored as a hindrance to El Paso's
progress. These racial and cultural misgivings were further distilled by
the experience of the World War, which had given Americans a new
blind faith in their national way of life, to the exclusion of anything
that appeared alien. Faced as they were with the prospect of a community that would become more and more dark-skinned and non-English
speaking, Anglo El Pasoans were increasingly apprehensive. Disturbed
by what was happening in his city, the anxious Anglo felt that some
sort of action had to be taken if American values and culture were to
remain dominant at the Pass. But from where would this action come?
From a local political machine that had traditionally kept itself in
power with Mexican votes? From the city's businessmen, the same ones
who had so effectively lobbied for permitting the continuance of Mex-

ican immigration? Clearly not. But then suddenly in 1921 an organization appeared that did offer a format of action, a means for Anglos to make their voices heard and to challenge the mad course that had been charted by the local establishment. Within the fantasy world of the Ku Klux Klan, with its paeans to "the western races" and "Protestant civilization," and its solemn vow faithfully to "strive for the eternal maintenance of white supremacy," the unsettled El Pasoan could at least feel he was doing something to meet a growing threat to his community and way of life.[35]

El Paso's racial situation and the unusual problems posed by the city's border location were certainly important in laying the groundwork for the arrival of the Ku Klux Klan, but the case must not be overstated. Although El Paso clearly presented the Klan with an excellent opportunity to play upon racial fears, the local organization, as was true of most Klans across the nation, would primarily address itself to other issues.[36] In examining these issues, however, it should also be borne in mind that racism often permeated the controversies entered into by the El Paso Klan. Indeed, it is important to recall the Pass's unusual racial situation when examining almost any aspect of the city's Klan experience.[37]

If racial problems were not the primary reason that the Invisible Empire found a following in El Paso in 1921, then there was an ample supply of other troubles for the Klan to exploit. As has been related, the Texas Klan was primarily occupied with issues concerning law, order, and social morality. In no other Texas community were these issues of more relevance than they were at the Pass. This was in large part due to the recent enactment of prohibition.

Texas entered the decade of the 1920s staunchly committed to the prohibition of alcohol. In an election held in July 1919, the state's voters had signified their approval of such proscription, providing a public mandate for the passage three months later of the Dean Law, a powerful act which provided for the vigorous punishment of all liquor offenders. At the end of the year, the Dean Law was supplemented by federal legislation, as the 18th Amendment went into effect, ushering in the era of national prohibition.[38]

Due to the fact that it was an urban border community, the Pass was almost uniquely affected by the prohibition of alcohol. Situated as it was next to a "wet" nation where bootlegging operations could be organized without fear of official harassment, the El Paso area was soon filled with hundreds of potential lawbreakers who anticipated a future in smuggling activities. At stake were enormous profits; the simple act of transporting grain alcohol across the border might reap the smuggler a five-hundred-percent profit in good times.[39] And such lawbreaking entailed little risk, as factors of topography, an inadequate number of prohibition agents, and the presence of several good roads leading out from El Paso made the Pass a premier location for the introduction of contraband liquor.[40]

By 1920 the ease with which the prohibition laws could be violated had created great disorder along the border in El Paso. In the summer of that year, a federal marshal noted that, despite the best efforts of the region's prohibition agents, the Pass was under "a veritable reign of crime" that included widespread trafficking in drugs.[41] A few months later the head of the El Paso prohibition district acknowledged that the situation was deteriorating, citing "the great need of additional men" if smuggling was to be contained. By early 1921 at least one federal agent had come to the conclusion that "Enforcement of the prohibition and narcotics laws presents a harder problem in El Paso and this federal district than perhaps any other in the United States."[42]

The problems of prohibition enforcement along the border were keenly felt by the El Paso community. Most traumatic of all was the atmosphere of violence created by the "almost nightly battles between Mexican liquor smugglers and American customs and immigration officers." To one local newspaper it appeared that "The casualties on both sides are greater than in the old days of border lawlessness. The flying bullets . . . recall to El Paso residents the days of revolutionary battles in Juárez."[43]

The struggle became bloodier and bloodier through the early months of 1921. In March a prohibition agent was fatally wounded near El Paso, prompting his district chief to suggest that the military might have to be called in to halt the "army" of smugglers coming from Mexico.[44] Less than three weeks later, two federal agents, Stafford E. Beckett and C. A. (Arch) Wood, were killed while searching for liquor on a Lower Valley ranch.[45] The following month two more prohibition officers were shot, this time near Anthony, New Mexico, where they fell victim to deadly "dum-dum" bullets.[46] Obviously, the liquor smugglers were serious. But federal officers were equally determined, and their efforts produced scores of arrests related to smuggling, bootlegging, and the illegal possession of alcohol. Soon the local federal commissioner's court was hearing a record number of cases, the majority of which involved liquor violations, and the county jail became home for an unprecedented number of new inmates, most of whom had been incarcerated on prohibition charges.[47]

The crowded condition of the county jail in 1921 was not solely the result of El Paso's prohibition woes. The difficulties of enforcing the 18th Amendment had the additional misfortune of coinciding with the phenomenon of a national and statewide crime wave. "There is sweeping over Texas, as never before in her history, a wave of crime," announced Governor Pat N. Neff in February 1921. "Murder, theft, robbery, and hold-ups are hourly occurrences that fill the daily press. . . . Criminals fill the land with terror and make unsafe both life and property."[48] This was certainly true in El Paso, where local newspapers daily revealed a fresh assortment of crimes against persons and property. Much of the problem was caused by recent arrivals, petty criminals and transients from both sides of the border who had been attracted to the Pass by the chaos created by prohibition. "To our city within the past two years there has drifted the filth and offscouring of the whole country," lamented one pastor early in 1921.[49] Included among the undesirables were hundreds of drug addicts who were, according to one federal official, "now living in El Paso for no other reason except that they can go into Mexico and secure their favorite narcotic."[50] The large number of "hop heads," "snow birds," and "drug fiends" produced one of the most serious narcotic problems in the nation. During 1920 and 1921, drug raids in the city resulted in the seizure of thousands of dollars worth of morphine, codeine, cocaine, heroin, and opium.[51]

Narcotic problems, the presence of criminals attracted by liquor smuggling activities, and general lawlessness all combined to make El Paso the scene of continual crime and violence throughout 1921. Burglaries became so rampant that one woman suggested that the city newspapers cease printing society columns because this informed prowlers when homes would be unoccupied. Such fears were probably well founded; by year's end, thieves had set a new record for stealing in El Paso, taking more than half a million dollars in property, including 349 automobiles.[52] In addition to crimes against property, numerous acts of personal violence plagued the city. In one incident, an El Paso real estate broker was shot in the head while he slept.[53] A few months later, an elderly blacksmith was knocked unconscious and viciously pelted with rocks by a gang of Mexican boys.[54] The summer of 1921 proved especially violent and was marked by a series of sensational murders and murder trials, one of which involved the killing of a young woman by a mental defective known as the "moon-eyed moron."[55] Other local women were also the victims of violent crime. In one instance, an El Paso socialite was lured from her home, drugged, gagged, and driven away in a mysterious black automobile before she managed to escape unknown kidnappers.[56] In a separate incident, yet another local woman claimed to have been drugged, after which she was assaulted by a Juárez chauffer.[57] And on and on it went, an almost endless litany of assaults, burglaries, holdups, and murders in El Paso that could not help but fuel emotions of rage and frustration in law-abiding citizens.

Certain residents acted to protect their community. Following the tradition of vigilantism established during the World War, El Paso's American Legion post offered the services of 250 members as reserve policemen who would aid local law officers in "combatting burglars and crime."[58] By this time El Paso Rotarians had already started a cleanup campaign that they hoped would rid the city of "petty grafters, pickpockets, and other undesirables."[59] The local police force also initiated a crackdown on crime, proclaiming a midnight curfew, after which no one could legally walk the streets except for urgent business.[60] But such efforts met with little success, and the wave of lawlessness continued. At times it looked as if El Paso law officers might be overwhelmed. In January two policemen were the victims of assaults by criminals, and a deputy sheriff suffered the indignity of being forcibly relieved of his money, pistol, and deputy's badge.[61] Two months later, an El Paso policeman was also held up, and in following weeks two more police officers were physically attacked, one being struck with a metal pipe.[62] In August, the same month that a police detective was shot in the arm, local officials were moved to comment upon the city's exceptionally large number of "attacks upon officers representing organized society."[63] By this time the most spectacular display of open contempt for El Paso law officers had already taken place when two Mexicans shot and killed Police Chief Harry P. Phoenix.[64] Quite a number of city residents must have agreed with a local minister's assertion that the question, "Shall it be law or chaos [in El Paso]?," had to be decided on shortly.[65]

The exceptional violence of 1921 was upsetting to almost all El Pasoans, but it by no means produced unanimity of opinion as to how the community should react. To many local residents, blame for the crime wave could be placed on the 18th Amendment, a conclusion at which the local newspapers were slowly arriving. Resentment towards both prohibition and prohibitionists was especially strong because city voters had twice rejected the "noble experiment," first in the local option election of 1918, and then in the statewide referendum of 1919.[66] Now El Paso, which had voted to remain "wet," was being forced to bear an unfair share of the problems that derived from prohibition. There was also considerable concern over the heavyhanded tactics of federal prohibition agents. When armed customs men searched his automobile without a search warrant, one local man complained that "Meddlesome officers have to pry into a man's personal affairs these days. A man has no liberty anymore."[67]

If there were those who felt that the increase in crime during the early 1920s signaled the failure of prohibition, there were also those who felt equally strongly that the answer to the problem lay in more vigorous enforcement of the laws. "I fought the saloons before prohibition, and I am going to fight the bootleggers as long as I have breath in my body," declared the Reverend Percy Knickerbocker.[68] Other El Pasoans were also determined to deal forcefully with lawbreakers and those who abetted lawbreaking. As the problems of 1921 unveiled themselves, this attitude hardened in some people into an almost fanatical intolerance that immediately branded all opponents of the 18th Amendment as un-American "anarchists" and "traitors." One local anti-prohibitionist noted the development of this hardline stance, citing the "fanatical attitude taken by the 'Holier Than Thou' class of citizens in regard to prohibition."[69] But in their new determination to uphold law and order and force strict observance of the prohibition statutes, the city's moral reformers found themselves thwarted. This was most glaringly demonstrated during the trial of C. Peter Shearman and three others who were charged with the murders of prohibition agents Stafford E. Beckett and Arch Wood. When a local jury acquitted one defendant and was unable to decide on the guilt of the other three, local prohibitionists were incensed. One El Paso clergyman noted that during the trial a "large part of the crowded [court] room was clearly antagonistic to the prohibition officers," creating an atmosphere that undermined justice. Percy Knickerbocker went even further and flatly declared that the defendants were guilty. "The result of the trial," he announced, "is due to the unpopularity of the prohibition law."[70]

Confronted with considerable public sentiment against the 18th Amendment and finding little satisfaction in the courts, El Paso's moral reformers were also faced with the predicament of receiving little, if any, support from local public officials. The city government was still controlled by the same Democratic machine that had evinced so little enthusiasm for prohibition during the 1918 election. El Paso's law officers were doing the best they could to enforce the law, but were slowly crumbling under a massive tide of brigandage. Worst of all was the attitude of leading businessmen, who seemed determined to make a profit from the unusual situation that prohibition had created at the Pass. And that attitude was closely connected with the touchy matter of the entertainment industry in Juárez, an interesting subject in itself.

If national prohibition had had an exceptionally disturbing impact on the city of El Paso, this impact paled in comparison with what the 18th Amendment had effected across the Rio Grande. As a result of American prohibition, Ciudad Juárez underwent an incredible transformation, from a relatively quiet Mexican town into a gaudy, sinful tourist mecca, a bustling city of over 20,000 residents dedicated to providing thirsty and lustful Americans with whatever they wanted.[71] And the tourists did come. With the cessation of hostilities in Mexico and the advent of prohibition in the United States, Americans began a veritable stampede across the border. Many of these tourists came through El Paso, and during the winter season the city was home for as many as 10,000 visitors a month.[72]

The new flood of tourist dollars was very welcome at the Pass, especially in Juárez, where the recent fighting from the revolution had greatly disrupted the economy. Such prosperity entailed a high cost, however, as Juárez now became almost exclusively dependent on Yankee tourism. Symbolic of this unhealthy trend was the city's main street, which was lined with bars "nearly every twenty feet for six long blocks."[73] In addition to the proliferation of saloons, Juárez was also the scene of widespread vice, most wantonly displayed along the notorious Calle de Diablo, described by one El Paso newspaper as "possibly the most sordid, poverty-stricken, evil-smelling, and uninviting 'red light' district in the world."[74] Many gringo tourists, nonetheless, found the *mexicanas* far from uninviting, as was reflected by Juárez police records that showed that most of the trouble involving Americans in that city was related to women.[75] If the tourist in Juárez managed to steer clear of the prostitutes, there were other sinful pleasures to be discovered. Open gambling was frequently available, although it was occasionally closed down by state and federal authorities.[76] Drugs of all kinds could also be found, and the American addict could choose from a wide selection of narcotics in the city's "drug dens," small rooms filled with "Sloe-eyed women and pasty faced men . . . puffing placidly on amber mouthed pipes."[77]

Saloons, nightclubs, gambling casinos, open prostitution, drug marts — all of these Ciudad Juárez provided in abundance, a brazen citadel of moral horrors in the view of all upright El Pasoans. After having crusaded so long to clean up their own city, the flagrant display of so much sin and decadence just across the river was infuriating to concerned citizens. In the words of one local minister:

> We vote the United States dry, we clean up El Paso, and we think 'now my daughter will never marry a drunkard, my son will never be a gambler,' and the first thing we know, right here at our door is a wide open gambling city and a wide open saloon. And our daughters are going with young men who are drinking and our sons are fast becoming gamblers.[78]

And more than moral issues were involved. The fact that Juárez was an entertainment center meant that an unending assortment of criminals, con men, drug addicts, and alcoholics would be coming through El Paso. "If we get this town full of a low class of people," declared one El Pasoan, "our home-loving husbands will be afraid to leave home at night for fear wife and daughter will be besmirched in their absence."[79]

Those El Pasoans who saw Juárez as being a danger to their community received little comfort throughout 1921. For one thing, it became much easier for both Mexicans and Americans to cross the border. In March the United States government lifted all crossing card and passport restrictions for Americans who desired to enter Mexico, thus nullifying the regulations that had been in effect since the World War.[80] Five months later, an international agreement lifted all passport requirements for Americans and Mexicans living within a forty mile zone on both sides of the border. The only requirement that remained in effect was that residents of the zone procure a border identification card before going across the river, a relatively easy procedure with which more than 33,000 El Paso residents had complied by the end of the year.[81]

With the border more accessible than it had been in years, tourists and El Pasoans alike made greater use of the forbidden attractions of Juárez in 1921. In June a record heat wave sent hundreds of thirsty gringos across the river in search of cool drink, causing Juárez barrooms and cabarets to overflow with visitors.[82] A similar exodus took place in September, as a huge crowd that included 10,000 El Pasoans crossed the border to help celebrate the centenary of Mexican independence.[83] Once again, at year's end, American crowds could be found in Juárez saloons and nightclubs, packing the dancefloors to the extent that the dancers appeared to be engaged in "wrestling matches."[84] Nor did El Pasoans confine their trips to Mexico to special occasions; often families or groups of friends would go to Juárez to imbibe or to dine and imbibe. As one city resident later remembered, there were "better cafés there [in Juárez]; the food was superior and the drinks were good and the hospitality was greater."[85] With inducements such as these, Ciudad Juárez attracted a steady clientele.

The fact that so many El Pasoans could and did go to Juárez to indulge in activities that were illegal in the United States placed unique strains upon moral reformers. Probably nowhere else in the United States was there more opportunity to flout openly the prohibition laws and the entire code of Protestant morality. And in searching for some way to remedy this infuriating situation, El Paso's reformers could anticipate little help from community leaders. What could be expected, for example, from a city administration headed by a mayor who stated: "The most important thing that faces us now is the opening of our trade territory in Mexico."?[86] The attitude of the local business establishment was even more hopeless. "I regard, from several angles, Juárez as El Paso's greatest asset," declared Adolph Schwartz, leading merchant and vice president of the local Chamber of Commerce. Schwartz backed up his statement by noting that Juárez brought conventions to El Paso and attracted the tourist dollars that sustained the local hotel trade and other businesses.[87] R. Burt Orndorff, one of the city's most prominent businessmen, agreed with this assessment and also labeled El Paso's sister city as "our great asset."[88]

The El Paso business community's determination to realize a profit from the liquor and vice in Juárez appalled city residents who believed that moral considerations should take precedence over economic advancement. "I am opposed to making the open conditions of booze, gambling, and licentiousness in Juárez an asset to El Paso in the sense of drawing people here," stated the Reverend Percy Knickerbocker, who later claimed that Juárez was a "menace" to El Paso and that those who defended vice across the river would later regret it. The Reverend Dr. Floyd Poe of the First Presbyterian Church was even more outraged, declaring, "Juárez is doomed! Doomed! Unless licensed sin is banished. It is not my word, but the word of Eternal God."[89]

Poe could perhaps be excused for becoming exercised. Having fought for so long to rid El Paso of gambling, lewd women, and liquor, the spokesmen for morality were now faced with the same problems that were to be found only a streetcar or short automobile ride away. But this did not mean that they were going to forego the effort. By 1921 the moral crusaders were determined to take corrective action and they would brook no interference — not from corrupt politicians, not from the mammon-worshipping business community, not from the "anarchists" and "traitors" who still refused to accept the 18th Amendment. "I'll strike evil wherever it puts up its head, whether that head is made of gold or mud," vowed Percy Knickerbocker. "I'll fight anything that hurts or harms any man, woman or child in El Paso."[90] Notice was thus given that there would be no more compromising with sin, no more toleration of evil.

The presence of an unabashed vice and entertainment industry adjacent to their city, acute problems concerning the enforcement of the prohibition laws, a severe crime wave, and the large number of immigrants arriving during a period of general nativist intolerance were the particularly stressful conditions that El Pasoans faced in 1921 as the Ku Klux Klan spread throughout Texas. Though other American cities might have shared similar problems, the situation at the Pass was especially unsettled, primarily owing to El Paso's location on the border. It should be emphasized that El Paso's problems were very *real*, that the city's troubles were rooted in fact and were not simply the result of paranoid fantasizing by a group of ultramoralistic and reactionary zealots. The increase in crime was real; the presence of exceptional vice in Juárez was real; and the relative flood of Mexican immigrants into the city was equally based in reality. Decent, progressive-minded people, filled with an active concern for the welfare of their community, daily came face to face with these problems and were deeply perturbed. Finding little satisfaction forthcoming from their local governmental and business leaders, there was a growing impulse on their part to take matters into their own hands and set things right. All that remained was to find a suitable means of doing so.

Although El Paso did indeed have its share of troubles in 1921, those problems were manifesting themselves within a rapidly growing community that was becoming increasingly prosperous. That the mood at the Pass was not altogether despairing was reflected by the musing of a local newspaper editor:

El Paso is ever a delight to the confirmed booster. There are so many things hereabouts that stir enthusiasm — climate, business,

past performances, and future prospects. One cannot breathe the
air and absorb the sunshine these January days [of 1921] without
a desire to indulge in superlatives. Almost any time one picks up a
newspaper he will find some new reason for boosting the town.[91]

As the decade of the 1920s unfolded, El Pasoans had much to be both
proud and optimistic about. In an age where growth and prosperity
were practically worshipped, the Pass's advancements during the previous ten years were nothing short of remarkable. The total population
of the city had skyrocketed, climbing from 39,279 in 1910 to over
80,000 by the end of 1921.[92] When this figure was added to the adjacent
populations of Ciudad Juárez and Fort Bliss, El Paso found itself at the
center of a metropolitan community of well over 100,000, by far the
largest urban area for hundreds of miles in any direction.[93]

Accompanying the Pass's population boom was an equally impressive upsurge in business growth. Benefiting from better transportation
systems, the ready financing provided by seven local banks, and the
general rise in the nation's prosperity, El Paso industries increased their
production 450 percent between 1909 and 1919.[94] Other indices of economic growth were also very encouraging. Aggregate city bank clear-
ings had steadily risen, the 1920 figure representing a three-fold increase over the total for 1915. Housing construction was booming and
building permits were granted each month for thousands of dollars
worth of new residential property. The first half of 1921 was an exceptionally prosperous period: the total value of local bank deposits was
up, and the city's wholesale and shipping businesses were operating on
a scale larger than ever before, particularly in the category of exports
to Mexico. It appeared certain that El Paso would make good on its
claim of being "The Wonder City of the Southwest."[95]

As a rapidly growing urban community, the Pass shared fully in the
dramatic social changes that swept across the nation during the years
after World War I. Though El Paso may have earlier conjured up a
"wild-west" image in the minds of Americans in other parts of the
country, this was no longer the case, as motion pictures, phonograph
records, newspapers, magazines, and thousands of new residents and
visitors helped to bring the emerging Jazz Age to the Southwest. By
1919 El Pasoans could purchase locally a recording of "Yelping Hound
Blues," by the Louisiana Five Jazz Orchestra, and the following year
the Rialto and Wigwam theaters offered moviegoers films such as *Why
Change Your Wife?* and *The Tiger Girl*, "the story of a man who lis-

tened to a siren's song."[96] At the same time, both of El Paso's newspapers consistently headlined spectacular divorce cases and relayed the latest gossip from Hollywood, as well as thoroughly informing El Pasoans about the revolution in women's fashions.

Not only were El Paso residents fully aware and interested in the social changes that were transpiring across the country; they also shared in the technological developments that had helped bring about those changes. By 1921 El Paso was in large part a community on wheels, with nearly 10,000 motor vehicles traveling along the city's eighty-five miles of paved streets.[97] Home for more than thirty car dealerships, the city was especially well-stocked with automobiles, due to its role as a major railroad shipping center.[98] In addition to motor vehicles, the latest in domestic appliances were available in the city, including electric washers, irons, curling irons, hair dryers, heaters, toasters, percolators, grills, ranges, and vacuum cleaners.[99] The impact of modern film technology was also strongly felt in El Paso, where nineteen movie theaters displayed the cinematic talents of Clara Bow, Mary Pickford, Charlie Chaplin, Fatty Arbuckle, and a seemingly limitless assortment of sultry vamps.[100]

As throughout the rest of the United States, the heady combination of the automobile, motion pictures, a sensational press, and the liberation of the American woman from the drudgery of unrelieved domestic chores produced unsettling results. Soon, local school girls were being sent home from classes due to dress code violations that included "Bobbed hair and vampire dresses, manufactured curls and overdone fluffy frocks." In 1921 a local policewoman noted that, although most El Paso girls avoided the more daring fashions, she still on occasion found "girls, usually 17 or 18 years old, attending public dances and wearing rolled down stockings and extremely short skirts."[101] A considerable number of the mothers and older sisters of these girls proved to be no more resistant to modern trends. "Bobbed hair may be a fad, but it is still in fashion," remarked a local barber in late 1921. "We trimmed the hair of a woman here the other day who must have been 45 years old. Her hair was gray."[102] By this time El Pasoans had already been given the incredible news that three hundred local women had had their little toes amputated just in order to wear the latest style in small shoes.[103] Women at the Pass engaged in other shocking behavior: they gambled in Juárez, drank to excess alongside male companions, and proved more willing than ever to get divorced.[104] Many females also began to smoke during the 1920s, as was observed by a city tobacco vendor who cited "an unprecedented increase in the number of sales of cigarets [sic] to women," among whom he included "working women, society girls, and housewives."[105]

The new behavior of American women after World War I was very upsetting to many El Pasoans who had been raised to expect certain strict standards of deportment from the fair sex. To the middle and older generations, "Women were the guardians of morality; they were made of finer stuff than men and were expected to act accordingly."[106] As these Victorian values began to crumble, parents became apprehensive as to the type of world in which their daughters were being raised. The situation appeared especially perilous in El Paso, where unbridled sin of all kinds was only a joyride away, in Mexico. In order to keep local adolescents from straying onto the wayward path, border crossing cards were not issued unless the applicant was at least twenty-one years of age or had the approval of his or her parents. As one official noted in the case of the many underaged girls who applied for cards: "We simply cannot issue these 'young things' permission to visit Juárez, some of whom would cross the river against their parents' consent."[107] Nevertheless, some young girls did make it across the river, and God-fearing El Pasoans could only shudder when they read about the mother of "one of El Paso's fairest debutantes" searching Juárez "dens" for a daughter fallen victim to "the bright lights of the halfworld — the gay orchard of forbidden fruit and stolen pleasures."[108]

The young men in El Paso could also, and perhaps more easily stumble into trouble during the 1920s. To the weak and dissolute, the widespread availability of alcohol and drugs offered a quick trip to perdition, and, on at least one occasion, local high school boys were discovered drunk in Juárez.[109] The old problem of social diseases, that had been so highly publicized during the war, was still a very real threat, especially during the era that was prior to the discovery of penicillin. Indeed, any type of sexual encounter seemed threatening with the spectre of the conniving vamp haunting the national psyche. It was not surprising that one local minister chose to describe sin as "a beautiful woman, with all the allurements, grace, and attractiveness of a siren, whose call has lured men to ruin and death through all time.."[110]

Of course, not all of the young people in the 1920s were flappers, hellraisers, or weakminded crowd followers. This was particularly true in a basically conservative and mildly provincial community like El Paso. One city resident who came of age in this period later recalled that the El Paso youth of his generation drank sparingly and rarely abandoned the prevailing moral code.[111] But to the unnerved older generation, there was enough flouting of traditional standards to give the distinct impression that (in the words of a local minister) "The world is going to the devil."[112] To the city's spokesmen of morality, almost every aspect of modern life seemed threatening. "The automobile of today," declared the Reverend Percy Knickerbocker in 1920, "is replacing the red light district of yesterday."[113] That same year, the Reverend George McCall of the Central Baptist Church included public dance halls and movie theaters in his enumeration of the "cesspools of El Paso."[114] In following months the city's clergymen continued to spout invective at alarming trends. Evangelist Jack Linn informed El Pasoans in March 1921 that men and women who used tobacco were "by their example and influence sending others to hell."[115] The pastor of the Government Hills Baptist Church asserted a few weeks later that "the modern dance is sending more souls to hell than ever."[116] Early in June a visiting Methodist dignitary announced that motion pictures were leading to immorality among children and promoting the current trend towards immodest clothing.[117] Everywhere, El Pasoans seemed to be surrounded by invitations to damnation. To those who were preoccupied with moral issues, life had never been so fraught with peril.

By the summer of 1921 the groundwork had been laid in El Paso for an auspicious reception for the Ku Klux Klan. Suffering from very real and uniquely severe problems of crime and vice, serving as the site of increasing foreign immigration, and beset by the unsettling social developments that were typical of urban America during the 1920s, the Pass was an ideal location for the expansion of the Invisible Empire. In retrospect, it is not so surprising that the Ku Klux Klan came and established itself in El Paso, as it is that the organization was fated to be decisively rejected.

Exactly when the Ku Klux Klan arrived in El Paso is not clear. As early as May 1921, however, there was a Klan recruiter in the city, a certain C. M. Kellogg. Kellogg set up headquarters in the Sheldon Hotel, where he held numerous "mysterious conferences" and received a large number of phone calls.[118] It was later reported in the *New York World*'s exposé of the Ku Klux Klan that Kellogg was the "King Kleagle" for the "realm" of New Mexico.[119] Whether Kellogg recruited Klan members in El Paso is unknown, but the fact that he operated out of the city for a while tends to direct speculation in that direction.

Throughout the summer of 1921 there was great interest in El Paso as to whether a branch of the Ku Klux Klan had been or would be orga-

nized in the city. Articles concerning the activities of the Klan in other
parts of the state and nation frequented the pages of the local newspapers, and the KKK was a topic of lively discussion. As in other Texas
communities, uncertainty as to whether the Invisible Empire had arrived produced unsavory pranks. In July, Ciro M. Garcia, an unem-
ployed boilermaker, received a note that stated: "Ku Klux Klan. Watch
Out! Warning! I will get you or your wife or child."[120] A few weeks
later, Herbert Strasser, a Canadian who worked as a mechanic in a filling station, received two phone calls from a man who warned him to
"get out of town before tomorrow afternoon, or the Ku Klux will be
after you."[121]

Recognizing that anonymous threats would only be but one of the
many dangers posed by the existence of a local society of disguised vigilantes, certain influential El Pasoans prepared to take a stand against
the Klan in 1921. Chief among the enemies of the Klan was James
Black, editor of the *El Paso Times*, who was to prove to be unswerving
in his deep and abiding hatred of the KKK. Through the medium of his
newspaper Black lashed out strongly and early at the Klan, denouncing
its members as "anarchists and public enemies" who "usurp the purpose
of the state."[122] The *Times'* attitude was shared by many local officials,
especially the city's highest-ranking law officers. "The Ku Klux Klan, at
its best, is a form of mob rule," declared Claud T. Smith, captain of city
detectives, in July 1921.[123] Police Chief Peyton J. Edwards agreed,
promising to "do all that is within my power to suppress the activities
of the Ku Klux Klan or any other secret order that would attempt to
mete out punishment to citizens of El Paso."[124] County Sheriff Seth B.
Orndorff was also quick (at least initially) to take a strong and uncompromising stand against the KKK.[125]

Less vehement in its opposition to the Ku Klux Klan was the *El Paso
Herald*. The *Herald*, under publisher Hughes D. (H. D.) Slater, was
staunchly pro-Republican and had crusaded for local reform for decades.[126] Though it gave sporadic lip service to denouncing the Klan, the
newspaper also displayed a large degree of understanding as to why
Texans were becoming Klansmen:

> . . . while condeming mob activities such as these, one wonders
> whether something is the matter with the laws or the courts,
> court procedures, officers or juries in these places where men have
> so little confidence in them that they go to the trouble of consti-

tuting themselves vigilantes and take whatever risks there may be in so doing.

In investigating the lawlessness of the masked bands, it would be well, perhaps, to look into the administration of law by its legally constituted agents of enforcement.[127]

But though the *Herald* might sympathize with some of the aims of the Klan, the paper simply could not accept the organization's methods. H. D. Slater was a longtime city resident who found the order's secrecy repugnant and cowardly. In his view, the KKK failed to meet the southwestern standards of manliness: "The old-time vigilantes of the west did not disguise themselves or attempt concealment; they had ugly work to do but they performed it as men."[128]

Despite the scorn directed at it by the city's newspapers and law enforcement officials, the Ku Klux Klan went about busily recruiting members in El Paso during the late summer of 1921. The community proved receptive, and in early September it was announced by the *Herald* that "A Klan has been organized in El Paso, but it has not as yet made any public announcement of its existence, nor has it yet held a parade of any sort, as in some cities where it has been found."[129] Credit for the organization of the local Klan was given to an unknown outsider who had subsequently left town.[130]

In a pattern typical of most other Texas Klans, the El Paso chapter of the Invisible Empire directed much of its early recruiting efforts towards prominent men in the community. The sales pitch varied from person to person. County Judge Ed B. McClintock, who refused to join, was approached by a "soft-pedalling kind of man" who declined to state which organization he represented — only that it was "an American secret society for the assistance of law enforcement agencies." The Klan recruiter told McClintock that many of the judge's best friends had joined the society, and he stressed the patriotic aspect of the organization. "He was strong on the 'American' part of it," recalled McClintock.[131] A more straight-forward approach was tried on Acting Mayor R. C. Semple: "This man came into my office and told me he would like to have me become a member of the organization [Ku Klux Klan]. When I declined, he walked out without further conversation." Almost all of the city council members received similar offers, and at least one decided to join.[132] Dr. Herbert E. Stevenson, post commander of the American Legion, was the object of more subtle techniques and could only say that he believed that he had been "felt out" for membership.[133]

In the midst of its recruiting drive, the Ku Klux Klan received a firm rebuff from city officials. On September 15, as rumors began to circulate that the fledgling El Paso Klan might attempt to parade, the city council approved an ordinance prohibiting "assemblages, parades and processions of masked people within the city of El Paso. . . ." The only council member to vote against the ordinance was William T. Griffith, who believed the anti-Klan law would be declared unconstitutional, an assessment with which the city attorney concurred a week later.[134] On September 29, however, a substitute ordinance that imposed a permit requirement for all parades in El Paso was passed unanimously. Under the new law, at least three responsible people would have to file for the parade permit. Dr. J. Hal Gambrell, a reserve army officer and member of the school board, attended the council meeting at which the ordinance was passed and protested that it restricted activities such as military troop movements and spontaneous parades by high school students. City Attorney Victor Moore admitted that the ordinance was broad in scope but said that the law should not be changed "if the city wanted to get the organization it was after."[135]

The city government moved quickly to squelch the possibility of any public demonstration by the local Klan, but the mere fact that the KKK had organized in El Paso angered the society's enemies. Included in this group was Sheriff Orndorff, who had vowed to arrest parading Klansmen even in the absence of a city parade ordinance. Asked by a reporter if he had been asked to join the Klan, Orndorff said no, but if he should be he would "take that fellow's name and address down and have him under surveillance for a long while."[136] El Paso Times editor James Black was even more offended by the arrival of the Klan at the Pass, and warned the city's Klansmen that if they had paraded "it is quite certain some of the paraders would have been identified, even though it were necessary to identify their bodies in the morgue."[137] In subsequent issues of the Times, Black called for "able-bodied citizens" to join with authorities in halting any Klan demonstration, and a reporter for the paper speculated that "the Ku Klux Klan would probably be on the receiving end of any barrage that took place beween civilians and officers here."[138] Implicit in almost all the Times' editorials was the threat of violence if the local Klan made a public appearance. One longtime city resident who gave full support to this belligerent stance was Judge Walter D. Howe of the 34th district court, who pointedly informed a new grand jury a few weeks later that an individual had the right to use homicide in defending himself from disguised parties.[139] El

Pasoan W. L. Rider was also angered by the formation of a local branch of the Klan and dubbed the group the "Kowardly Kurs Klan." "When it comes to a showdown, these masked pharisees will learn that the punishment of delinquents is everybody's business," declared Rider, "and that the sane majority of our citizens will not broach any interference with the orderly processes of law and justice. We are not in the bigoted belt."[140]

Although many El Pasoans were disturbed by the presence of the Ku Klux Klan in their community, there was a significant number of city residents who did not see what the big furor was all about. To those persons already at odds with the local establishment's handling of El Paso's problems, the outcry against the Klan probably made the KKK that much more attractive. The fact that the Texas legislature had decided not to take any action against the Klan seemed to have proved that the organization was not overtly dangerous.[141] The apprehensions that remained were possibly eased in August when the *Herald* printed a full page message from Imperial Wizard Simmons that claimed that there was nothing in the Klan constitution that "any honorable, law-abiding, conscientious, clean-hearted and pure-spirited, hundred percent American could not subscribe to and swear to uphold."[142] County Attorney Will H. Pelphrey shared this opinion and stated: "I have seen nothing in the published oath of the Ku Klux that I think a good citizen could not take."[143] Certain civic groups also remained open-minded on the subject of the Klan, including El Paso's American Legion post, which decided to take no official position on the KKK pending its future actions.[144] That local Protestant churches had remained especially mute was pointed out in October by Rabbi Martin Zielonka, who noted that he had "failed to see in print a single line from a Protestant pastor of this city against this organization [the KKK] or its claims to represent Protestant Christianity."[145]

The failure of El Paso to present a solid front against the Ku Klux Klan and the nature of the troublesome problems facing the community combined to allow a thriving branch of the KKK to be established at the Pass. By late September there were more than three hundred Klansmen in the city and the number was growing.[146] Little is known about the actual operation of the group or its membership at this time, but it can be reasonably speculated that much of the local Klan's recruiting was now done through contacts in the city's fraternal societies, particularly the Masons and the Shriners.[147] Additionally, it is known that the group desired to be respectable. Towards this end, a Houston Klan representative was brought to the city to explain the purposes of the organization to city officials. The representative asserted that the Klan was nothing more than a civic group that provided "moral support for officials who were more or less bound by political environments."[148] These assurances were somewhat undercut in early October when County Attorney Pelphrey announced that he had received a threatening note signed "K. K. K." that demanded that he resign his office. A few days later, Leandro Nielo, an employee of the Mexican customs house in Juárez, was also threatened in a letter and warned to "leave the country [presumably the United States] at once." The letter was signed "Ku Klux Klan" and bore a fake postal mark. These notes were probably not authentic but they demonstrated, nonetheless, the problems that the presence of the Klan was bringing to the community.[149]

At the same time that the Klan was establishing itself in El Paso, the entire Invisible Empire was fast becoming a national sensation. In early October 1921, the Congressional House Rules Committee held public hearings on the Ku Klux Klan, during which Imperial Wizard Simmons was called to testify. Though his testimony was marked by considerable obfuscation and cheap theatrics. Simmons emerged from the hostile questioning in surprisingly good form, and in subsequent months the Congress failed to take any action concerning the Klan.[150]

In El Paso the new nationwide interest in the Invisible Empire generated by the Congressional hearings supplemented the already considerable excitement over the local chapter of the order. That El Pasoans had the Ku Klux Klan on their minds expressed itself in curious ways throughout late 1921. In September the El Paso Salesmanship Club held a parody of the "Coo Coo Clan" during which six robed men warned members to "put El Paso first."[151] A few weeks later, the day after Halloween, the *Herald* noted that some local boys had costumed themselves as Klansmen.[152] In November, Schumann Photo Shop ran an advertisement headed by a large "K. K. K." The ad explained that the K's stood for "Kodak Kan Katch'em."[153] Even the *El Paso Times* could not resist mentioning the Klan in its advertising: "Why run your business like a Ku Klux Klan? Why shroud it in mystery? . . . That's exactly what you are doing if you don't advertise."[154] Similarly, in December, five sheet-attired horsemen paraded down Montana Avenue as part of a recruiting stunt for the Eighth Cavalry at Fort Bliss. Each of the robes was emblazoned with a red "K. K. K.", which the Fort Bliss commandant later explained stood for "Keep Khaki Kicking."[155]

Amid the surge of local interest in the Ku Klux Klan, the El Paso chapter of the Invisible Empire decided in early November to make its first public announcement. In identical letters sent to the *Times* and *Herald*, the Klan announced that it had been organized and chartered four months before and had recently been "quietly gathering information for future reference." The letters denied that the Ku Klux Klan was racist, religiously intolerant, or desired to serve as a "moral correction agency." Rather the local Klan asserted that it was composed of "decent, respectable American citizens" from "practically every walk of life," whose sole purpose was "to make El Paso a better and cleaner city . . . a better place in which to live and rear our children, in which purpose we feel we will receive the cooperation of all good citizens." The letters were signed "Frontier Klan No. 100, Knights of the Ku Klux Klan" and were affixed with a Klan seal.[156]

Enemies of the local Klan remained unimpressed by the group's temperate announcement of its goals in El Paso. "Like all associations of bigotry, its aims are clothed in fair words," warned the *Times*. When subsequent letters from the KKK were sent to the *Times*, the paper refused to print them, requesting that "the Klan Klopper or whatever its treasurer is called, please get our rate list hereafter and inclose checks with future communications. . . ."[157] The *El Paso Herald* proved a bit more accommodating than the *Times* and printed one more letter from Frontier Klan No. 100. In this letter the Klan listed problems in the community that the organization felt needed immediate attention:

1. The running openly of a large number of houses of prostitution.

2. Approximately 500 women of immoral character on the streets, and some of them residing in our best residential districts, openly plying their trade.

3. Approximately 1000 males here being supported by the above mentioned females.

4. Automobile thefts averaging nearly one each day. On account of such condition the automobile insurance companies have nearly doubled their rates; some of them have withdrawn from the city entirely and the others have threatened to do so, leaving car owners without protection whatever.

5. Burglaries of private residences are of such frequent occurrence and committed with such boldness as to put many good people

in constant fear, and to the extent that insurance companies have nearly doubled rates covering these risks.

6. The United States government maintains, at great expense, the largest force of prohibition enforcement officers on the border, because smugglers, bootleggers, highjackers, and confidence men without number have made El Paso their headquarters.

At the end of the letter the Klan struck its first ominous note, stating that "we expect to see that our fair city is rid of these cancers. How? That is our business." Once again the letter bore the official seal of Frontier Klan No. 100.[158]

After printing the second Klan message, the *Herald* declined to publish anymore letters from the organization. In following days the *Herald* letter column bore the note: "No attention is paid to anonymous letters. Editor." H. D. Slater had no intention of allowing his paper to become the publicity organ of the local Klan.[159]

Deprived of an outlet for its views in the local press, Frontier Klan No. 100 decided to demonstrate its respectability in other ways. Accordingly, on November 10, the organization donated fifty dollars to the local Associated Charities fund drive. Six days later, however, the gift was rejected and returned to the post office to be claimed. The Klan did not take kindly to this rebuff and accused the Associated Charities of taking money "from gamblers and other vicious characters."[160] An unsigned letter to Dr. W. Launcelot Brown, director of the Associated Charities, warned that Klansmen intended to boycott the association's annual charity ball in late November:

> Folks have concluded you don't need money and a shower of tick-ets [for the ball] is being returned. Glad you came out in the open. We are always glad to know who are our friends, our enemies likewise.[161]

The feud between the Associated Charities and the local Klan delighted the *El Paso Times*, which hoped that a successful charity ball would humiliate Frontier Klan No. 100. Unfortunately for the *Times*, events did not work out this way. The day after the ball, editor James Black made reference to those who "semi-apologize" for the Klan, and he later threatened that if the local Klan proved violent, his newspaper would be forced to draw attention to their comments.[162] What had happened at the ball was not made clear, but evidently some prominent El Pasoans had openly defended the Invisible Empire.

At the same time that it was squabbling with the Associated Charities, Frontier Klan No. 100 made a bold move to ally itself with El Paso's Protestant clergymen. "We have planned a great mass attack on his satanic majesty," announced the Klan in a letter sent out to several local ministers. Assuring the clergymen of "the support of worthy citizens," the Klan called for the city's pastors to devote one Sunday to urging a new moral cleanup campaign in El Paso. Special mention was made of the corrupting influence of motion pictures in the community.[163]

The Klan's open appeal to El Paso's Protestant men of the cloth met with mixed success. The Reverend Dr. Fuller Swift of St. Clement's Episcopal Church turned down Frontier Klan No. 100's overtures, stating in a public letter that he was inclined to agree with Judge Howe's opinion of the KKK. Dr. Swift did admit, however, that he believed that some of his friends were Klansmen.[164] Other local ministers proved more receptive to the Klan's appeal. The Reverend Dr. Floyd Poe of the First Presbyterian Church stated, soon after receiving his letter, that "It is refreshing, quite so, to find the Ku Klux Klan interested in a better El Paso." Two weeks later, Poe was even more impressed by the Klan and announced to his congregation: "The Ku Klux Klan is a mighty engine and it is on the right track. We like its destination. . . . I want right now to declare myself in sympathy with the purposes of the Ku Klux Klan as published in El Paso."[165] The Reverend Percy Knickerbocker also spoke well of the Klan's aims, and stated in a sermon at Trinity Methodist Church: "I am not a Ku Kluxer, but if the Klan wants to see decency and righteousness enthroned, why raise such a muss about the Klan?"[166] A fellow Methodist of Knickerbocker's, the Reverend Henry Van Valkenburgh of the First Methodist Church, echoed these sentiments and declared that he was "not on the warpath against the Ku Klux Klan as long as it stands for decent principles."[167]

As El Paso entered the final weeks of 1921, both Frontier Klan No. 100 and many of the city's Protestant ministers were marching to the same tune. This new moral alliance, informal though it was, was fully felt by the community. By year's end, quiet pressure was being exerted in El Paso to close the international bridge at an earlier hour. In connection with this pressure, the *Times* noted that "hidden interests have been at work in a small way in our community against any attempt at better understanding between the citizens of Juárez and El Paso."[168] At the same time, as will be discussed later, religious tensions in the city were reaching unprecedented heights. The forces of intolerance had been let loose, and there was no telling where this would lead.

By 1922 it appeared to many El Pasoans that local Klansmen were respectable and not subject to the violent tendencies of their east Texas brethren. The local KKK was being praised from Protestant pulpits and had initiated a new cleanup campaign. Klan charges that the city was a moral disgrace seemed confirmed in February 1922, when a team of federal hygiene inspectors declared El Paso the "most corrupt city" in the Eighth Army Corps area.[169] Established civic groups had already begun to jump on the cleanup bandwagon. In January 1922 the Chamber of Commerce was leading a drive to bar minors from Juárez's saloons.[170] A month earlier, El Paso club women declared "war on jazz" and vowed to swing public sentiment against it.[171] In early 1922 Chief of Police Edwards was appointed the city's literary expert in order to protect El Paso youngsters from "immoral literature."[172] The moral crusaders were out in droves again, but this time with a new twist. Beside them marched Knights of the Invisible Empire.

Conclusion: There is nothing remarkable in the fact that the Ku Klux Klan managed to establish itself in El Paso. Despite the region's tradition of tolerance in regard to racial and moral matters, events of the past ten years had strained El Paso, making it in many ways an ideal location for the expansion of the Invisible Empire. Nevertheless, the appearance of the Klan almost instantly divided the community. Most vehement in their stand against the hooded order were members of the entrenched political establishment (who moved quickly to dissuade the KKK from any public demonstrations), the media voice for these politicians and leading businessmen, the *El Paso Times*, and long-time southwesterners who were repelled by the Klan's secrecy and methods. Thus, from the beginning, Frontier Klan No. 100 was forced to assume the mantle of insurgency; the organization would prove most attractive to those citizens who were unhappy with the management of local affairs.

CHAPTER 5

The Klan Triumphant –
Part One

vents in the national headquarters of the Invisible Empire
were a vital influence in the course of Frontier Klan No.
100. By late 1921 considerable in-house opposition had developed to Imperial Wizard Simmons, who was being variously condemned for heavy drinking, financial ineptitude,
and an unswerving defense of Edward Young Clarke and Elizabeth Tyler in the aftermath of a morals scandal. Simmons managed to retain
control of the Klan for several more months, but in May 1922, worn
down by the endless squabbling in his Atlanta headquarters, the ex-
hausted Imperial Wizard took a six-month vacation. During Simmons'
absence, control was seized by a group committed to a drastic change
in direction.[1]

Leader of the coterie was a successful Dallas dentist, Hiram Wesley
Evans. A flashy dresser and an impressive speaker, Evans had quickly
risen through the ranks of the hierarchy, holding high office in Dallas

Klan No. 66 and the "realm" of Texas, before being appointed to the position of Imperial Kligrapp (national Klan secretary).[2] Once ensconced in Atlanta, Evans placed himself at the head of the anti-Simmons faction and began the deft political maneuvering that eventually enabled him to replace Simmons.[3]

Hiram Wesley Evans' ascendency signaled a redirection toward politics. In line with his intent to shape the Invisible Empire into "a great militant political organization," he schemed to shuttle Klan funds back to candidates in his home state.[4] Beyond the mere acquisition of power, the Klan's involvement in Texas politics was to serve another purpose. Throughout 1921 the Texas Klan had proved exceedingly violent; in one six-month period there had been forty-three reported tar-and-feather "parties" and the entire year had produced scores of assaults, beatings, and violent threats. At times there was no doubt as to the source of the violence, as in an incident where the initials "K. K. K." had been branded into the forehead of a Negro bellhop.[5] Although his own hands were by no means clean, Evans understood that such outrages must cease. It was his hope that the movement into politics would serve to moderate violent impulses.[6]

Even without the change in the national headquarters, it seems probable that the KKK would have been drawn (almost inevitably) into politics. As a leading historian noted: "The character of the Klan, with its unified membership and revivalistic spirit, bred political ambitions and made the entrance of the organization into politics seemingly inescapable."[7] In addition, the KKK's recruiting among elected officials, lawyers, and other prominent citizens brought many politicians into its ranks. An El Pasoan later recalled that the Klan "attracted a lot of people who liked to be joiners, and who thought they would get some political backing out of it. . . . Certain individuals saw a chance to get a power group behind them out of the Klan."[8] In fact, even before the shift in the national Klan, Frontier Klan No. 100 had decided to involve itself in El Paso elections. As the entire KKK became more involved in political matters, the course taken by the local Klan received the full blessing and support of the national organization. Thus, throughout 1922, El Paso was confronted by an increasingly politicized Klan which issued forth to battle the entrenched establishment.

Fundamental to any understanding of El Paso politics in 1922 is a recognition of the changes at that time in the local electorate. To a large extent these derived from the impact that the Mexican Revolution and World War I had had upon the Pass.

Probably the most important trend in El Paso politics in the early 1920s was the declining importance of the Mexican vote. As racial resentments had intensified during the revolutionary period and the patriotism of local Hispanics was frequently impugned, El Paso politicians came to the realization that any candidate who used the Mexican vote as his primary power base was courting disaster. Such had been the case in the mayoral election of 1915, which pitted incumbent Mayor Charles E. Kelly, leader of the "Ring," against self-styled reformer Tom Lea. Advocating the removal of undesirable Mexicans from El Paso, Lea carried the Anglo precincts north of the railroad tracks and won.[9] When Lea declined to run for re-election two years later, a decision he credited to "a lot of yapping coyotes at your heels all the time," the city's brief flirtation with reform was over. However, the new Ring that came to power under Mayor Charles Davis had learned a valuable lesson and was reluctant to rely too heavily on the Latin vote.[10] With the approach of war and the accompanying spirit of superpatriotism, even El Paso politicians felt obligated to support moves to "Americanize" the electorate. Indeed, local state representatives Robert Ewing (R. E.) Thomason and Richard M. Dudley were at the forefront in sponsoring a state constitutional amendment that would bar aliens from voting. Dudley approvingly observed that "El Paso has had enough of the practice that is resorted to in the cities along the border, and especially in El Paso, [whereby] Mexicans are voted in herds."[11] It was not until 1921 that the new exclusion became law, but by then a rough consensus in favor of such a move had emerged among local Anglo leaders. The *El Paso Times*, firm supporter of the Davis machine, endorsed the change, citing the "many scandals and abuses . . . in the border communities where people from across the line were 'planted,' often in numbers sufficient to sway elections."[12]

By 1922 the El Paso electorate was disproportionately Anglo. Of the 19,040 residents paying poll taxes for that year, nearly 15,000 were Anglo.[13] A majority of these resided north of the railroads that bisected the city, many having recently purchased homes in the expanding suburban additions. It is important to note that most of these were new arrivals who had migrated to the Pass within the previous decade. In 1910 there were probably only slightly more than 10,000 native-born Anglos in El Paso (among a total population of nearly 40,000). Ten years later, the Anglos exceeded 30,000 and the numbers were rapidly increasing. When deaths and departures from the city are taken into consideration, it can be seen that a very large majority of the adult resident

Anglo population in 1922 had arrived after 1910.[14] As had been noted, this was a period marked by continual tensions that stood in sharp contrast to earlier relaxed and tolerant traditions. It was predictable that this electorate would be less culturally and racially accommodative than earlier electorates.

Contributing to the intolerance was the fact that many of the Anglo newcomers were natives of the southern states. The exact percentage of southern migrants cannot yet be determined (since the unpublished 1920 manuscript census schedules remain confidential), but the electorate's general preference for the Democratic party, the large memberships of the city's southern Protestant churches, and such census data as has been made available, leave little doubt that a large proportion of the new arrivals had originally come from the South.[15] Having only recently arrived, these residents were naturally imbued with their region's special outlooks and preferences in religion, morality, and race. It can be reasonably speculated that, because of their southern origins, this group was especially susceptible to Klan overtures.[16]

Although the local Anglo population was characterized by close ties to southern culture, this did not signify that they were typical southerners. For one thing, El Paso Anglos were usually members of the middle class. One study has estimated that perhaps as much as two-thirds of all non-Spanish-surnamed workers in El Paso in 1920 were white collar employees; only slightly more than three percent of this group were unskilled laborers or menial workers.[17] The heavily middle-class nature of the Anglo population was a direct result of the Pass economy, with its vast supply of cheap Mexican labor that squeezed whites out of the lower-class job market. Consequently, El Paso Anglos were an exceptionally affluent group that included unusually high percentages of professionals, businessmen, and clerical workers. Due to their above-average education and social standing, these residents were generally averse to southern-style nightriding and lynching. Many were married, the parents of children, and deeply interested in the type of community in which their progeny would grow up. Most would have described themselves as "progressives," or at least as believers in fair elections, good schools, and civic improvements.[18] Upon arriving in El Paso, they found much that worried them: a large non-white population who seemed ready to plunge the city into bloodshed; local officials who utilized illegal alien votes; open and bloody defiance of prohibition laws; a Godless entertainment mecca within sight across the river. Spurred by the tradition of civic activism that had intensified

during the war years, and confident in the new strength of their numbers, recently arrived Anglos were determined to play a dominant role
in local affairs and thereby correct these problems.

Another change in the El Paso electorate must not be overlooked. In
June 1919 the Texas legislature ratified the 19th Amendment, which
provided for the enfranchisement of women. The following year, the
amendment became national law and women took their place as full-
fledged members of the electorate.[19] It was commonly hoped and expected that woman suffrage would inaugurate a new enlightened spirit
in politics. One southern woman stated that through female suffrage,
"The ideals of democracy and of social and human welfare will un-
doubtedly receive a great impetus."[20] Of course, this expectation
proved to be largely unfounded. Among the major disappointments
was the fact that many women did not exercise their new entitlement.
Of the 12,238 El Pasoans who paid their poll taxes in 1921, for example,
only 2,816 were women. Noting the low turnout, the *Times* regarded
this as "the cause of no little amazement, to say nothing of disappointment. . . ."[21] Moreover, it was overly optimistic to presume that women would prove less susceptible to political passions and prejudices
than men. This was especially true at the Pass, where women had long
lived under particularly stressful conditions.

Life in El Paso had never been easy for Anglo women. Widespread
vice and violence had marred local society throughout its history; the
weather was extremely harsh at times, and geographic isolation and
economic backwardness required that women often forego refinements
that were customary elsewhere. The Pass's peculiar biracialism was
also disturbing to many local women, especially those arriving from
the South. In articulating her feelings concerning the Mexican population, one El Pasoan averred in 1911 that ". . . I would prefer sitting on
top of a [street] car rather than sit or stand by them [Mexicans] for, being from the South, I am not used to such close contact with this disturbing element."[22] In the ensuing decade, as racial resentments resulting from the Mexican Revolution swept over the city, other Anglo women acknowledged similar misgivings. Julia A. Sharp, a society reporter for the *El Paso Times*, objected to donations of baby clothes to Mexican refugees, insisting that charity efforts should be reserved for the
"worthy poor of El Paso," such as the "American women [who had]
come out of Mexico, with only the clothes on their backs. . . ."[23] Another El Paso woman described Mexicans as a "disturbing element"
who laughed behind the backs of American soldiers and customs

officials, but who were nevertheless happy to "live here and pander off the American people."[24] Still another female El Pasoan was persuaded that "the beautiful quality of gratitude is something left entirely out of the character of the Mexican" and lamented that "our sidewalks, streets, amusement places, and street cars [are] thronged with [Mexicans] to overflowing, to the discomfort of every good citizen."[25]

Although most El Paso women had become less outspoken in demeaning the local Mexican population by 1920, this did not mean that they had become a force for racial tolerance. Just as was the case for Anglo males, most Anglo women were recent arrivals at the Pass, and many were from the South. With their male counterparts, they had experienced the disturbing impact of the Mexican Revolution and had actively participated in homefront activities during World War I. The advent of the "Roaring Twenties" provided El Paso women additional causes for concern. Chief among these was a new social morality that challenged Victorian values to which most older women were committed. As hemlines were raised and jazz music began to blare, many grew increasingly apprehensive, particularly those with children to rear. The presence of nearby Juárez and a wave of postwar lawlessness did nothing to lessen the uneasiness. Partly because of these stresses — almost surely — local women at times behaved in boorish and bizarre ways. One El Paso girl complained in 1921 that local females were "meddlesome, jealous of each other, and treacherous."[26] A member of the Salvation Army held a similar view, commenting that "Women are relentless in passing judgement on the guilt of their own sex. Their sympathy for one another is very rare and they are absolutely merciless in their criticisms of one another."[27] A local waitress asserted that a woman customer was typically less polite than men and quick to "protest with a knife and a clinking glass if you don't report to her table at once."[28] Similarly, an El Paso policeman noted that men were generally more careful and courteous when driving automobiles than were women.[29] On occasion, local women even resorted to aggressive physical violence. In one incident, the spouse of a prominent businessman assaulted a rival for her husband's affections in a downtown department store, bludgeoning her victim senseless with a blunt instrument wrapped with newspapers.[30] Not even the city's Klansmen were ever to prove this violent.

Apparently as prone as men toward intolerance, insensitivity, and unpleasantness, women were destined to play a very important role in the El Paso elections of 1922. Though many women had failed to pay their poll taxes in previous years, a new state law required that the poll tax for 1922 be automatically assessed against all property owners. This had the effect of bringing into the electorate many who had avoided the tax in the past. Whereas only 2,816 El Paso women paid their poll tax in 1921, this figure rose to 6,098 the following year. It can be surmised that the bulk of the new female voters came from the city's middle-class districts north of the railroad tracks.[31] Most had only been in El Paso for a few years, and a large percentage came from the South. Fully infected with the intolerant spirit of the times, they would form an essential element of Frontier Klan No. 100's successes in politics.

As the first El Paso election of 1922 approached, there was much to ponder concerning the course of community affairs. The recent transformation of the electorate was naturally a topic for speculation; with so many Mexicans now disfranchised and the introduction of thousands of new Anglo voters, who could tell what direction local politics might take? This uncertainty was intensified by two other developments. One, of course, was the recent establishment of the El Paso Klan. Although the Klan would take care not to involve itself too overtly in the elections of 1922, its presence seemed to hang mysteriously about the city's political affairs and there was great suspicion that prominent men had affiliated with it. Closely associated with the Klan was an even more ominous development, one that seemed at times to poison the very air that El Pasoans breathed. Religious intolerance had come to the Pass and had managed to insinuate itself into almost every aspect of civic life, including politics.

The issue of religion would be frequently raised during the El Paso elections of 1922, and this was a curious and rather sudden development. Living in an isolated frontier community, El Pasoans had generally been preoccupied with matters other than religious disputation. Generally, the "wide-open" nature of Pass society had attracted a breed of people who gave only cursory acknowledgement of spiritual concerns. As historian Owen P. White has noted, the mere organization of churches had been a "colossal" task because of the extraordinary "sinfulness" of the town.[32] As late as the 1920s a surprising number displayed little interest in religion. The Reverend Percy Knickerbocker observed in 1921 that there were two types of El Pasoans: "Men in El Paso are either making 100 miles an hour for the devil, and having a good time, or else they are making 100 miles an hour for the Lord, and having a better time."[33] That same year, the Reverend Henry Van Valkenburgh noted that the local Protestant churches were still handi-

capped by "some of the old-time traditions carried over, though rapidly disappearing." He emphasized that "we are a long distance from
other great [religious] centers, which necessarily means isolation,
somewhat, from the inspirational contacts with their enthusiastic religious workers."[34]

Though difficulties remained, El Paso's churches were not as incon-
sequential in community affairs as they earlier had been. This was especially true of the Protestant fellowships, whose congregations were
swollen by new residents, many from the singularly religious South.
On November 13, 1921, records indicate that 6,906 El Pasoans attended Protestant Sunday schools, whereas one year before the figure had
only been 4,585.[35] By the end of November 1921 an all-time Sunday
school attendance record of 7,325 had been reached.[36] In September of
the same year, it was reported that 981 had joined Baptist churches in
the city within the past twelve months.[37] The Central Baptist Church
announced in early 1922 that it had acquired 250 new members during
the past year, while the First Baptist Church and the First Methodist
Church cited increases of 100 and 120 respectively during the same interval.[38] Other Protestant churches experienced similar growth, one
pastor estimating that the city's total number of church members was
increasing thirty to forty percent annually.[39] This rapid expansion in
turn set off a flurry of building activity, as old churches were enlarged
and new ones erected.[40]

Nor was the growth of El Paso's Protestant churches solely the result
of more Anglo residents. The troublesome years following World War I
caused many Americans to doubt both themselves and society in general. Amid disillusionment, many turned to religion for comfort in a mass
movement about which the El Paso *Times* commented in 1921:

> Even pastors and church workers are somewhat at a loss to ac-
> count for the recent and tremendous revival of interest in things
> spiritual. . . . Still the phenomenon is not difficult of explana-
> tion. A large part of the world is chaos. In other parts, like our
> own favored country where peace prevails, men are fearful for
> the future. They see a breaking down of moral standards, a
> growth of selfishness and of evil. Rejoicing over the triumphant
> ending of the great war is quickly checked by the thought the war
> we so fondly hoped was to end war has done nothing of the kind.
> There is ever present fear it may prove but the prelude to strife
> more terrible and devastating.[41]

Perhaps because the times seemed so bleak, clergymen were often disposed to expound upon the issues of the day. Imbued with the zeal that had characterized their wartime activities and their role in the prohibition crusade, local ministers were at the forefront in discussing civic problems in the 1920s. "That preacher is a bigger fool, who keeps silent on the immoralities of his time than the one who is 'in politics,'" declared the Reverend Floyd Poe, who went on to assert that "a cowering, silent pulpit is obnoxious to God Almighty."[42] The Reverend Percy Knickerbocker held a similar view: "I will not deal in dead issues. I will deal with the tragedy and pathos of life today."[43] One minister who was particularly outspoken on secular matters was the Reverend Henry Van Valkenburgh, who frequently warned his congregation of the dangers posed by foreign immigration and political intrigue in the public schools.[44]

As was the case in other parts of the nation, the social activism of the Protestant clergy in El Paso sometimes took a dark turn. Surrounded by exceptionally acute moral and social problems, some ministers felt compelled to crusade against anything that did not seem to meet the peculiar standards of Protestant morality and Protestant verities. By 1921 this included open condemnation of Roman Catholicism. The spirit of "100 percent Americanism" generated by the war was still very strong and still demanded denunciation of anything foreign. In this context, the Catholic Church, with its international hierarchy and Latin mass, seemed patently alien. Of course, bigots could easily relate Catholicism to bootlegging, vice, the evils of Juárez, corruption in politics, and the problems resulting from Mexican immigration. By attacking the Catholic religion, Protestants to some extent struck back at the particular problems that plagued their community.[45]

Apprehensions concerning Catholicism increased in El Paso throughout 1921. The local Catholic diocese had recently completed an ambitious building program that included the construction of Saint Patrick's Cathedral and a new parochial school, and both Mexican immigrants and new Anglos helped swell the membership of local parishes.[46] A vivid demonstration of the strength of Catholicism at the Pass occurred in June, when more than 50,000 spectators and participants turned out for a massive Corpus Christi parade. The procession was an international affair; marchers carried Mexican and American flags side by side, and presiding over the event were the Bishop of El Paso and the Bishop of Chihuahua.[47] This impressive display did not go unnoticed by the city's Protestants, one minister warning that "We [Protestants] are decidedly in the minority, with only a membership of little more than 10,000 in this city of nearly 100,000."[48]

Other Protestant clergymen were already publicizing their reservations concerning Catholicism. In January 1921 the Reverend Floyd Poe asserted that the Catholic clergy:

> . . . obey orders as they receive them — and this is a frightful handicap for a clergyman in these United States. It is a sad handicap for any group of leaders in the United States to receive orders from abroad which cause them so frequently to thrust a discordant note into our national song.[49]

A few weeks later, Poe continued his discussion of the un-American nature of Catholicism:

> The Roman Church has the genius of a hierarchy, while Protestantism has the genius of liberty. Romanists are bound, Protestants are free. . . . Protestantism says to the American government, 'We are Americans and we stand by the government first, last and all the time.' Roman Catholics understand that with them it is the Church of Rome first, last and all the time.[50]

Early in 1922 the Reverend Percy Knickerbocker went even further in denouncing Catholicism, implying that it could not properly be called a Christian faith:

> What makes infidels here in El Paso? Principally misrepresentation of the teachings of the Bible and Jesus Christ. The same thing that has made 90 percent of the men of Italy infidels! The same cloak of hypocrisy of religion that handicaps Spain, France, and Mexico! We know better in this country.[51]

With ministers making such intolerant statements and both Protestant and Catholic churches expanding their memberships, it was probably inevitable that religious feuding would intensify. One of the more volatile issues was the zealous missionary effort by Protestants in El Paso's predominantly Catholic southside. Looking back on recent troubles in the spring of 1922, the *Herald* provided an excellent summary of the problem:

In latter years, various protestant denominations have become very active in missionary work among the Spanish-speaking population; this work takes the line of social service, schooling, vocational training, athletics, care for health, home betterment, and 'Americanization,' but it is also directed toward proselyting [sic] members of Roman Catholic families, especially the younger element of both sexes, and toward directing into the protestant churches such persons as may have no close affiliation elsewhere. . . .

From the start it has been in the main a matter of attack by the protestants and defense by the Catholics in the papers, though sometimes the tables have turned. Notice has been taken by 'north side' churches, and church weeklies in various parts of the city have entered into the fight.[52]

The religious tensions generated in El Paso's southside first came to a head in early December 1921. Asserting that "a good Catholic must be a criminal, a hypocrite, a traitor, and a liar," the Reverend Ezequiel B. Vargas, pastor of the Church of the Messiah (a Methodist church) and editor of *The Mexican Evangelist*, issued a challenge to El Paso Catholics to debate publicly the tenets of their religion. To Vargas' surprise, the challenge was accepted. Selected as the Catholic participant in the debate was the Reverend Romauld Benedet of the Society of Jesus, editor of the *Revista Católica*. Father Benedet held doctoral degrees from the University of Barcelona and the Jesuit Theologate in Woodstock, Maryland, and was a specialist in Oriental studies; he spoke several Biblical languages, being especially fluent in Biblical Greek. Pastor Vargas' formal theological studies were limited to a few months at Southwestern University, in Georgetown, Texas.[53]

After the debate had been agreed to, strict rules of procedure were drawn up. The debate was to be held in Liberty Hall and was to extend over three evenings. The following topics were to be addressed:

1. Whether the Catholic Church is the only true Church.

2. Private interpretation of the Bible.

3. Whether the Catholic Church is infallible.

Stenographers were to be present, and at no time were offensive phrases to be allowed. The debate was to be presented in a formal syllogistic fashion, after which a winner would be selected by a panel of five judges.[54]

As the date for the first round approached, Vargas began to have second thoughts about the rules. When only four debate judges could be found, the minister claimed that there was no sense in holding a formal debate, that the two participants should simply give speeches. Father Benedet refused to accept this proposal and stated that any fifth judge would be satisfactory to the Catholics, even a member of Vargas' own church.[55]

The day before the debate was scheduled to begin, representatives from both the Catholic and Protestant communities were called before the county commissioners' court. A spokesman for the Protestant Ministers' Alliance, the Reverend Watson M. Fairley of Westminster Presbyterian Church, was in favor of canceling the debate, as was Percy Knickerbocker, who claimed that the proceedings would be "bad public policy." But El Paso Catholics, represented by former County Attorney William H. Fryer, decried the last-minute Protestant hesitations. Despite considerable misgivings, the members of the commissioners' court sided with the Catholics and gave permission for the event to be held in Liberty Hall, but stipulated that the debate take place on one evening only and that no future debates were to be held in that building.[56]

On the evening of December 12 over ten thousand El Pasoans converged upon Liberty Hall. Only six thousand could be seated, and some were turned away, but this was still "easily the largest assemblage ever attending a public meeting in Liberty Hall." To the disappointment of the crowd, however, the proceedings quickly turned into a nonevent — the Reverend Ezequiel Vargas declining to appear. In a written statement, Vargas later explained that he had been unalterably opposed to the syllogistic format of the debate and also wished to respect the county commissioners' reservations about the event. Finding himself without an opponent, Father Benedet decided to address the crowd and gave a lecture on Catholicism in Spanish. Standing nearby were members of a Catholic men's league, armed with shotguns. There was no disturbance and the large crowd quietly dispersed after the address.[57]

In the aftermath of this episode, religious tensions remained strong. Fearing that violence might result from Protestant activity in the southside, Mayor Davis requested the Reverend Charles D. Daniel of the First Mexican Baptist Church to quit distributing copies of *La Verdad*, a vehemently anti-Catholic sheet. Daniel continued to hand out religious literature, however, prompting the mayor to have the pastor and three other Baptist missionaries arrested in early January 1922 on the dubious charge of "distributing handbills."[58] Davis later explained that such action was necessary in order to avert "a religious war among the Mexican population of El Paso, and no doubt bloodshed."[59] Many local Protestants refused to accept this explanation and viewed the incident as certain evidence of a Catholic plot. The Reverend Percy Knickerbocker declared that Daniel had been arrested "through the efforts of the Roman Catholics," and the Protestant Ministers' Alliance vowed that Protestants would continue "to prosecute their programs of service among the Spanish-Americans without apology to the Roman Catholic Church or any other body."[60] Rallying to the cause of Pastor Daniel, a large and sympathetic crowd packed the courtroom during his preliminary hearing on January 10. When all the charges were dismissed, Daniel's supporters gave hearty shouts of "Amen."[61]

The arrest exacerbated the worsening situation. The uncompromising attitude of the local Protestant clergy was also less than helpful. When a statewide "Tolerance Week" was announced early in 1922, the Reverend Henry Van Valkenburgh snorted that "I believe the Tolerance movement is propaganda and I will have nothing to do with it."[62] By March, tensions had again reached the breaking point, the *Times* declaring that "A situation exists which may at any moment plunge us into riot and bloodshed. . . ."[63] Southside Catholics were particularly incensed by the continuing incendiary appeals of *La Verdad* and by rumors that Protestants planned to bring in a former priest for a series of religious lectures.[64] The recent activities of the Ku Klux Klan (which will be discussed later) had also contributed to an atmosphere of hysteria, one city resident observing that "Many of the Catholics in south El Paso have the idea that the Protestant ministers are connected with the Ku Klux Klan and this idea is wrong. It is the fear of the Klan that is stirring the people up so much now."[65]

Hoping to avoid a religious riot, Mayor Davis called together twenty-eight prominent El Pasoans, who in turn formed a religious tolerance committee. The committee hoped to initiate a dialogue between the city's Protestant and Catholic clergymen, but the plan met with little success. Claiming that the city owed Charles Daniel an apology, the local Baptist Pastors' Conference refused even to meet with the tolerance panel, let alone any Catholic leaders.[66] Because Baptists had figured prominently in the southside disputes, this meant that there was little hope of ending El Paso's religious problems in the near future. What the *Times* referred to as the "moral miasma" of religious intolerance seemed destined to be around for a long time.[67]

Early in 1922, with religious tensions mounting and new opportunities being proffered by the recent changes in the electorate, the local
chapter of the Ku Klux Klan decided to make its first entry into politics.
On January 28, Samuel J. (S. J.) Isaacks, a well-known local attorney
and former state district judge, announced that he would seek a position on the school board. Shortly thereafter, Isaacks was joined on a
three-man ticket by Charles S. Ward and Dr. J. Hal Gambrell, both incumbents. Ward was a leading member of the El Paso local of the International Typographical Union and had been employed for the past
fifteen years as the foreman of the *Herald*'s composing room. Gambrell
was a practicing physician, also an active member of the El Maida
Shrine, and an officer in the Army Reserve.[68] Although there was no
public announcement to this effect, all three candidates were members
of Frontier Klan No. 100.[69]

As a new and insurgent force in El Paso politics, the Klan had cleverly involved itself with a topic that was calculated to provoke great controversy — the public schools. Because of the region's generally depressed border economy, the city lacked an adequate tax base with
which to support a first-class school system. Whereas other Texas cities
such as Houston and Dallas could expend nearly seventy dollars per
pupil per year, only forty-nine dollars were expended for each El Paso
student annually.[70] This level of expenditure resulted in large part from
the city's sizable Mexican population, which provided the schools with
thousands of children, yet contributed only a small amount of the tax
money needed to maintain the system. This problem had first become
acute during the Mexican Revolution, as was noted by a local taxpayer
in 1915:

> More than half of the children of school age [in El Paso] are of
> Mexican parentage (most of whom are probably not American
> citizens) and probably nine-tenths are non-taxpayers.
>   It is easy to conceive of a condition whereby the proportion of
> non-taxpaying families would be so large and their children so
> numerous that the tax-paying element would no longer be able to
> support enough schools for all.[71]

Inundated by the early 1920s with additional thousands of students,
the El Paso school system could no longer adequately serve the community. Partially as a result of this, perhaps as many as thirty per cent of
the city's school-age children were not enrolled.[72] Children who did en-

roll faced serious problems of overcrowding and substandard facilities. This was especially true in the predominantly Mexican southside, where half-time and double-sized classes were common. In early 1922 at Aoy School, for example, there were only 1,240 seats available for a student body of 1,960. During the same period, both Alamo and Beall schools were forced to place hundreds of children in half-time classes.[73]

Although overcrowding in the Mexican districts was far the worst in the city, schools north of the railroad tracks also had problems. Because they were more politicized than the Mexican population and expected higher standards from the educational system, Anglos were particularly forceful in airing their complaints. Referring to the shortage of classrooms at Manhattan Heights School, one irate mother stated: "It's a shame to have children struggling for an education in such turmoil. This is the sort of thing that makes Bolsheviks and I'm almost converted myself." Other patrons of the same school registered their dissatisfaction in an open letter to the *Times:*

> It is not our purpose to urge that the Manhattan section, by reason of the larger amount of taxes paid into the city treasury, is not at least entitled to as much consideration as our Mexican and colored citizens, but we do claim, and it cannot be gainsaid, that this very important section of the city should not have its educational facilities neglected, even to the extent of omitting authorized and needed school rooms, while new projects affording no special relief to present emergencies be given all the money.[74]

In an appearance before the city council, members of the Manhattan Heights Parent-Teacher Association complained that "Pupils at Manhattan School study on the stairs, many lower grade pupils are shifted about the building three times a day before finding a roosting place, and there is only one desk for each three students in the [Manhattan] junior high school."[75] El Pasoans with children attending Morehead School were equally angry, one parent claiming that conditions there were "a disgrace to a civilized community. . . . One hundred and sixty little children are attending classes in basement rooms. On account of poor ventilation, the odor becomes so vile there that it is almost unbearable."[76] Additional resentment could be found in elite Kern Place, not because of poor conditions, but because the neighborhood had no school of its own despite the large amount of taxes collected in that area.[77]

Concern over the public schools was not confined to worries over crowded classrooms and the lack of facilities. With religious passions flaring, there was the fear that the Catholic Church might be attempting to exert control over the schools. Among the first to warn of this danger was the Reverend Henry Van Valkenburgh, who said in March 1921 that the public should be on guard against the schools becoming the "tool of sectarian greed."[78] Similar fears were held by the highest officials in the El Paso public school system. During the summer of 1921, the school board (including Charles Ward and J. H. Gambrell) voted to dismiss, without explanation, Mrs. Edith Coyne, a school librarian. A dissenting trustee, William T. (W. T.) Power, angrily asserted that the dismissal occurred because Mrs. Coyne was a Catholic and had dared to protest the recent removal of a Catholic encyclopedia from a school library. In Power's view, School Superintendent Allen H. Hughey was the main force behind the unfair removal of Coyne. In response, Hughey explained that Coyne had threatened that her dismissal "would start a religious war in El Paso."[79] Thus, even before the developments of 1922, the school board was fully embroiled in religious controversy.[80]

With the dissatisfaction over the schools running high, the Ward-Isaacks-Gambrell ticket launched its campaign in February 1922. From the beginning it was clear that the W-I-G slate hoped to achieve victory by promising more money and attacking the city administration's fiscal restraint.[81] Throughout 1921 Charles Ward, as president of the school board, had vigorously sought more funds for the schools, advocating a higher tax rate as the only way the system could avoid bankruptcy.[82] The city political machine consistently tried to pare down the school board's funding requests.[83] The machine's control over the schools' budget angered many El Pasoans who believed their children were being victimized by career politicians. In Pastor Van Valkenburgh's opinion, it was ridiculous "that the board of education is not 'capable' of determining the needs of the schools, but must be advised by the political organization."[84]

Other residents had serious reservations about the schools being so dependent upon politicians who had often taken unacceptable stands on moral issues, such as prohibition and vice. Apprehensions were reinforced in late February of 1922 when a team of federal "social hygiene" inspectors declared that local conditions were "very much worse than they were during the period of the World War. It [El Paso] is by far the worst city that we have run across in Texas, New Mexico, Arizona, Col-

orado, and Wyoming." The problems were credited to a lack of law enforcement.[85] City officials were outraged by these indictments, with
Mayor Davis declaring:

> I am not going to get excited about 57 women [prostitutes detec-
> ted by the inspectors] in a town of 100,000. I would rather the
> chief [of police] arrested the man who killed that old Mexican the
> other night [a recent murder case] than arrest 200 prostitutes.[86]

But Davis' pragmatic attitude was not shared by others, such as the acting pastor of Asbury Methodist Church, who commented;

> If officials in some cities had said [such things] they would have
> been dragged from office. The idea that a man who takes a few
> dollars out of our pockets or steals our watch is more dangerous
> than 200 prostitutes, who are liable to wreck the physical and
> moral lives of hundreds of our boys and girls, is ludicrous.[87]

In early March, with only a little more than three weeks remaining
before the election, the city was filled with rumors that the Davis administration would soon field its own slate. Anticipating that the Ring
might revert to corrupt practices that had marred past elections, concerned citizens formed a "non-partisan" organization to oversee polling. The new group at first called itself the Purity Ballot League, but
then settled on the more refined title of Good Government League
(GGL). The League's founder, George B. Oliver, proprietor of a local
fuel yard, stated that the main purpose of the organization would be to
"keep aliens, illiterates and others who have no right to vote, from entering the polls at the coming school election and all future elections."[88]
    The first meeting of the Good Government League, held on the sixth
of March, shattered any illusions that the group might truly be nonpar-
tisan. Temporary secretary Clifford L. Sirmans warned that the city
would try to influence the election and that an employee of the municipal water department had "opened an office in the Trust building with
the evident intention of playing school politics." State Representative
John E. Quaid noted that special attention should be given to the selection of election judges, because such officials in the past had been chos-
en solely on the basis of their ability to "carry the election regardless of
the methods of voting aliens." These concerns were echoed by the
League's temporary chairman and future president, George B. Oliver,
who stated: "I have watched El Paso elections for the past 20 years and

realize fully how much work is necessary to purify our politics. I firmly
believe that only 100 percent Americans should be allowed to vote."
Most vehement in his denunciation of the city political machine was
James H. Peden, a local attorney, who railed at "low-down, dirty politicians seeking graft in El Paso and getting it."[89]

Few knew at first what to make of the Good Government League. A
hooded, secret order like the Klan was easy to vilify, but a group advocating honest elections did not make a convenient target. Even the *El
Paso Times*, generally a mouthpiece for the local establishment, felt
obligated initially to announce that the GGL deserved "and doubtless
will be given the support of all good citizens."[90] However, the fact of
the matter was that the League was rife with Klansmen committed to
the W-I-G ticket.[91]

On March 9, a second slate of candidates for the school board was
announced. Included on it were three of the most prominent members
of the El Paso establishment: William H. Burges, Ulysses S. Stewart,
and Dr. James B. Brady. Burges was one of the city's most distinguished
lawyers, a past president of the Texas Bar Association, and former re-
gent of the University of Texas. Ulysses S. Stewart was president of the
City National Bank and a leading figure in the local Chamber of Commerce. Dr. Brady was a dentist with business concerns throughout the
city. All were longtime El Pasoans; Burges and Stewart had resided in
the city for over thirty years, and Brady had arrived in 1898.[92] Although the Burges-Brady-Stewart (B-B-S) ticket claimed to be "non-political," it was no secret the Davis administration looked upon it with
favor. Soon it was charged that Burges and his running mates were
controlled by city politicians and that municipal employees were being
"lent" to organize their campaign. It was said that former Mayor
Charles E. Kelly and notorious ward heeler Joseph (Joe) Dunne had
promised to give their influence to the effort.[93]

The appearance of a slate of city-backed candidates spurred the
Good Government League to new activity. On March 13 more than
two hundred leaguers assembled for another meeting dedicated to la-
menting the state of local affairs. Among those in attendance were
George B. Oliver, Clifford L. Sirmans, John E. Quaid, R. E.
Thomason, Dan M. Jackson, *Herald* publisher H. D. Slater, S. J.
Isaacks, the Reverend Henry Van Valkenburgh, El Paso Central Labor
Union President Frank H. Balt, and Mrs. Robert Townshend of the
League of Women Voters. Once again, James H. Peden proved the live-
liest speaker, claiming that conditions in El Paso were "rotten and a

disgrace to any city — even one in the heart of Mexico." "Vice is flourishing here," he declared, "and if you raise your voice against it, you are accused of being disloyal to the city's best interests." There was general denunciation of corruption in past elections, and S. J. Isaacks carefully explained the provisions of recently-enacted legislation that excluded aliens from the franchise. It was decided that the League would submit a list of recommended election officials for the school board's consideration.[94]

In the days that followed, the GGL remained active. After receiving news that in the past week there had been a mysterious increase in poll tax receipts in the Mexican districts of east El Paso (the area of Joe Dunne's influence) and that many Juárez residents held such receipts, the League vowed to "investigate."[95] Shortly thereafter, the GGL announced its intention to expand countywide and possibly seek affiliation with the recently founded Civic and Commercial Club of Ysleta. The Ysleta club was greatly distrusted by Lower Valley Mexican-Americans, who claimed it was a front for "anti-Mexican and anti-Jewish" activities.[96] Nevertheless, by the end of March a branch of the Good Government League was functioning in Ysleta.[97]

Additional plans were formulated on March 20. James H. Peden was assigned to compile a list of all aliens who had paid their poll tax, and it was agreed that rewards would be offered for information leading to the arrest of illegal voters. Expressing concern that local officials might not arrest or prosecute such offenders, Frederick C. Standish suggested that "If the law isn't at hand there is one organization that hasn't made any mistakes so far." George Oliver replied, "I don't think there will be any call for the K. K. K." One official the League did not have to worry about was County Attorney Will H. Pelphrey, who used the occasion to declare that "any person who contribute[s] to illegal voting is un-American and not a good citizen," and to further assert that any candidate who failed to join the GGL "does not deserve a vote in the community."[98]

The following evening, both the Good Government League and the Ward-Isaacks-Gambrell ticket scored a major victory. At a meeting of the El Paso School Board, two lists of recommended election officials, one from the GGL and the other from representatives of the Burges-Brady-Stewart ticket, were submitted. Without a reading or discussion, the board adopted the League's list. Board member Mrs. William R. Brown objected to the hastiness of the decision but was unable to convince her colleagues to reconsider or even discuss their action. The remainder of the meeting was dominated by Charles Ward, who called for funding new additions to the Manhattan and Morehead schools and the construction of new schools in east El Paso and Kern Place.[99]

With less than two weeks remaining, the school board campaign was marked by increasingly fierce electioneering. In a series of speeches, the W-I-G candidates continued to hammer on the same issues: the Burges candidates were mere lackeys for the city administration; the schools needed to be divorced from the machinations of politicians; the W-I-G ticket would insure more and better schools. Accusing Mayor Davis of trying to prop up his "rotten political machine" by "obtaining control of the city schools," S. J. Isaacks asserted that the city and all three B-B-S candidates were implicated in a scheme to make unethical profits from a school bond issue.[100] It was also noted that since members of the Burges ticket were not patrons of the school system, "They cannot possibly have the intimate sympathy for the affairs of the public schools that men of families have."[101] This line of reasoning was shared by Pastor Van Valkenburgh, an ardent and open W-I-G partisan, who saw the campaign in a populist light: "In this race, all the moneyed powers have lined up behind Burges, Brady, and Stewart. It is the common people who must educate their children in the public schools, who are most vitally interested in the school system."[102]

The W-I-G ticket received two important endorsements during the final week of the campaign. One was from H. D. Slater and the El Paso Herald, a not too surprising development since Charles Ward was a Herald employee and two members of the B-B-S ticket were directors of the rival Times. The Herald's backing demonstrated that the city's older reform element was inclined to support the anti-establishment challengers.[103] Ward's prominence within the local labor movement was responsible for the other endorsement, that of the Central Labor Union's Non-Partisan Political Conference. Unhappy with the Davis administration's support of an anti-picketing ordinance and long aggrieved by the local business establishment's commitment to cheap Mexican labor, union members eagerly took part in the assault on the old order. This included an active role in the Good Government League; both Central Labor Union President Frank Balt and William Moran, editor of the El Paso Labor Advocate, were GGL officers. Definitely not a force for cultural or racial tolerance, organized labor constituted yet another part of the W-I-G ticket's formidable coalition.[104]

With their opposition gathering strength, the Burges-Brady-Stewart ticket realized that it must campaign more actively. Despite William

H. Burges' earlier assertion that "There is little to be accomplished by making speeches and we will leave that to our adversaries," a series of nighttime rallies was scheduled for the last week of the campaign. On March 28 a Liberty Hall crowd of two thousand heard an assortment of speakers deny that the B-B-S candidates were controlled by city politicians. Burges himself denied that there had been a conspiracy to profit from school bonds and then directed a few words towards the local Klan:

> I haven't anything but contempt for an organization that parades in a night shirt and wears a mask. And if there is one in here tonight I want him to take the news to his kind that I cordially invite them to vote against me. We do not want them because we do not stand for the same things. Good men got into that organization but got out when they found out what they had joined.[105]

In subsequent rallies, Burges and his running mates continued to stress their platform of a professional and business-like administration of the schools that would be "non-political and non-sectarian." Unlike the W-I-G ticket, they refrained from making specific promises in regard to new school construction. Special attention was drawn to religious tensions, Burges citing a recently distributed pamphlet which accused his ticket of being nominated in the Knights of Columbus Hall: "[We] were not nominated in that hall and we were not nominated in the camp of the Ku Klux Klan. . . . I am not so sure that our adversaries can say [that]." A link between the Good Government League and the Invisible Empire was also hinted at, it being questioned whether a recent GGL proclamation had "originated with the Ku Klux Klan itself or the executive committee of the league. . . ."[106]

As polling day approached, the Davis administration abandoned all pretenses of noninvolvement. On March 29 Burges announced that Mayor Davis was a close friend of his and would vote for the B-B-S ticket.[107] The following day, Davis stated that "The city administration is backing the Burges-Brady-Stewart ticket to the limit," and soon municipal employees were frequenting B-B-S headquarters, manning phones and helping plot strategy.[108] On election eve the mayor made a final appeal to city workers to vote for the Burges slate, "because there can be no choice between these two tickets in the mind of any thinking person."[109]

The Davis Ring's overt involvement in the school board contest was not unanticipated by the Good Government League. On March 24

George Oliver mailed letters to all election judges, advising them to go early to the polls: The League had information that "certain persons interested in continuing the practices heretofore prevalent of illegal voting, [and] voting of aliens and floaters" were planning to impersonate GGL officials over the phone and tell the judges their services were not needed.[110] Clifford Sirmans warned that if the judges failed to show up, a "crooked faction might have a lot of its followers on hand the minute the voting was set to begin and put in their own officials."[111] When it appeared that the Burges ticket might seek a court order removing a number of League-approved officials, Oliver proclaimed that his followers were prepared "to die, if necessary, that the greatest bulwark of our American liberty, the purity of the ballot, may be safeguarded and insured."[112]

Additional action was taken by the Good Government League to prevent corruption at the polls. Letters were mailed to suspected aliens and illiterates [!], warning them not to vote, and a reward of one hundred dollars was offered for information leading to the conviction of any illegal voter.[113] It was announced that a list had been compiled of immoral women and their "hangers-on" who had recently been removed from precincts in the city's "rooming-house districts" and were thereby temporarily disfranchised. The old practice of using "municipal garbage wagons and auto trucks to haul persons to the various polling places" was formally denounced, and it was charged that "members of the police force, health department, and water department are being used to check poll tax lists for the coming school board election, thus neglecting their work for which they are paid." On a more personal level, George Oliver warned Joe Dunne that if he did "the things in this year's election that he has done in the past, he is either going to hell or to the peniteniary."[114]

Confident that everything possible had been done, W-I-G supporters and officers of the Good Government League gathered at Odd Fellows Hall on March 30 for a final rally. Once again the city administration was soundly criticized for everything from poor garbage collection services to forcing firemen to work in the current campaign. The religious issue was also openly discussed. "We are being supported by Presbyterians, Methodists, Jews, Lutherans, by members of the Christian church, Christian Scientists, and other denominations I can think of except one," asserted S. J. Isaacks, who reminded his listeners that

"This is a country of religious tolerance, but not a country where any sect can come in and run our educational system." It was averred that the Catholic clergy were urging their flocks to support the B-B-S ticket and that priests had already meddled in the election by helping "ignorant citizens" register to vote. Thus, by election eve, El Pasoans had been given ample indication of what to expect in the event that the W-I-G ticket was elected.[115]

The school board election was expected to be a lively affair. Noting that the contest had been "the most bitter of any school election I have ever seen," Police Chief Edwards assigned seventy policemen and city detectives to extra duty monitoring the polling.[116] As had been feared by the Good Government League, representatives of the Burges-Brady-Stewart ticket gained an eleventh-hour injunction that prevented some election judges from assuming their duties. The great majority of precincts remained in the hands of W-I-G partisans, however.[117]

As polling began on April 1, local politicians were amazed by the unprecedented turnout. After touring the city, a worried Mayor Davis noted, "They are certainly flocking to the polls in the districts north of the tracks. And in the southern part of town the voting is not as heavy as we expected."[118] Wary of any last minute influx of pro-B-B-S votes, W-I-G workers remained vigilant throughout the day. At the 47th precinct in southeast El Paso, the election judge turned back forty Mexican voters because they could not speak English. The Good Government League stationed a photographer at precinct 14 with the hope of gathering evidence of illegal voting, and George Oliver himself arrived to inspect the suspect proceedings. Unintimidated, Joe Dunne and a group of B-B-S adherents were also present at the site when the photographer was chased off, threatened with a large rock, and relieved of his camera. Joe Dunne warned George Oliver to "quit butting in where you don't belong," and when Oliver refused to leave, he fumed that "You have been doing a lot of talking about sending me to hell or the penitentiary lately. Let's start now." A short fist fight ensued, but without serious damage.[119]

Even before the polls closed, there was little doubt that the W-I-G ticket had prevailed. One Good Government League member accurately summarized the situation when he stated: "It's all over but the shouting, for the Northside precincts are so heavy for the Ward-Isaacks-Gambrell ticket they will swamp the Mexican vote south of the

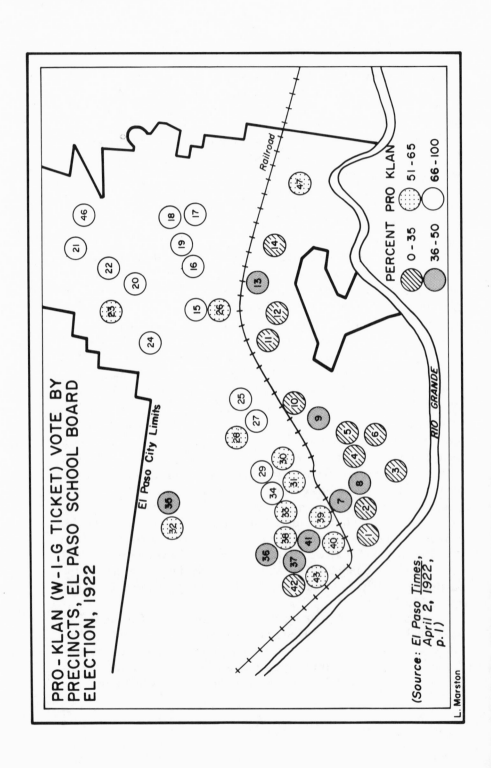

PRO-KLAN (W-I-G TICKET) VOTE BY PRECINCTS, EL PASO SCHOOL BOARD ELECTION, 1922

El Paso City Limits

Railroad

RIO GRANDE

PERCENT PRO KLAN

0 - 35   51 - 65

36 - 50   66 - 100

(Source: *El Paso Times*, April 2, 1922, p. 1)

L. Marston

tracks.[120] The final vote tallies for the three seats on the school board were: Ward, 5,959; Isaacks, 5,712; Gambrell, 5,686; Stewart, 4,860; Burges, 4,542; Brady, 4,362.[121] Despite the vigorous opposition of the local establishment, an imposing coalition of recent Anglo arrivals, organized labor, and old-time reformers had emerged victorious. For the first time, "progressivism," albeit of a definitely intolerant cast, had triumphed at the Pass. In the process, three members of the Invisible Empire had been elected to the school board, including the Exalted Cyclops of Frontier Klan No. 100.

CHAPTER **6**

The Klan Triumphant –
Part Two

lthough Frontier Klan No. 100 chose not to assume an open role in the school board election, its presence in the city became increasingly overt and pervasive during early 1922. As in the previous year, the Klan continued to seek public forums and promotional opportunities. Toward these ends, two letters accompanied by advertising-fee payments were sent to the *Herald* in February. Perhaps the anonymous writer or writers believed that the *Herald's* support of the Ward-Isaacks-Gambrell ticket signaled a favorable change in attitude concerning the Invisible Empire. If so, they were disappointed, for the editor refused to print the documents and returned the payments to the post office. A subsequent editorial declared that the Klan "will not be afforded space for its dubious discourses" and reiterated the assertion that "There is no place in El Paso for the Ku Klux Klan. . . ." At the same time, it was revealed that the *Herald's* offices had been visited by a "[Klan] organizer of high rank" who attempted to "explain" the KKK, but that he had been sent on his way.[1]

Though rejected by the press, Klansmen could take comfort in increasingly cordial relations with Protestant ministers. During January 1922, only a few weeks after the Klan's flamboyant appeal for sermons on the need of a moral cleanup, several clergymen spoke out against decadence in the city with unusual vehemence and specificity. Foremost among them were the Reverends Arthur W. Jones of the Austin Park Christian Church, George McCall of the Central Baptist Church, Henry Van Valkenburgh of the First Methodist Church, and Percy Knickerbocker of the Trinity Methodist Church.[2] And at least a limited alignment with Klan goals was signified in other ways as well. During a revival at the First Baptist Church, a visiting evangelist declared that "If the Ku Klux Klan stands for 100 percent Americanism and for clean living, and is opposed to immorality, I'm for it." This incendiary statement drew no public rebuttal from *any* local Protesant clergyman.[3] Nor was there an adverse response when the Reverend Dr. Hubert D. Knickerbocker, brother of Percy Knickerbocker and reputedly "the highest paid Methodist pastor in the South," proclaimed from the pulpit at Trinity Methodist Church that:

Justice may sometimes be rightfully administered outside the law. Jesus Christ did this when He took the cat o' nine tails and drove the thieves and money changers from the Temple. . . . In this respect He was the first Ku Klux Klansman.[4]

There can be no doubt that the friendly stance of the Protestant clergy and the enthusiasm generated by the school board campaign served to embolden Frontier Klan No. 100. Early in March, Claude O. Borcherding, a barber residing at 2910 Aurora Avenue, was the recipient of a letter warning him to discontinue trips to Juárez with his wife. Without signature, but bearing the official seal of the local Klan, the missive ominously pointed out that "Dynamite has been handled by many men for many years, but it has been known to explode." When Borcherding informed the police, Captain of Detectives Claud T. Smith urged him not to worry, because "If the Ku Klux cowards haven't got nerve enough to parade in El Paso it is not likely that they will try to start anything that they know they can't finish." It was conjectured that "scores of El Pasoans" had received similar warnings, for the message had been mimeographed, and it was further speculated that Klansmen were watching the bridges to Mexico in order to identify those who habitually visited Juárez.[5]

Such threats took on added significance on the evening of March 10, when the organization offered local journalists a specific indication of its strength. Proceeding according to directions from an anonymous telephone caller, three *Herald* reporters drove to the foothills just west of the city, near Kern Place, where they were halted by a group of robed Klansmen. After being led on foot to a nearby hill, they were placed under close guard and permitted to witness a meeting of Frontier Klan No. 100. The gathering was well attended: There were more than one thousand Klansmen in white hoods and robes, and nearly three hundred recruits stood nearby awaiting initiation. Automobiles of the participants were double parked in a line extending nearly five hundred yards. Perhaps anticipating a raid by their adversaries, the throng was widely dispersed; small groups clustered around scattered fires that radiated out from a central bonfire for a distance of more than one mile. In due course an initiation ceremony was conducted, after which the recruits were admitted into a large circle of costumed Klansmen. Then five new fires suddenly flared up, as clumps of kerosene-soaked cactus were ignited. Confused by the proceedings, one reporter asked his guard to explain the spectacle. "They are scalping the pope," the Klansman replied.

Shortly after ten o'clock, the ceremony concluded, and the reporters were released to tell their story. Throughout the entire affair the greatest secrecy had been maintained: license numbers of cars had been covered, incoming roads had been guarded, and secret signals had been relayed by whistles and flashlights.[6] It had been an eerie evening, but it was not quite over.

Following the initiation, six Klansmen motored up Scenic Drive on Mount Franklin. After reaching the parking space at the drive's summit, the men erected and ignited a wooden cross. Four of the Klansmen departed before the cross burned out, but two who lingered heard laughter coming from a nearby automobile. One of the duo looked into the matter and found a man and a woman in the parked vehicle. Resenting the intrusion, the seated man served notice that "If you don't get away from this automobile, mister, I'll burn my initials into you in hot lead." The two Knights of the Invisible Empire rapidly exited, and the first local cross-burning was over.[7]

But the Scenic Drive encounter did not dissuade the Klan from other similar demonstrations. On March 14 and 15, with the school board campaign heating up and religious tensions nearing the breaking point, Klan fires blazed again on Mount Franklin. On the first night, bonfires arranged into the pattern of a giant cross were ignited on the side of the mountain. The following evening, lanterns were used to produce the same effect. On both occasions the displays were visible in the city and were a source of considerable speculation.[8]

Reports of a large membership and these increasingly overt activities revived apprehensions that the organization might attempt a parade. The day after the *Herald*'s reporters witnessed the westside gathering, the paper predicted that the "next big step in the local organization will be a public parade of the masked and robed members through the streets of El Paso." But local authorities remained determined that no such parade would take place. Despite warnings from his friends not to interfere with the KKK, Chief of Detectives Claud Smith announced that if the Klan "tries to take the law into its hands or attempts to parade, nothing will be left undone to see that the law is enforced."[9]

On the evening of March 13 the city was suddenly filled with rumors that the Klan was assembling at the smelter in preparation for a procession through downtown El Paso. Anonymous phone calls to Mayor Davis and Sheriff Orndorff asserted that a parade would indeed take place. In response, the entire police force was placed on alert and a detachment of armed officers was sent to the municipal power house to guard against any tampering with the electrical generator and lines. As police assembled, Chief Peyton Edwards admonished them to arrest any Klansmen who dared to parade: "Stop them at all hazards . . . . Whatever you do, bring back your man."

A large number of citizens were eager to assist authorities. One local attorney called Sheriff Orndorff and offered the services of sixty-three men as special deputies. Other El Pasoans, many with "suspicious bulging of hip-pockets," congregated at Fifth and Oregon streets. By eleven o'clock the assemblage had grown to five hundred, some with clubs, bricks, and shotguns, while heavily-armed, anti-Klan vigilantes cruised the streets in cars.

Happily, this spontaneous display had no opportunity to develop into something more serious. Motorcycle patrolmen returned from the smelter with the news that there had been no gathering there, that the rumors of a parade had been false. By midnight the anti-Klan crowd had dispersed and the excitement had subsided.[10]

But the police department remained wary during the days that immediately followed. Policemen worked twelve-hour shifts, and three-fourths of the force was kept on call at night. To improve the department's ability to cope with any eventuality, fourteen new policemen were added to the force. The *Herald* questioned the hiring of the additional men, reporting that they were "from the Knights of Columbus membership chiefly," but a polling of the recruits revealed that they were predominantly non-Catholic.[11]

The manifest determination of authorities to forestall any unauthorized Klan parade obviously impressed the leadership of Frontier Klan No. 100. With the school board election pending, the Klan simply could not become an issue in itself without damaging its favored candidates. If a parade were held, there was little doubt that Klansmen would be arrested and subsequently unmasked. This might ultimately lead to the exposure of the local Klan's entire membership and to untold political damage. A parade would almost certainly provoke a violent clash. Reflecting about the rumors of a parade on March 13, one opponent later observed that "If that parade had showed up that night, with the excited condition, there would have been some shooting, plenty."[12] The *El Paso Times* held the same opinion, noting on March 18, "If [the Ku Klux Klan] attempts a parade there will be serious trouble. That is certain. There is no getting away from it."[13]

For the next several weeks, the local Klan practically disappeared from public view: there were no additional cross-burnings on Mount Franklin, and the furor over a possible Klan parade subsided. When a phoned report told of a Klan gathering at the smelter on March 22, Sheriff Orndorff and two motorcycle patrolmen dashed out there, only to discover a group of hobos sprawled around a campfire.[14] It can be surmised that during this period Klansmen were too preoccupied with the Ward-Isaacks-Gambrell campaign and the Good Government League to dedicate much time to "Klankraft."

But, two weeks after its victory in the school board election, the El Paso Klan again made its presence known. A number of letters bearing the Klan seal were mailed to parents of high school students, informing them that their children had recently been in Ciudad Juárez. Dr. Frank H. H. Roberts, principal of El Paso High School, announced, "I know that high school children have been watched and their movements have been checked." He also noted that as a result of one of the letters, a fifteen-year-old girl had received a "severe whipping" from her father.[15]

During the interval when it systematically monitored the activities of carousing juveniles, the Klan decided to renew efforts for social acceptance. In a letter to Adjutant Louis Carl of the Salvation Army, Frontier Klan No. 100 announced its desire that the fifty dollars which it had sought to contribute to the Associated Charities be turned over to Carl's organization.[16] When the Associated Charities responded by repeating its earlier announcement that the donation had been returned to the post office, the Klan warned that "We never sleep, we never rest, and we never fail."[17]

Other charitable overtures were more successful. In one incident, an ill and impoverished citizen, Mrs. Jack Brennan, received ten dollars from the Klan. An accompanying letter explained that "We are informed that you are a victim of unfortunate circumstances and we are always ready to assist the unfortunate. . . ."[18] One month later, on May 12, it was announced that the local branch of the Young Men's Christian Association had received fifty dollars from the Klan and intended to accept the gift.[19] On the evening of May 16, a sum of two hundred dollars was donated to the Salvation Army via the Klan-dominated school board. New board member S. J. Isaacks declared that the contribution was "a very generous act," and a majority of the board voted to accept the money with thanks. However, an opposing trustee, W. T. Power, charged that the donation was "tainted money."[20] No such reservations were heard a few weeks later when the Klan donated two hundred and sixty-five dollars to the local chapter of the United Confederate Veterans. The money was intended to enable eight El Paso veterans to attend their organization's national convention in Richmond, Virginia. The old Confederates were so delighted that they gave the Klan a rousing "rebel yell."[21]

Throughout the spring and summer of 1922, Frontier Klan No. 100 remained on guard against its enemies' discrediting efforts. In late April, letters bearing the Klan seal informed Sheriff Orndorff and Police Chief Edwards that:

> We have what we consider reliable information that the enemies of the Klan are banding themselves together for the purpose of perpetrating outrages upon El Pasoans in order that they may point to such acts as the work of the Klan, thus hoping to bring us into disrepute and impair our usefulness in this city.

The letters offered five hundred dollars for information leading to the felony conviction of any Klan imposter.[22]

Despite the Klan's worries, El Paso remained peaceful during the following months, in large part because of the organization's genuine desire to be law-abiding. An illegal Klan parade was never attempted; there were no tar-and-feather parties; and no El Pasoans were spirited away or flogged. On occasion, however, the Klan continued to involve itself in private affairs. In late April, Frank H. Morris, a clerk at the Union Drug Store, reported that the Klan had ordered him over the telephone to withdraw his pending divorce suit. Morris was unnerved and said he would do as he had been told: "I wasn't exactly scared, but . . . I remember reading about the Ku Klux setting fires all over the mountain and meeting around here. It made me nervous when he [the caller] told me who he was with." The phone call was probably not a hoax — District Clerk Clarence Harper (who was himself a Klansman) later informed Morris that his office had been telephoned by an anonymous party inquiring into the status of the divorce case.[23]

At least two other residents attracted the attention of the Klan. On July 19 John E. McAllister informed the press that he had received a note from the KKK relative to his "personal affairs." McAllister was far from being intimidated and challenged the Klan to meet him face to face.[24] In another incident, Charles Clark, an American residing in Juárez, was advised by two men bearing KKK cards to return to the United States or face deportation. Clark later learned that a $250 bribe had been offered to the Mexican immigration service to effect his ouster.[25]

As unsavory as such episodes were, the Ku Klux Klan in El Paso continued to draw new members to their organization. On May 30 a "starlight gathering" of the Klan was held outside the city limits in the Upper Valley. Present were over one thousand Klansmen, including two hundred and twelve new recruits who took their oath "around a blazing cross [that towered] high above the heads of the weird, fantastic gathering." After the ritual was completed, the Klansmen removed their masks, shook hands, and proceeded to enjoy a barbeque dinner. At the end of the festivities, members piled into three hundred and twenty-seven automobiles, each of which carried three to six Klansmen. In the confusion of departure a Klan costume was left behind and subsequently recovered by some *Herald* reporters. The number "2,706" was stamped on the back of the outfit, a possible indication of the minimum strength of Frontier Klan No. 100.[26]

By mid-1922 the Ku Klux Klan had managed through active recruiting to insinuate itself into many of the organizational mainstays of local Anglo society. S. L. A. Marshall, who was a member of the *Herald's* editorial staff at this time, later recalled:

It [the Klan] was in control, for instance, of the American Legion
here. It was in control of the Masonic Lodge. It was in control of
the National Guard. I had been an officer in the National Guard
and practically every other member of the Guard was in the
Klan.

Marshall also recalled that, of the twelve members of the *Herald*'s
editorial staff, he alone was not a Klansman.[27]

The presence of Klansmen in local organizations led at times to bitter
confrontations. At a "stormy and prolonged" meeting of the American
Legion post in June 1922, Samuel Dreben, a Jew who held the Croix de
Guerre and the American Medal of Honor, shouted that:

I'm a member of this legion and I do not see how I'm going to get
a square deal from any K. K. K. outfit. They didn't ask me when
I was on the front line in France whether I was a Jew. They didn't
ask me if I was a Catholic.

Subsequently, the post decided that no Klansman could hold office in
the local branch of the Legion. However, a formal motion to question
members concerning their affiliation with the Invisible Empire was
tabled indefinitely by a vote of nineteen to fifteen.[28] Dissension could
also be found among members of the League of Women Voters, which
had divided into "'pro' and 'anti'-Klan factions." As to the school
board's acceptance of the Klan donation to the Salvation Army,
League member Julia Sharp said that "the school board should be com-
mended for taking money from any source." Another member,
Elizabeth Mundy, vehemently disagreed, stating that "Public-spirited
citizens should turn down the Klan at every opportunity; it is a
cowardly, un-American institution."[29]

In early April 1922, as the Klan was beginning its new drive for social respectability and was attracting hundreds of additional members,
the organization's victorious candidates were sworn in for their two-
year terms on the school board. As was only appropriate, George
Oliver, notary public and fellow Klansman, officiated over the ceremony. Almost immediately after taking office, the new trustees moved
to fulfill their campaign promises, voting numerous improvements and
additions for northside schools. Under the leadership of board president Charles Ward, the trustees also managed to secure from the city a
record appropriation of $715,672 for the school system, a large portion
of which would fund new schools in the Cotton addition and Hadlock

Place.[30] The ease with which Ward, Isaacks, and Gambrell dominated the board's affairs increased in early May, when board member E. Gordon Perry resigned. Selected by incumbents to succeed Perry was James A. Borders, President of the American Trust and Savings Bank, who was recommended by S. J. Isaacks. Borders was a member of Frontier Klan No. 100, and his presence gave the Invisible Empire a majority of four among seven trustees.[31]

Having consolidated its hold on the school board, the Klan was now free to effect certain changes in the system. One interesting innovation was new names for schools. At the suggestion of S. J. Isaacks, the names of Texas heroes were used — thus the origin of Bowie, Austin, Crockett, Burleson, Fannin, and Rusk schools.[32] The name of El Paso High School was changed to Sam Houston High School (temporarily as it turned out), a move which provoked considerable controversy.[33] Shortly thereafter, the board made its stand on the Klan clear by accepting the KKK's two-hundred-dollar donation to the Salvation Army. Voting in favor of acceptance were Charles Ward, S. J. Isaacks, J. H. Gambrell, James A. Borders, and Mrs. Herbert E. Stevenson. Opposed was W. T. Power.[34] It was the opinion of the *El Paso Times* that the action "justifies the worst fears of the opponents of these board members [Ward, Isaacks, and Gambrell] in the election."[35]

But, in the Klan's view, additional actions were needed. On May 26 the school board met for the purpose of voting on the re-election of teachers and principals for the forthcoming school year. The proceedings were conducted in secret in what the *Times* referred to as a "star-chamber session." After the meeting, it was announced that five of nineteen current school principals were not rehired for the next year. These included Maria J. Gallagher of Alamo School, Frances S. Culligan of Grandview School, and Alberta Heep of Sunset School. All three women were Roman Catholics. Due to the fact that there had been only four Catholic principals in the first place, the cry of religious bias was immediately raised. Board member W. T. Power explained that:

The whole thing simmers down to Ku Klux Klan and the anti-Ku Klux Klan. The majority of members of the school board are in sympathy with the Ku Klux Klan — I would not say they are members — and some of the principals they refused to re-elect are Catholics and are opposed to the Klan.[36]

Mrs. William R. Brown also felt that bias had been manifest, and on the evening of the controversial session she confronted J. H. Gambrell with her suspicions:

> "I have had many persons come to me and urge that I vote against Miss [Maria J.] Gallagher," said J. H. Gambrell, trustee, prior to voting.
> "They came to you, doctor," said Mrs. Brown, "because they know you are anti-Catholic."
> "Do you mean to say," asked Dr. Gambrell, "that I am not honest?"
> "I mean to say," retorted Mrs. Brown, "that you are anti-Catholic."[37]

The failure of the board to rehire the Catholic principals became an item of great public discussion in the days that followed. Even the *Herald* expressed disapproval, noting that Charles Ward's role in the affair had "surprised and disappointed those who had supported him in the recent school board election."[38] Especially outraged was the Reverend Father Malachi O'Leary, pastor at Saint Patrick's Cathedral; he decried the school board's partiality to the "Ku Klux Klan, an organization of cowards and fanatics." Father O'Leary went on to list what the board had recently effected: out of four Catholic principals, three had been dropped or held up for further consideration; out of eight high school teachers who were Catholic, four had had their salaries reduced and one was held up for appointment; out of thirty Catholic teachers in the grade schools, seven had been dropped. El Paso Catholics were determined not to accept the situation passively, O'Leary observing that "nothing is to be gained by silence. . . . We intend, therefore, from now on, to meet these attacks as they arise."[39]

The dismissal of Maria Gallagher was especially controversial because she had been in the El Paso schools for over twenty-five years and was fondly remembered by former students.[40] Teachers from Alamo School petitioned for her reinstatement, and residents began appearing at school board meetings to register dissatisfaction. One of Gallagher's suporters stated;

> I do not believe this is a religious question. I am a Protestant, as far as that is concerned. . . . There is an injustice being done this good woman. In justice to all, the public should know why this action has been taken.[41]

There was also resentment over the dismissal of Frances Culligan and Alberta Heep, one petition in Mrs. Culligan's behalf asserting that "the board of school trustees has seen fit to disregard the wishes of the patrons of this district, and have removed this faithful and efficient principal. . . ."[42]

On June 5 a number of petitions requesting reinstatements of Gallagher, Culligan, and Heep were presented to the school board. On motion to reconsider their earlier action, however, Ward, Isaacks, Gambrell, Borders, and Stevenson voted negatively, and the subject was closed.[43] At a later meeting, Mrs. Brown and W. T. Power were prevented by a parliamentary technicality from reopening the issue. Power claimed that the technicality had arisen because the minutes of the previous meeting had "been monkeyed with."[44] Whatever the reason, by the summer of 1922 there was good reason to credit the *Times'* allegation that the Ku Klux Klan had "seized the schools."[45]

As religious intolerance gained ground on the school board, the Good Government League began fulfilling its promise to prosecute illegal voters. On April 4 Francisco Fierro, a homeowner resident of El Paso for twenty-three years and the father of four school children, was brought before officials of the GGL for interrogation. When it was learned that Fierro had voted in the school board election but was not a United States citizen, League Secretary Stuart F. Loughborough had him arrested on the charge of illegal voting, an offense which carried a maximum penalty of two to five years in prison. Fierro explained that he had thought he was an American citizen, but now realized that he had only taken out the first papers toward naturalization.[46] Other such initiatives followed. In one instance, Mrs. Eufracia Zubia and her husband were arrested for illegal voting after being subjected to "severe grilling" at League headquarters. When the complaint against the Zubias was presented in court, the judge warned the GGL "to follow the strict legal procedure in filing charges instead of calling suspects to the league's office before having warrants issued."[47] To the *Times* the League's actions appeared "a good deal like invisible government."[48]

Despite the criticism, the Good Government League continued to file complaints against those suspected of voting illegally. In many of the cases the information had been provided by William P. Hawkins and Jesús Pérez, both of whom had at one time served on the El Paso police force.[49] Hawkins noted that in investigating the cases he had been instructed by the GGL only to secure evidence that could be used against *alien* voters, that the League was not interested in instances where American citizens might have violated the election laws.[50] Jesús Pérez, who assisted Hawkins as an interpreter, seemed ashamed of his own role: "I have hated [this job] and if I had a job I would quit it. I have my wife and two children to support . . . but I have not found one."[51]

In some instances, league initiatives resulted in unwarranted arrests. This was true in the case of Victor Payan, who was interrogated by the GGL and then turned over to authorities. It was later discovered that Payan had not even voted, and he was released.[52] In another episode, the charges against Mrs. Paula González were dismissed. She had been accused of being an alien, but it was revealed in court that she was a widow who had been married to an American citizen and was thereby qualified to vote.[53] Tomás Montes was also wrongly charged with illegal voting, the League asserting that he had been disfranchised by a felony conviction in 1912. When it was shown that the conviction had only been for a misdemeanor, the court dismissed the charges.[54] But the GGL pressed on, and by the middle of May the county grand jury had indicted eight men and two women, all Mexicans, on charges of illegal voting.[55] When those who had been indicted went to trial in early June, four were convicted. Among these was Francisco Fierro, who received a two-year suspended sentence.[56] In three other cases, defendants were given five-year suspended sentences.[57] Ballot slips retrieved from the jury room showed that some jurors had favored five-year sentences with *no* suspension.[58] Evidently satisfied with the proceedings, the Good Government League expended four hundred dollars for the four convictions, most of the money going to William P. Hawkins and Jesús Pérez.[59]

Having successfully prosecuted illegal voters and having so convincingly triumphed in the school board election, the Good Government League looked forward to a bright political future. The ultimate goal of the League was stated by member Charles H. Kirkland: "[One] victory is not enough. We will have to remake the political fabric of our city."[60] However, enemies of the League were becoming more defiant. In April, George Oliver began carrying a gun "in view of the fact that certain politicians opposing me have threatened to 'get' me."[61] League Secretary Stuart Loughborough was informed of the opposition's enmity through a letter that stated: "Go you shall. All the powers on earth and hell cannot deter us from our object. We are out to get you."[62]

Unswayed by such threats, the GGL made preparations for El Paso's next important political contest — the state Democratic primary on

July 22, wherein nominees for state and county offices would be selected. Once again, the League vowed to be on the lookout for alien voters and would this time be assisted by local immigration records that would help the organization keep better track of suspects. "In this way," explained George Oliver, "if we have trouble with alien voters again, we can expect to have several hundred indictments next fall where we had nine or ten this spring."[63]

It was also decided to draw up a list of suggested election officials and submit it to the County Democratic Executive Committee.[64] But there was dissension within the League. George Oliver advocated that the GGL investigate "graft among elected officials," an undertaking which probably would have resulted in the League officially endorsing or opposing specific candidates. League member William Pelphrey, himself an elected official, was against such activity, stating: "Nearly everyday I am called on to defend the league to persons who accuse it of being a political faction with 'clean-up' and 'lift-up' as its aim. It is the league's purpose solely to insist on clean elections." However, Oliver remained committed to his suggestion and said, "If I find that I have not time to carry on the work of the Good Government League and to investigate existing political rottenness, I may resign as president and carry on investigations personally."[65]

By the end of June, eighty Democratic candidates, "the largest number ever participating in an El Paso county primary [up to that time]," had announced. Of particular interest was the race for nomination as United States Senator: it was here that the Ku Klux Klan was making its first bid for national power. United States Representative Robert L. Henry was running openly as a Klansman, but the real support of the Klan hierarchy was behind Texas State Railroad Commissioner Earle B. Mayfield.[66] Mayfield's major opponents were incumbent Senator Charles Culberson and former Governor James E. Ferguson. Though Culberson enjoyed considerable support in El Paso, he had let his political base erode elsewhere in Texas. He had not set foot in the state during the past six years and he would not make a single speech during the campaign.[67] James Ferguson had political troubles of his own — he had been impeached and removed from the governor's office in 1917 for financial improprieties. Both Culberson and Ferguson took strong anti-Klan stands. Insisting that the KKK was not an issue, Mayfield refused to say whether he was a Klansman.[68]

The members of Frontier Klan No. 100 knew that Earle Mayfield belonged to their organization. Earlier in the year, he had secretly attended and addressed a local gathering of the Klan.[69] In late April, Mayfield was again in El Paso, this time praising the Good Government League's work to "obliterate forever the gang that for so many years ruled the politics of the city and county by unclean methods."[70] Upon his arrival, Mayfield had been enthusiastically greeted by El Paso's State Representative John E. Quaid, another Klansman.[71]

The Invisible Empire's other senatorial aspirant, Robert L. Henry, also made an appearance at the Pass. Henry, who described himself as "a natural born Klansman," originally planned a rally in Cleveland Square, but Mayor Davis withheld his permission, claiming that Henry represented a society which was "an organized enemy of organized constitutional government. . . ." The Reverend Henry Van Valkenburgh did not share the mayor's misgivings and proffered Henry the use of his pulpit at the First Methodist Church. The candidate accepted and was personally introduced by Van Valkenburgh, who later explained: "I am not a member of the Ku Klux Klan, but the time has come when we need the Klan or some other organization if free speech and free thought are to be abridged by the actions of a chosen few."[72]

Although the issue of the Klan figured prominently in the senatorial contest, lower-level races did not revolve as much around that controversial matter. There were some exciting races, nonetheless, one being the contest for county school superintendent, the first all-woman race in El Paso's history and one that revived the religious question relating to the school board's recent purge. The contestants were Frances Culligan, one of the fired Catholic principals, and Lillian Huggett, a high school teacher and daughter of the Reverend William D. Huggett of the Highland Park Methodist Church.[73] The Culligan campaign was based primarily on evoking sympathy for its candidate, Culligan's campaign manager noting that "She needs the place. Unlike her opponent, if defeated, she will not have the assurance of a position in the schools, as Miss Huggett has, in case she is not elected." A card distributed in Culligan's behalf portrayed her as "A widow supporting an invalid soldier son who receives no compensation."[74] An appeal was also made to the electorate's regional loyalty, it being pointed out that, while Lillian Huggett had been born in England, "Mrs. Culligan is not an adopted citizen of the United States, but a Southerner of the type of which you are proud. A daughter of Dixie, from the good old Southland, born in Mississippi. . . ."[75] The Huggett campaign emphasized the religious issue. Though Miss Huggett generally refrained from overt religious bigotry, her supporters were not so tactful. Pastor Van Val-

kenburgh accused the "Democratic machine" of trying to "place a religious organization known to be out of harmony with our public
school system in complete control of our county schools." "It is to be deplored," Van Valkenburgh inveighed, "that the superintendency of
schools must be mixed with partisan politics, but I am on safe ground
when I declare that Protestantism walks in accord with our public
school system."[76] The Reverend William H. Elfring of the First Congregational Church was also a Huggett partisan, declaring that "Religion
undefiled and pure is never the enemy of education, but sectarianism
may be."[77]

In addition to the Culligan-Huggett contest, there was a spirited
fight for the district attorney nomination. Contending for the position
were Charles L. Vowell, currently an assistant district attorney, and
James H. Peden, former assistant county attorney and outspoken member of the Good Government League. Peden's supporters characterized
their candidate as a "fearless prosecutor" and charged that Vowell was
reluctant to pursue prostitution cases. Peden claimed that, when he
and his opponent had worked together as prosecutors, Vowell had refused to dismiss a case against a man who was clearly innocent. Vowell
denied the charge in a public confrontation:

> "Tell us his name [the man who had been falsely accused], and if I
> can recall the case and recall the circumstances I will admit it if I
> was wrong. What was his name?"
> "I'll tell it later," Mr. Peden replied from the crowd.
> "Tell it now; tell it now," Mr. Vowell said. "Don't be a George
> Oliver in politics; be a man."[78]

Despite the spirited politicking in the races for United States Senator, county superintendent of schools, and district attorney, it became
evident that local voters were not as interested in the July primary as
they had been in the school board contest. The *Herald* sensed the increased apathy, speculating that it might be due to "the great amount
of fireworks used in the school board election last April." The failure of
the numerous candidates to divide neatly into pro-establishment or
anti-establishment tickets confused the voters.[79] Nevertheless, a flyer
listing an anonymously sponsored ticket appeared in early July. The
flyer urged the nominations of Earle Mayfield for United States Senator, James H. Peden for district attorney, J. E. Anderson for county
clerk, Frank D. Scotten for county tax assessor, Asa R. Webb for county

treasurer, Lillian Huggett for county superintendent of schools, and Robert H. Oliver for county commissioner, precinct one.[80] Almost without doubt, the flyer was drafted by Frontier Klan No. 100.

In contrast to the situation in April, the Klan's prospects for electing favorable candidates in the Democratic primary suffered from a variety of problems. One of these was that organized labor endorsed a ticket that differed substantially from the Klan's. Included among the candidates recommended by the Central Labor Union's Non-Partisan Political Conference were Frances Culligan, Charles Vowell, and Robert Lyons, candidate for county commissioner, precinct one.[81] These endorsements demonstrated that labor had considered its own interests before committing itself to any pro-Klan coalition. In the case of Mrs. Culligan, labor endorsed her because her deceased husband had been a member of the machinists' union. A labor spokesman explained that "If a man has been a member of union labor, his family is not forgotten after his death. Mrs. Culligan is labor's choice and labor is unqualifiedly for her."[82]

The *El Paso Herald*, whose support had contributed to the Klan victory in April, also proved less than reliable. Although the paper strongly backed Lillian Huggett, it failed to endorse any other Klan-supported candidate who was involved in a contested race. The *Herald* was particularly fervent in urging the re-election of Charles Culberson, who was openly anti-Klan.[83] Thus, despite its many Klan employees, the *Herald* could not be counted on in every instance to support KKK candidates.

Nor did the Klan, in the guise of the Good Government League, find it easy to install sympathetic election officials in the Democratic primary. A recommended list of election judges was drawn up and then submitted to the County Democratic Executive Commiteee for consideration, it being stressed by the League that "We wish especially to request that those officers named for precincts No. 1 to 14 and No. 47, lying south of the tracks, be appointed to act."[84] However, the Executive Committee, under Chairman Frank J. Lyons, was uncompliant and selected a list of officials that greatly differed from the GGL slate. In the end, only eighteen of the League's fifty-five recommendations were utilized. At the GGL's suggestion, the committee did, however, resolve that all voters in the primary be required to read and speak English.[85] The *Herald* gave hearty approval to this action, stating that ". . . the fact is, that if a native of the United States can't read and speak English, it is high time he is learning."[86]

Beyond the activities of its members within the Good Government League, the El Paso Klan proved reluctant to endorse publicly any candidate or to participate actively in any of the primary's campaigns. There is some evidence, however, that the KKK was interested in ascertaining where candidates stood on the issue of the Klan. A few days before the election, Coy R. McDowell, who was running for county treasurer, was approached by a man who was apparently a Klansman. According to McDowell:

> He said he had something that he wished to tell me in private. He took me to Cleveland Square and after making sure no one was about told me, speaking in a low tone, that 1600 members of the Klan are out to defeat all candidates not friendly to them.

McDowell was then advised to take a stand on the Invisible Empire, which he subsequently did, announcing that he was against the organization.[87] It is interesting to note that McDowell lost in the primary to incumbent County Treasurer Asa R. Webb, who, unbeknownst to most voters, was a member of Frontier Klan No. 100.[88]

Balloting began as scheduled on the morning of July 22. At first the voter turnout was very light and the eventual vote total would be more than two thousand less than that of the school board election. This delighted Ring politicians, Art Woods, superintendent of the city water department, noting, "With a light vote north of the tracks our chances are much better." "Sh-h!," admonished Mayor Charles Davis, who had noticed that a reporter was taking down Woods' comments; "Don't say anything about it."[89] As in the last election, the Good Government League was on guard, claiming to have received information that three unscrupulous politicians were planning to "deliver 800 votes in the three boxes they work in."[90] Anti-League partisans were also out in force, and the GGL became involved in numerous clashes at polling places. Police were called in to restore order at precinct 47, where there were rumors of "gun play." Hearing of the trouble, William H. Burges commented, "I hope there was a killing if they got the right man." At other polls, particularly on the northside, designated election judges failed to appear. In response, George Oliver and Clifford Sirmans, assisted by Sheriff Orndorff, dashed from precinct to precinct helping to elect substitute officials. Accompanying them were deputies armed with pistols and rifles, and the rumor began to circulate that Orndorff had become a Klansman.[91]

When the primary's results were tallied, the Klan had little reason for despondency. Out of fifteen contested races, seven "anti-Ring" candidates won, gaining the Democratic nominations for county attorney, county tax assessor, county treasurer, justice-of-the-peace place two, county commissioner precinct two, and justice of the 8th Court of Civil Appeals.[92] Lillian Huggett won her contest for county school superintendent by an impressive margin of 1,176 votes. However, Charles Vowell trounced James H. Peden 4,864 to 2,909. State races proved interesting also. El Paso County went heavily for Charles Culberson, giving him 3,466 votes compared to 1,630 for Earle Mayfield. But pro-KKK governor Pat Neff easily carried the county, and rabid Klansman Billie Mayfield trailed the leading vote-getter in the lieutenant governor's race by only 126 votes. As the results had come in, El Paso politicos had openly discussed the KKK and dubbed pro-Klan precincts north of the tracks as "dynamite precincts."[93] It had not been a repetition of the stunning victory in April, but there was no denying that the Klan had amply demonstrated its clout.

After the totals were announced, a rally was held at Highland Park Methodist Church to celebrate the nomination of Lillian Huggett. The gathering opened with a prayer: "Our great victory for the welfare of the community — may it be the beginning of a mighty overwhelming influence of the gospel of the son of God over the land, and we pray that the gospel of the son of God be inculcated in our schools." Pastor Huggett explained that his daughter's victory was due to "the fear of God [being] put in the hearts of some people who didn't care how they won a victory so long as they got it." Texans in other parts of the state also seemed to think that the time had come for a change. Klan candidates had won big in many elections, including those in Dallas and Travis counties.[94] Earle Mayfield led in the race for United States Senator and would face a runoff with James Ferguson. Billie Mayfield had also finished first in his contest and would face T. W. Davidson.[95] At the end of July, influential El Pasoans lunching at the Hotel Paso Del Norte heard the Lieutenant Governor of Texas argue that "there is a perfectly proper place in our social life for the Ku Klux Klan."[96] It appeared that the KKK was here to stay.

The weeks after the Democratic primary were relatively quiet. George Oliver's brother, Robert H. (Bob) Oliver, who had apparently lost a close race for one of the county commissioner's seats, initiated proceedings that eventually resulted in his name being placed on the general election ballot in November.[97] An investigation by county

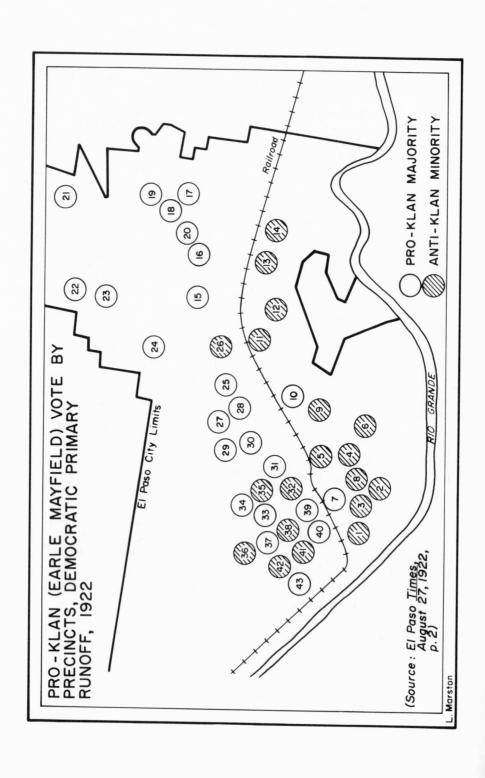

PRO-KLAN (EARLE MAYFIELD) VOTE BY PRECINCTS, DEMOCRATIC PRIMARY RUNOFF, 1922

PRO-KLAN MAJORITY

ANTI-KLAN MINORITY

El Paso City Limits

Railroad

RIO GRANDE

(Source: El Paso Times, August 27, 1922, p. 2)

L. Marston

Democratic authorities revealed that some of the people listed as having voted in precincts that went for Oliver's opponent had been deceased or out of town on election day.[98] The statewide runoff election
on August 26 was marked by extreme apathy. At one point it appeared
that the runoff would not be held in El Paso, due to a lack of funds;
ironically a five-hundred-dollar donation from former Mayor Charles
E. Kelly made the election possible.[99] James Ferguson, running on an
anti-Ku Klux Klan, anti-prohibition platform, was soundly defeated
by Earle Mayfield. In El Paso County the ex-governor lost to Mayfield
by 1,631 to 1,245.[100] Once again El Paso had voted pro-Klan.

By early September, El Pasoans traveling along Upper Valley roads
ran the risk of being stopped and told to turn back by hooded Klansmen conducting initiation rites.[101] The Invisible Empire was now at the
peak of its power in El Paso.

Conclusion: In September 1921, shortly after Frontier Klan No. 100
had been founded, the *El Paso Times* stated:

> [It] is doubtful if such an organization could get very far in El
> Paso or that any considerable number of our citizens could be in-
> duced to ally themselves with an order that is founded upon the
> presumption that the government is a failure, the law enforce-
> ment officers incompetent and the courts useless.[102]

Less than a year later, events had proven that the *Times'* evaluation
had been overly optimistic: hundreds of El Pasoans had joined the
Klan; three Klansmen had been elected to the school board; and a
number of candidates supported by the Invisible Empire were assured
of high office in county and state government. Almost every sphere of
community life was influenced by the presence of the Klan. The city
had been severely divided along religious lines, one clergyman noting
that:

> Catholics and Protestants have become suspicious of one another;
> friendships of long standing are either strained or broken, and
> business associations are daily being dissolved to the destruction
> of peace and the detriment of the prosperity of the city.[103]

Social and civic organizations were also divided by dissension over the
Klan. As city resident William J. Hooten later remembered: "Almost

every organization and club had its pro-Klan and anti-Klan factions."[104]

Though the state of local affairs in the late summer of 1922 was indeed ominous, the situation did proffer a certain degree of hope to the Klan's enemies. Despite the electorate's surprising willingness to support candidates who were sympathetic to the hooded order, it was still unclear what most voters thought of the Klan itself. Frontier Klan No. 100 had not openly involved itself in the 1922 elections, and locally, pro-KKK candidates had successfully avoided making the Invisible Empire a campaign issue. Instead, the El Paso establishment, saddled with a record of corruption and indifference towards moral issues, was the focus of debate. Initially opposing the establishment was an imposing coalition of new Anglo arrivals (many of them women), organized labor, and the city's older reform element. This coalition triumphed in the school board election, not so much because of widespread support for the Klan but because of the electorate's general dissatisfaction with the management of public affairs. During the Democratic primary in July, when voters were not as clearly presented with pro and anti-establishment tickets, the Klan-backed coalition began to disintegrate; organized labor left the fold, as did the *Herald*. Nevertheless, Klansmen managed to score a number of victories, and after the primary they looked forward with confidence to future political successes. Few of them could anticipate that in less than six months Frontier Klan No. 100 would be consigned to permanent political oblivion.

CHAPTER 7

The Defeat of the El Paso Klan

During the late summer of 1922, the activities of Frontier Klan No. 100 became intertwined with the reform efforts of a religious revival. In early September evangelist Bob Jones, a renowned "fighting parson" from Montgomery, Alabama, arrived in El Paso for five weeks of daily religious services. For weeks this prospect had stirred intense excitement among local evangelicals, who conducted a series of preparatory "cottage prayer meetings" and constructed a three-thousand-seat tabernacle at the corner of Virginia Street and Wyoming Avenue. Most of the city's Methodist, Baptist, Christian, and Presbyterian congregations officially endorsed the revival.[1] These efforts were well-rewarded: Jones proved to be a dynamic and entertaining orator who energetically assailed the despiritualizing trends of the day. He especially deplored "painted-faced, frizzled-headed high school girls," who could "give an old toper lessons in cussin'," and "half-dressed actors and half-naked actresses on the stage, ridiculing the Constitution."[2] To curb the sinful influence of Juárez saloons and nightclubs, he called for an early-hour closing of the international bridge: "Why, as a business proposition, don't you close the Juárez bridge?. . . . Why, every night thousands of dollars are spent in drinking and gambling across the river. That money might be kept in El Paso."[3] After visiting Juárez himself, Jones confessed that "When I crossed to Juárez I felt like I had gone to hell. Never in my life have I seen anything like it. I don't believe there is a spot on God's earth where there is more degeneracy, depravity, [or] more sin."[4]

Such attacks were music to the ears of moral reformers, particularly the Protestant ministers who had called for a concerted moral cleanup earlier that year. And other elements were similarly activated — pressure was soon being exerted within the most influential quarters of the business community to close the bridge every day at sundown. At a luncheon of the El Paso Real Estate Board, Horace B. Stevens, one of the city's most prominent realtors, introduced a resolution endorsing a 6 p.m. closing time.[5] When the realtors failed to take action, Stevens carried the fight into the El Paso Chamber of Commerce, where a "heated discussion" ensued.[6] Eventually, the Chamber decided to poll its members as to suggested closing times, and appointed a committee to conduct the referendum. One of those selected to serve on the committee was S. J. Isaacks. Isaacks had already given his opinion on the bridge issue, stating: "The Juárez saloon is bleeding El Paso of the money that ought to be spent for dry goods, shoes and groceries, and is detracting from the prosperity of El Paso."[7]

The results of the Chamber of Commerce referendum, released on September 30, proved enlightening. A total of 495 votes were cast in favor of the current closing time of 12:30 a.m., while 471 were for a variety of earlier closing times. A subsequent examination of the polling revealed that a preponderance of the votes for the status quo were cast by small businesses.[8] This element in the Chamber was no doubt concerned that an early closing time might reduce the profitable tourist trade. Another major consideration was the possibility that the Mexican government might be provoked into some form of retaliation, the chief fear being that Mexico might again establish a free trade zone along the border. A Chamber of Commerce report, released shortly before the referendum took place, concluded that such a zone would be disastrous, allowing Juárez merchants to undersell American wholesalers, and ruining United States importing concerns.[9] Confronted as always with an economy which was scarcely prosperous, businessmen were unwilling to risk the reimposition of a free trade zone.

The referendum displeased Evangelist Jones, who angrily declared that "The members of the Chamber of Commerce who voted for the 12:30 closing [time] did just what Lot did when he cast his vote for Sodom."[10] By this time, moreover, he had moved to ally himself with a group that was at odds with the business establishment. At a special Good Government League Night observance at the tabernacle on September 20, Jones rejoiced that "the Good Government League stands behind the movement to close the bridge."[11] He announced a list of League members who had pledged to lobby for an early bridge closing, including S. J. Isaacks, Dr. J. H. Gambrell, Charles S. Ward, George B. Oliver, Bob Oliver, and R. E. Thomason.[12] Earlier in the day, it was revealed that GGL President George Oliver was taking an active role in the bridge controversy, posting himself near the international bridge for the purpose of recording the license numbers of automobiles that went to Juárez.[13]

It became apparent that members of the Good Government League who were also Knights of the Ku Klux Klan had decided that Bob Jones was one of their kind. During the evening of September 29, the evangelist was an invited guest at a gathering of the El Paso Klan in Odd Fellows Hall. As Jones later described it:

> I went to a hall in this city that was built to accommodate 200 people and I found nearly 500 men packed in that little building. These men told me that they were members of the K. K. K. I found ministers and many of the outstanding, consecrated, Christian laymen of the city there.[14]

The meeting had been a lively affair, punctuated by occasional "loud cheering." Exactly what was said is not known, but Bob Jones was impressed, and the compatibility was mutual. After the meeting, Clifford L. Sirmans, Good Government League member, past potentate of the El Maida Shrine, and recently designated Klan spokesman, announced that the revivalist had invited Frontier Klan No. 100 to attend services at the tabernacle on October 2.[15] Jones confirmed the invitation, informing his audience two nights later:

> [Tomorrow] night we are going to have the Ku Klux Klan of the city of El Paso as our special guests. That organization seems to be

growing, so you will just tell your friends there will be something
doing that night. A great many of your friends want to know who
the Ku Klux are, so they will have an opportunity to find out some
things about them.[16]

The news rekindled fears among city fathers of an unauthorized
Klan parade. Reiterating his warnings against any such procession, Police Chief Edwards placed the entire police force on alert.[17] As events
transpired, however, this precaution was unnecessary. The Klansmen
decided to go to the revival as individuals and did not march *en masse*.
The fact that the meeting was open to all comers and that several other
"patriotic" organizations, such as the American Legion, the Veterans of
Foreign Wars, and the Red Cross, had been especially invited to attend
on the same evening, made positive identification of the individual
Klansmen almost impossible.[18] Nevertheless, it was clear that many El
Pasoans were curious to glimpse those who belonged to the hooded order, for the "Klan Night" crowd of over four thousand was the largest
of the entire five weeks of the revival. The throng spilled out onto adjacent sidewalks, and many who could not be seated listened to the proceedings from their parked automobiles.[19]

Almost all of Jones' oratory that evening related to the Ku Klux
Klan. He expounded at length on Colonel Simmons' views of Catholics
and Jews, and admitted that he had attended the Klan meeting on September 29. On the basis of his observation, he was persuaded that:

> The K. K. K. is here to stay. There is no question in my mind
> about this. When newspapers and men talk about killing the or-
> ganization, they are raving. . . . I am sure the crowd of last Fri-
> day night I saw in El Paso are not anarchists. They are as good
> men as ever walked the dirt of El Paso. I feel safe with the organi-
> zation in the hands of men of that kind.[20]

Jones advised his audience that at the Friday night meeting he had
found himself in the company of "most of the ministers [of] the leading
churches [in El Paso] . . . who informed me that they stood for enforcement of the law only through constitutional authorities."[21] This
was the extent of the evangelist's revelations concerning the Klan, however, and the crowd quietly dispersed after the benediction. During the
service, a Klan circular was distributed which showed a secret oath
that was purportedly taken by members of the Knights of Columbus.[22]

When the revival ended less than a week later, Jones received a five-hundred-dollar donation from Frontier Klan No. 100, with an accompanying letter that praised stands he had taken for "Christianity, law enforcement by constituted authorities, Americanism, and his efforts to make El Paso a better place in which to live."[23]

By the time that the Bob Jones revival left the Pass, Frontier Klan No. 100 was in serious disarray, the victim of unrelenting assaults on the tight secrecy it had previously maintained. The primary instigator of these assaults was William (Will) H. Fryer, former county attorney and prominent Catholic layman.[24] Fryer despised what the KKK was doing to El Paso and was determined to expose the organization's membership. His animosity also had personal overtones: he had at one time been the law partner of S. J. Isaacks. The partnership had ended acrimoniously in August 1921, at just about the time that the local Klan was being organized.[25] Almost from the beginning, Fryer and Isaacks had apparently disliked each other, and they were to remain "bitter enemies" for the rest of their lives.[26] The conflict was not so much over religion or politics as it was a clash of differing personalities. Stern and uncompromising, Isaacks was a basically reserved individual, while the flamboyant Fryer reveled at being in the public eye.[27]

Whatever his precise motivation, Will Fryer had, by the summer of 1922, begun compiling extensive information concerning the local Klan. During the county Democratic convention in July, he advocated (unsuccessfully, as it turned out) a formal repudiation of the Ku Klux Klan, noting that the organization was "otherwise known as the National Business Men's Association."[28] Following through on this piece of information, the *El Paso Times* dispatched a reporter to the offices of the National Business Men's Association (NBMA) in the First National Bank Building. The association's representative, Clifford L. Sirmans, insisted that the NBMA was merely a business organization which handled credit references. But it was later discovered that no local banks or businesses had previously heard of the NBMA.[29] The first crack had appeared in Frontier Klan No. 100's ultrasecrecy.

By September 1922 the *Times* had become fully involved in efforts to determine which El Pasoans had joined the Invisible Empire. On September 8, the Klan held still another initiation west of the city, somewhere between the Courchesne bridge and the El Paso Country Club. The *Times* posted "watchers" near the scene, who took down the automobile license numbers of those attending. The meeting was marked by two interesting innovations. Instead of the usual wooden cross,

Klansmen assembled beneath an electrically lighted "fiery cross" which received power from a truck generator. The same generator also supplied a large spotlight which "played over the scene of the almost weird and awe-inspiring ceremony." Unfortunately for the participants, a sudden rainshower shorted out the generator: "Klansmen, their robes flapping and their pants legs showing at the bottom, made an undignified rush for their machines [cars] and in a few minutes, silence and the rain reigned supreme." Standing nearby and untouched were two truckloads of sodas and sandwiches, the latter ruined by the downpour.[30]

The *Times*' investigative reporting eventually resulted in an extensive compilation of members of Frontier Klan No. 100.[31] Of course, the Klan resented this and reacted accordingly. When the *Times*' city editor personally attempted to investigate a report of Klansmen taking down the license numbers of automobiles going to Juárez, he was accosted by a city policeman (apparently a KKK member) and struck down.[32] The newspaper man's wife later received a telephone call from a self-described "klanswoman," who warned:

> We know all about the Times [*sic*] and we would have gotten its editor [James Black] long ago, but instead of going to his business alone and unafraid, he chose to nightly ride from his work in a city auto at city expense, escorted by two of El Paso's "finest officers." But we will get him yet, for he does not know that he often rides home with two policemen who are active members of Frontier Klan No. 100.[33]

As was indicated by this threatening call and the assault on the *Times*' man, the local Klan had managed to recruit members from among the El Paso police force. City officials were aware of this, having been notified that the personal automobiles of policemen had been seen near Klan gatherings. When the suspected officers were questioned by their superiors, they proved "evasive."[34] In response, the city civil service commission adopted a resolution forbidding Klansmen from serving as city policemen or firemen, and began a probe into the extent of the Invisible Empire's influence within the police department.[35] The first step was to require all officers to sign the following affidavit:

> I hereby most solemnly swear and state under oath that I am not now a member of an organization or order known as the Ku Klux

Klan and I am not a citizen of the Invisible Empire, and I further
swear and state under oath that I have not been within six months
next preceding this date a member of the Ku Klux Klan, nor a citizen of the Invisible Empire.[36]

Every member of the police department signed the affidavit, with the
exception of Police Sergeant Stanley Good, who admitted that he had
been a Klansman within the past six months.[37] Mayor Davis, however,
was not satisfied. He had acquired a list of suspected KKK members
and knew that, despite what their affidavits said, certain officers had
recently attended Klan meetings. In Davis' view, this was an intoler-
able situation which posed a grave threat to his political machine.
With the city Democratic primary only five months away, the municipal administration had to be purged of any disloyal employees who
might supply damaging information to the opposition.[38]

The city moved quickly. On September 26, National Business Men's
Association representative Clifford L. Sirmans was subpoenaed to appear immediately before Justice of the Peace Clark Wright. Sirmans
was instructed to bring the membership list of Frontier Klan No. 100
with him. Realizing that further deception would be futile, he said he
would comply.[39] In court, Sirmans was questioned extensively by Assistant District Attorney Charles Vowell as to which police officers had
been members of the Klan. It was revealed that a total of fourteen policemen had joined the organization, including four charter members.
According to Sirmans' records, all of the men had eventually resigned
from the Klan, but four had been active members within the past six
months. Having supplied this information, the Klan secretary was
released.[40]

The news that Clifford Sirmans had been interrogated and that city
officials had had access to the local Klan's membership list threw Frontier Klan No. 100 into a panic. After the story broke, forty-three men
entered the law office of S. J. Isaacks for a hurried conference. Steve
Lattner, Isaack's law partner, noted the next day that:

There were a number of visitors I suspected of belonging to the
Ku Klux Klan who called on my law partner, Judge Isaacks, yesterday morning. . . . Judge Isaacks is my law partner and my
business associate, and I would not care to be quoted as saying as
to what secret orders he may be affiliated with."

It was reported that resignations from the Klan were pouring in, most of them by mail and telephone because the resignees were afraid that the offices of the National Business Men's Association were being watched.[41]

In the days that followed, the El Paso city government took additional steps to cleanse itself of Klansmen. Mayor Davis suspended the four policemen who had signed false affidavits and ordered all municipal employees to sign sworn statements that they had not been members of the KKK within the past six months. Davis warned that he had seen a Klan membership list and knew that it included ten to twelve city employees. When Robert Koenig, a mechanic in the city automobile shop, and James M. Darr, a chain gang guard, refused to sign affidavits, they were summarily dismissed. City weights and measurements inspector Lucian T. Jones also failed to sign, but was allowed to keep his job after he admitted he had been a Klansman. Samuel L. Townshend surprised everyone when he announced that he had been a member of the Ku Klux Klan for sixty-seven years! It turned out that Townshend had belonged to the original KKK, and he was permitted to continue as watchman at the city corral.[42]

The Davis administration's anti-Klan crusade did not receive unanimous support. A gathering of seventy-five prominent local Protestants passed a resolution that condemned the mayor's firing of "Members of a certain Protestant secret organization," claiming that the action was "un-American and not in accord with the spirit of American institutions." The gathering was attended by a large majority of El Paso's Protestant ministers.[43] Other citizens also voiced sympathy towards the Klan. H. Walter Loggins contended that the only reason the KKK had been organized in the first place was "because of the non-enforcement of laws, and because of the failure of officials and courts to deal with vicious conditions effectively."[44] Members of the Klan itself were of course angered by the city's actions and were of the opinion that they were being treated unfairly. Noting that city detectives had been posted near Odd Fellows Hall while a Klan meeting was in progress, George Oliver angrily shouted, "You'd better watch some of your officials instead of spying on decent citizens, peaceably attending a meeting!"[45] In retaliation for the harassment, the Klan managed to cause the city administration a small degree of embarrassment. On September 27, the day after he had been interrogated, Clifford Sirmans revealed that former school board candidate and current city civil service commissioner Dr. James Brady had at one time belonged to Frontier Klan No. 100. Brady admitted this was true, but explained: "I had misunderstood the real nature and purpose of the organization and very soon realized that I was not in sympathy with them." Yet, in fact, Brady had continued to pay his Klan dues until April 1, 1922. Thus it appears that the school board election of 1922 involved *four* candidates who were members of the Ku Klux Klan.[46]

Having removed active Klansmen from the municipal work force, the Davis administration took no further action concerning the order. To a certain extent this is understandable; Frontier Klan No. 100 had proved to be law-abiding and there was no other way to attack the Klan through the courts. However, it would have been a relatively simple matter to have subpoenaed the KKK membership list once again (on almost any pretext) and then to have revealed the Klan roster to the press. The city Ring did not do this. Why is not known, though it can be speculated that the Davis administration knew that such exposure would reveal that certain influential businessmen, politicians, and community leaders had joined the Invisible Empire, even if only for a short time. With the city Democratic primary approaching, the Ring wanted to avoid taking any action that might alienate these important people. The same line of reasoning would also explain why the establishment's spokespiece, the *El Paso Times*, declined to print an extensive list of past and present members of Frontier Klan No. 100.

An El Pasoan who did not share the Davis Ring's reticence concerning a full exposure of the Klan was Will Fryer. It was his avowed intention to reveal the Klan's membership and thereby undermine its influence. Towards that end, the former county attorney filed a petition in 65th district court requesting that the names of four Democratic nominees be taken off the general election ballot in November. Named in Fryer's petition were John E. Quaid, nominee for state representative; Frank Scotten, Jr., nominee for county tax assessor and collector; Clarence W. Harper, nominee for district clerk; and Asa R. Webb, nominee for county treasurer. The petition asserted that these individuals had "forsworn allegiance to the constitution and laws of the state of Texas" through the taking of an oath of loyalty to a foreign power — the Invisible Empire. It was requested that certain witnesses be called who could give testimony as to the nominees' affiliation with the Klan. These were S. J. Isaacks, Dr. J. H. Gambrell, James A. Borders, George B. Oliver, the Reverend Paul G. Preston, pastor of the First Christian Church; William J. Moran, editor of the *El Paso Labor Advocate*; Charles H. De Groff, co-proprietor of the Hotel Orndorff;

C. Rutledge Isaacks, local attorney; Dr. William P. Rogers, local physician; George G. Franklin, president of the Tri-State Grocery Company; William E. Orr, secretary-treasurer of the Dudley & Orr Building Stone Company; John W. Wray, chief of the fire department; and John W. Mershon, railway conductor.[47]

In response to Fryer's petition, subpoenas were issued ordering the four nominees and the fourteen witnesses to appear in court on October 30. Clifford Sirmans and Mrs. Charles B. Winstead, secretary of the National Business Men's Association, were also subpoenaed and ordered to present the membership list of Frontier Klan No. 100. Eight additional witnesses later received summons: John P. Yearwood, president of the Standard Grocery Company; James J. Ormsbee, United States Postmaster; the Reverend Henry Van Valkenburgh, pastor of the First Methodist Church; the Reverend William H. Joyner, pastor of Government Hills Baptist Church; William Lankford, immigration officer; John B. Kilpatrick, deputy sheriff; John Boone, deputy sheriff; and John Wood, former captain of police.[48]

During the two days before they were scheduled to appear in court, a number of the respondents and witnesses named in Fryer's petition were questioned by reporters as to their membership in the KKK. Asked whether he was a Klansman, State Representative John E. Quaid said, 'I don't care to talk about that, as it is in the hands of my attorneys." Responding to the same question, Asa R. Webb replied, "That is my business," and Frank Scotten, Jr., would only say, "We'll discuss that in court tomorrow." When confronted by the press, S. J. Isaacks, George B. Oliver, the Reverend Paul Preston, and James A. Borders all refused to say whether or not they were Klansmen.[49]

On the afternoon of October 30 Will Fryer had his showdown with the local Klan. The packed courtroom crowd, more than half comprised of women, had a definite pro-Klan air about it. When S. J. Isaacks, Clifford Sirmans, Frank Scotten, Jr., and Dr. J. H. Gambrell entered, there was great cheering and applause. The appearance of Fryer brought forth only boos, hisses, and catcalls. As the proceedings began, W. M. Peticolas and Edward M. Whitaker, attorneys for the respondents, introduced a plea of abatement in behalf of John E. Quaid, and a general demurrer in behalf of the other three nominees, requesting that no injunction be issued barring their names from the general election ballot. The essence of the respondents' defense was that the Ku Klux Klan did not constitute a foreign power and that taking the Klan oath did not disqualify a person from holding public office. It was then

Will Fryer's turn to make an opening statement and he quickly launched into a vitriolic denunciation of the Klan:

> Counsel says that the Ku Klux Klan is not an empire. We are prepared to prove that the members claim it to be an empire. . . . The worst crime there is is treason. In the oath of the Klansman you will notice that the invisible empire is placed first and America comes second. Duty to the Klan comes first. . . . This is why I can face the hisses, the cowardice of those who think they can frighten the court by the thought [that]cowards in masks might visit you at night.[50]

After Fryer had completed his statement, the proceedings took a crucial turn. Judge Ballard Coldwell decided he would rule on the respondents' plea of abatement and general demurrer before hearing further evidence. This deprived Fryer of the opportunity of immediately questioning the witnesses who had been subpoenaed. As Coldwell left the courtroom to deliberate, there were shouts of "Hurrah for the Klan!"[51] It is not known what Fryer planned to ask the witnesses, but some indication is given in an *ex parte* depostion he had drawn up. One of the questions in the deposition asks whether any of the following men had ever attended a meeting of Frontier Klan No. 100: S. J. Isaacks, J. H. Gambrell, James A. Borders, Charles De Groff, Clifford L. Sirmans, the Reverend Henry Van Valkenburgh, the Reverend George McCall, pastor of the Central Baptist Church; James Dudley, president of Dudley & Orr Building Stone Company; Edward M. Whitaker, local attorney; Preston E. Gardner, local attorney; and Bob Oliver, candidate for county commissioner.[52] As is indicated by the deposition, it had probably been Fryer's intent to expose every prominent citizen who was currently a member of the Ku Klux Klan.

Fryer knew that Judge Coldwell would rule in favor of the respondents' plea of abatement and general demurrer. The entire case against the Klan had been based on unsound legal ground, the only purpose being to direct the spotlight of publicity on local Klansmen. Before Coldwell could deliver what would have been an unfavorable ruling, Fryer withdrew his petition for an injunction. He later explained, "I consider the results that I have gained in this instance gratifying, inasmuch as my petition served to smoke out many who denied they were Klansmen."[53]

Will Fryer's court case dealt Frontier Klan No. 100 a severe blow.

Many of the organization's most influential members were exposed, and, henceforth, their public actions would take place with the community aware that they were Klansmen. For those businessmen and politicians who had joined the Klan out of expediency, membership had become a liability: at any moment their name might appear in the papers or a court proceeding, thus bringing the wrath of anti-Klan partisans upon them. Moreover, it would be difficult from now on to recruit new Klansmen. The idea of joining a secret society which was being spied upon by city detectives, newspaper reporters, and former county attorneys was hardly appealing to most respectable citizens. The days of the large westside initiation ceremonies were gone.

Despite these problems, a significant number of Klansmen held firm. On October 30 Bob Oliver admitted he was a Klan member, declaring that he was proud to belong to "an organization which stands for everything good in this community."[54] The previous evening, Asa R. Webb, El Paso county treasurer, had stood before the congregation of the Government Hills Baptist Church, stating: "If you want to see a good Klansman, look at me." At the same meeting, the church's pastor, William H. Joyner, and a dozen other church members also revealed that they were in the Klan.[55] Five days later, the four candidates named in Will Fryer's petition, accompanied by Bob Oliver, candidate for county commissioner, and Arthur M. Horn, candidate for justice of the peace, held a political rally at the church. Asa R. Webb informed the gathering that "We are all Christian men. . . . Nobody here need get excited because we are Ku Kluxers." District Clerk Clarence Harper denounced Joe Dunne and Will Fryer, claiming: "They are fighting the Klan because the Klan stands for clean politics." Pastor Joyner promised the Klansmen his full backing in the pending election, stating that "It's time that we repudiate rotten politics in El Paso. It's time for the churches and preachers to get into the fight."[56]

By November 1922 the stage was being set for what would prove to be the last major test of strength between Frontier Klan No. 100 and the El Paso establishment. In less than four months the city Democratic primary would be held, and the Klan had already begun to field a full ticket. However, a number of developments boded ill for the Klan.

Throughout 1922 important sectors of the El Paso community had become increasingly apprehensive about the impact of Frontier Klan No. 100. One such group was comprised of El Paso businessmen. The past year had not been a good one economically: there had been a million dollar decline in new building permits from the previous year, and

El Paso's population had shrunk by six thousand. It appeared that at least part of the blame could be placed on sectarian discord. In March the president of the local Chamber of Commerce noted that "This religious controversy is hurting business," and in August, Zach L. Cobb declared:

> If we do not put a stop to this discord and the fight between people of different creeds and get together and come back in the old spirit that existed here, we might just as well pull our freight and move to some other community where such conditions do not exist.[57]

The election of a Klan-backed municipal government would probably mean a continuation of this disruptive animosity, and would probably intensify economic problems. After the Bob Jones revival (as has been discussed), it was clear that the Klan was in favor of an early closing time for the international bridge. Such a move would surely damage the tourist trade and the significant portion of the El Paso retail trade which was sustained by customers from Mexico. In addition, the Mexican government might be provoked into again establishing a free trade zone along the border.

Businessmen realized that even if a Klan city government did not attain an early closing hour for the bridge, the mere existence of such a government would damage the city's relations with Mexico. Delicate negotiations were currently underway for full United States recognition of the Obregón government, and local financial interests looked forward to a great surge in business activity south of the border when recognition had become a fact. The presence of a Klan-run city administration would hardly be a favorable inducement for Mexican businessmen and officials to direct business and trade toward El Paso. Apprehension concerning Frontier Klan No. 100 had already been manifested in the southern republic. In March 1922 a Mexico City newspaper, *El Universal*, ran a wildly exaggerated story that claimed that the El Paso Klan had threatened to dynamite Sacred Heart Church in Chihuahuita. The article said the church was currently being guarded by two thousand American soldiers and one thousand Mexican parishioners.[58] In August, following the incident in which Charles Clark was warned by men bearing KKK cards to leave Juárez, a newspaper in that city ran a front-page story under the headline, "First Attempt By Klansmen to Invade the City." Juárez officials were angered by the incident, one of them announcing: "We will not tolerate for a moment this thing of Klansmen meddling with Juárez residents. . . . If a Klansman comes over and announces himself as such, he may find himself behind bars, even though he is not molesting anyone."[59] Clearly, a Klan city government would not be conducive to good relations with El Paso's sister city.

Just as was the case with the business community, many other rank-and-file El Pasoans were developing serious doubts about the Klan. The postwar crime wave had abated considerably, and there no longer seemed to be as great a need for a society of extralegal vigilantes. Problems relating to prohibition continued, but the situation was not nearly as chaotic as in 1921.[60] The romantic appeal of the Klan had largely evaporated, particularly after the Fryer exposures in October. Unmasked, Klansmen no longer appeared as the mysterious embodiment of honor and reform. Moreover, El Pasoans now had ample evidence of what "invisible government" could lead to. Ever since April the school board had been divided into two bickering factions that availed themselves of almost every conceivable occasion to quarrel. At one point, a dispute over the dismissal of a truant officer nearly resulted in physical violence. After engaging in a shouting match with fellow board member W. T. Power, S. J. Isaacks picked up a chair and appeared ready to use it on his adversary. As Isaacks later explained: "I guess I got a bit excited and I did jump up from my chair. Then Powers [sic] reached for his hip. I sat down."[61]

Even more distressing than this unseemly behavior was the heavy-handed fashion in which the pro-Klan clique on the board of trustees had run school affairs. In defiance of an informal precedent in use since 1909, board president Charles Ward used his vote not only to break, but to *make* tie votes. Ward also reserved the right to single-handly fire teachers, confident that the other Klan trustees would back him up. On one occasion the arbitrary transfer of a popular school principal brought a sharp protest from the Morehead Parent-Teacher Association, a representative stating:

> Pardon me, but is this the way you usually treat your patrons?
> . . . Things are being put over by the board without considering the people. We are highly concerned with the business of the school because the patrons are our children, yet we are not consulted as we used to be.[62]

With the city primary approaching, El Pasoans seriously had to consider if this was the manner in which they wanted municipal affairs to be conducted.

Faced with an increasingly skeptical public, Frontier Klan No. 100 also had to contend with severe internal problems. The exposures in September and October had led to mass resignations, and there was little hope of making up for losses through new recruiting. Other resignations had come about simply because some members had become dissatisfied with the KKK, seeing it as a money-making scheme that had little hope of playing a positive role in the community.[63] By then it was evident that the Klan's political alliance had fallen apart: organized labor could no longer be counted upon to support pro-Klan candidates, and the press was uniformly hostile, including the new *El Paso Post*, which advocated keeping "hooded morons" out of public office.[64]

The friendly relationship that the Klan enjoyed with the city's Protestant ministers also suffered setbacks. By the end of October the Reverend Percy Knickerbocker, who had allowed the Klan to meet in the basement of Trinity Methodist Church (exactly when is not clear), had been transferred from El Paso, taking up new duties in Paris, Texas.[65] That same month, the Reverend George McCall, the pro-Klan pastor of the Central Baptist Church, resigned to accept a call from a Tennessee congregation.[66] Early 1923 saw the departure of the outspoken Henry Van Valkenburgh, who moved to Havre, Montana, where it was later reported that he was complaining that "a good man has no chance [in El Paso]."[67] Other Protestant pastors, perhaps sensing the shift in local attitude toward the Klan, moderated their vocal support for the Invisible Empire and began to extol religious tolerance. In mid-October, while addressing a Rotary luncheon, the Reverend Dr. Floyd Poe asserted:

> This is God's country and we are all His. There should be a bigger place in America for a real Catholic Christian than for a half-hearted Protestant. There should be a heartier welcome for an honest Jew than for a tricky Catholic.[68]

A similar stance was taken by other ministers, and the *Times* noted that: "The most encouraging matter of the season is the apparently unconcerted decision of several of the leading El Paso ministers to preach tolerance."[69]

Despite the change in heart demonstrated by some men of the cloth, others among them continued to support the Klan. On October 11 the *Herald* conducted a symposium among twenty-two of the city's prominent Protestant ministers and church officers, asking them:

1. Are you now, or have you ever been a member of the Ku Klux Klan?

2. If not a member of the Ku Klux Klan, are you in sympathy with the organization?

Revealingly, only two of those queried said they were decidedly against the Klan. "Of the remainder," reported the *Herald*, "ten expressed sympathy for the organization while the others gave answers so burdened with conditional phrases that they were practically evasive." Nine ministers refused to clearly state whether they were Klansmen. They included the Reverends Samuel J. T. Williams of the First Baptist Church, Charles D. Daniel of the Baptist Home Mission Board, Henry H. Vermillion of the Southern Baptist Sanatorium, William S. Vanderpool of the Asbury Methodist Church, Arthur W. Jones of the Austin Park Christian Church, Paul G. Preston of the First Christian Church, George McCall of the Central Baptist Church, Henry C. Schneider of the Altura Presbyterian Church, and William Elfring of the First Congregational Church. The Reverend William S. Huggett of Highland Park Methodist Church admitted that he supported the Klan, but pointed out that he could not be a member because he was foreign born. The Reverend Henry Van Valkenburgh continued to deny Klan affiliation, although he did admit, "I am in sympathy with the El Paso Klan, with apologies to no one."[70]

This, then, was the situation as El Paso prepared for the city Democratic primary that would be held in February 1923. After a number of remarkable political successes in 1922, Frontier Klan No. 100 had become afflicted with serious problems which undermined its influence. It was apparent, nevertheless, that considerable support for the Klan still existed. Protestant pastors generally persisted in their friendly stance toward the organization, and as late as November 1922, local voters demonstrated that they were not totally averse to recognized Klansmen: John E. Quaid, Asa R. Webb, Frank Scotten, Jr., Clarence Harper, Robert Oliver, and Arthur M. Horn all easily won their general election contests. In the same election, Earle Mayfield carried El Paso County by a two-to-one margin over an anti-Klan fusion candidate for the United States Senate.[71] The possibility that the Invisible Empire might win political control of the city still loomed large.

In late August 1922 Preston E. (P. E.) Gardner announced that he was a candidate for mayor. A resident of the city for twelve years, he was an attorney and the owner of the Gardner Hotel, in downtown El Paso.[72] During the weeks that followed, Gardner's association with the Ku Klux Klan became a matter of common knowledge. On October 29 Will Fryer informed the *Times* that a candidate for mayor had addressed Frontier Klan No. 100 a few weeks earlier.[73] Because there was only one candidate currently running for that position, the insinuation was clear. In addition, Gardner was one of those listed in Fryer's deposition (which had been published in the local press) as having attended meetings of the local Klan.[74]

In mid-December P. E. Gardener announced that he was running on a ticket with four aldermanic candidates. They were Robert Lander, owner of the Lander Lumber Company; J. Mack Crawford, operator of the Southwestern Planing Mill; Robert E. Ross, president of the El Paso Headlight Gas Manufacturing Company; and Roy Walker, owner of the Walker Electric Company. Three of these men were lay Protestant church officers, and all four were Masons.[75] They, along with Gardner, were also members of Frontier Klan No. 100, and they received the formal endorsement of that organization at a secret Klan meeting in December.[76]

The KKK was not to be without formidable competition in the city primary. On November 11 State Senator Richard M. (Dick) Dudley announced that he would run for mayor on a five-man ticket. Slated for the aldermanic positions were A. B. Poe, owner of Evergreen Cemetery; Harvey P. Jackson, owner of the Alamo Motor Company; Milton Tracey, railway conductor and active union leader; and Walter Clayton, former alderman under Mayor Charles E. Kelly.[77] The ticket had been carefully chosen so as to appeal to a wide range of voters. Jackson had worked under reform Mayor Tom Lea, and would draw the progressive vote; Tracey would attract union support; and Clayton would hopefully bring in the votes of the Kelly-Ring partisans. However, Clayton decided to leave the ticket and was replaced with William K. Ramsey, a local realtor.[78]

In many ways Dick Dudley was the ideal candidate to oppose the Ku Klux Klan. Plain spoken and scrupulously honest, he was one of El Paso's most respected businessmen and officeholders and was currently serving as the president pro tem of the state senate. Furthermore, he was not tied to the Davis administration; he was a "business progressive" who supported "prohibition, woman suffrage, all the war measures, and [who] fought for every kind of education from the little country school to the university." As has been related, Dudley had also been active in the movement to bar alien voters in Texas and he stood firmly in support of "clean election laws and permitting none to vote but American citizens. . . ."[79]

At first it appeared that there would be a three-way race for mayor. Strong support still existed for Mayor Charles Davis, who was completing his third consecutive term, and there is little doubt that he would have liked to remain in office.[80] Anticipating a Davis re-election bid, the Dudley campaign was originally prepared to take the middle ground between the Klan and the Ring, stressing that neither Klansmen *nor Catholics* were on their ticket.[81] However, Mayor Davis realized that his candidacy would split the anti-Klan vote, thus possibly resulting in the election of P. E. Gardner. In what must be credited as an admirably selfless act, Davis announced on December 9 that he would not seek re-election.[82] This was a crucial development which determined that the anti-Klan partisans would not be forced into the uncomfortable position of defending the past actions of the Davis machine. Davis' withdrawal also meant that the city primary would be a simple one-on-one contest — the Ku Klux Klan versus those arrayed against the Klan.

The differing stands of the Dudley and Gardner tickets in regard to the Invisible Empire were established early on in the campaign. On January 10 the *El Paso Post* submitted questionnaires to the two tickets, inquiring whether their respective candidates were members of the Ku Klux Klan or had ever solicited the support of that organization. Gardner campaign manager Charles H. Kirkland, a former vice-president of the Good Government League, refused to answer the questionnaire and would only say that "The Ku Klux Klan is not an issue." The Dudley ticket, on the other hand, announced that none of its members were Klansmen and that they did not desire the endorsement of Frontier Klan No. 100.[83] It was not acknowledged, however, that aldermanic candidate A. B. Poe and Dudley campaign manager Cleveland W. Croom were both former Klan members.[84]

The El Paso electorate was particularly interested in whether candidates were members of the Invisible Empire because of the recent and sensational Mer Rouge murders. The violence involved two Louisiana communities, one Klan-controlled, the other vehemently anti-Klan.

Bad blood eventually escalated into torture and murder after Klansmen kidnapped two of their adversaries. When the victims' bodies were
found in a swamp, it was discovered that their extremities had been
slowly crushed in a large, cogged "torture machine." The hands and
feet of both men had been amputated.[85]

The investigation of the Mer Rouge murders was headlined in the El
Paso press throughout the months of December and January. Though
Louisiana officials never indicted any Klansmen, these vile crimes
showed how the presence of the Klan could inflame community fears
and hatreds, and lead to senseless violence.[86] Mer Rouge served as an
example to many thinking El Pasoans who were now faced with the
possibility of a Klan-controlled city government.[87]

Needing to obscure the Klan issue, the Gardner campaign attempted
to direct the public's attention to a variety of other topics. P. E. Gardner called for reduced taxes, a better city water supply, and improved
street paving; and it was claimed that Dick Dudley was the puppet of
the Davis administration: "Henchmen of the present city ring put a
ring in his [Dudley's] nose and lead him around like a blooded bull." At
a series of political rallies considerable oratory was also dedicated to
vice, drug smuggling, bootlegging, and Joe Dunne, but the Klan issue
would not go away.[88] In desperation, Charles Kirkland charged that
Dudley had sought Klan aid in his recent senate bid and that the
senator's friends had once characterized him as "as good a Klansman as
ever wore shoe leather."[89] These assertions were not true, but they
demonstrated that even the Gardner forces realized that membership
in the KKK could be a political liability.

In contrast to the Gardner effort, the Dudley campaign was an impressive (and well funded) enterprise. Senator Dudley repeatedly cited
his progressive record and called for a reunited El Paso which would
"not be governed or controlled by any one class or sect, but rather by
broad-minded businessmen who represent its full citizenship. . . ."[90]
As did his opposition, Dudley advocated lower taxes, civic improvements, and better law enforcement.[91] Unlike Gardner, however, the
senator came out forthrightly on the side of racial and religious tolerance. In one speech, Dudley discussed the national tomb of the unknown soldier:

That hero might have been a native of New Jersey. He may even
have been an El Paso boy. He might have been the son of a rich
man or the son of a poor man. He may have been a Baptist or a

Catholic, a Jew or Gentile. He may have been a white boy, or a
Mexican or a Negro. I don't know. What I do know is that he was
a 100 per cent American.[92]

During the course of the campaign, the anti-Klan ticket gathered a
number of important endorsements. All three daily newspapers strongly backed Dudley, including the *Herald* (notwithstanding the fact that
its city editor and news editor were Klansmen).[93] After answering a labor questionnaire to the satisfaction of local union men, the Dudley
candidates also received the support of the *El Paso Labor Advocate*.[94]
Impressive personal endorsements came from former Mayor Tom Lea
and former Speaker of the Texas House of Representatives R. E. Thomason.[95] One group of Dudley backers was careful to maintain a low
profile. Wary of repeating their mistake in the school board election,
city government incumbents declined to play an active role in the campaign. This was difficult at times. Faced with a barrage of charges from
the Gardner forces, Mayor Davis angrily asserted that the Klan partisans were the "biggest bunch of liars I ever heard of."[96] Nevertheless,
the Ring held back from entering the fray, sparing Dudley the embarrassment of appearing to be allied with the old order.

As the campaign heated up, the enemies of the Klan initiated a fierce
two-prong attack on the Invisible Empire. Tom Lea (who unbeknownst to most of the public was a former member of Frontier Klan
No. 100) was in charge of assailing the past record of P. E. Gardner, la-
beling him a "smooth cunning hypocrite," whose legal career had mostly consisted of posting bail bonds for fallen women.[97] The job of attacking the Klan itself was given to District Attorney Charles Vowell, who
gave a series of brilliant speeches explaining why the KKK had no place
in El Paso:

> In this great southwest, we are used to meeting each other man to
> man and fighting it out. That's the way of the great southwest —
> we don't want to look at each other through the holes of a pillow-
> slip.
>   Let us say to them in this election, 'By the eternal Gods, you
> shall not crucify El Paso on a fiery cross!'[98]

The oratory of Lea and Vowell at large rallies at Liberty Hall, as
well as the strong anti-Klan editorials in the local press, helped distill

the city primary into a referendum on the exclusive issue of the Ku Klux Klan. As one El Pasoan explained:

> The only issue in this campaign is whether El Paso is a Ku Klux town or is not. No matter what may be said or written and regardless of the efforts that may be put forward to cloud this and befuddle the people, there will still be this only issue. . . .[99]

The primary campaign ended with a colorful demonstration by supporters of the Invisible Empire. On February 21 the city council was petitioned to permit a pro-Gardner parade through downtown El Paso. The council consented to allowing the parade, but only "with the understanding that there is [sic] to be no masked or hooded parties participating in said parade."[100]

On the evening of February 23 the El Paso Klan paraded. Included in the procession were over five hundred automobiles, some of them with license plates from McLennan and Ellis Counties in east Texas. The cavalcade assembled at the intersection of Montana Avenue and Stanton Street and slowly proceeded to Cleveland Square.[101] At the head of the parade were the Gardner candidates, walking on foot, followed by a band and truckloads of women and children singing 'Onward Christian Soldiers." Some of the Gardner supporters carried torches and signs that read "Joe Dunne is not in this parade" and "Gardner will close public gambling." The most lively participant was Mrs. Charles De Groff, who waved a flag back and forth, shouting, "My God, men, sing!"[102] Also prominent were El Paso City Tax Assessor and Collector William (Billy) P. B. McSain and County Commissioner Bob Oliver.[103] After the parade arrived at Cleveland Square, a crowd of three thousand heard P. E. Gardner and Charles Kirkland give short speeches. On stage with the speakers was an out-of-town stranger who gave KKK cheers through a megaphone:

> Ku Klux, Ku Klux
> Come blow your horn
> We're going to elect Gardner mayor
> Just as sure as you are born[104]

This was the extent of the hoopla, and the crowd quietly went home following the speeches to await the verdict of the voters.

Everybody expected the primary balloting to be extremely close. The

El Paso Drug Company held a straw vote and the results were 1,092 for Gardner and 1,002 for Dudley.[105] During the campaign Gardner had vowed that 4,000 "Christian soldiers" would vote for him and this did not prove to be an idle boast. On an election day marked by "much ill feeling," the Klan's candidate for mayor polled an impressive 5,452 votes. However, Dudley received 7,572 votes and brought in two members of his ticket (two still faced runoffs). Klansman Billy McSain was soundly defeated in his re-election bid, and an anti-Klan candidate won the race for city treasurer.[106] The only Klan-endorsed victor was Stewart Berkshire, candidate for corporation court judge, but this made little difference; his chief opponent had been incumbent Charles E. Pollack, a former member of Frontier Klan No. 100.[107]

The anti-Klan partisans were ecstatic after Dudley's convincing victory. To many it appeared that a terrible danger had passed, as indeed it had. In celebration the senator's supporters held a short parade downtown, and it was gleefully announced: "There will be an auction sale of sheets and pillowslips from Gardner headquarters. Feathers will be thrown in."[108] A crucial decision had been reached — El Paso would not be a Ku Klux Klan town. As the *Times* accurately pointed out, Dudley's triumph had been "a victory of the old El Paso spirit."[109]

The results of the city Democratic primary spelled the end of Frontier Klan No. 100 as a viable political force. Amid rumors of "considerable depletion in the Klan organization ranks," the two KKK aldermanic candidates who had qualified for runoffs withdrew their candidacies.[110] Enemies of the Klan, however, knew that the fight was not over. Four seats on the school board would be filled in April 1923, and the anti-Klan forces needed all of them to overcome the Ward-Isaacks-Gambrell bloc whose terms ran for one more year. In March a two-man and two-woman anti-Klan ticket was announced, and it appeared that the Invisible Empire would not field any opposition.[111] The *Times* declared that the election was an excellent opportunity to "break the Klan's grip on our schools and our children" and "put Judge Isaacks in the minority, where he will have to stop exerting his wizard-ordained privileges of absolute command and absolute rejection."[112] But the Klan still had a few tricks up its sleeve. Two days before the election, the name of James Borders was placed on the ballot, and Klansmen and members of the Invisible Eye (the Klan women's auxiliary) began a telephone campaign in his behalf. The Klan also endorsed Dr. Felix P. Miller, a prominent Mason and independent candidate who refused to tell the press whether or not he belonged to the KKK.[113] It was a des-

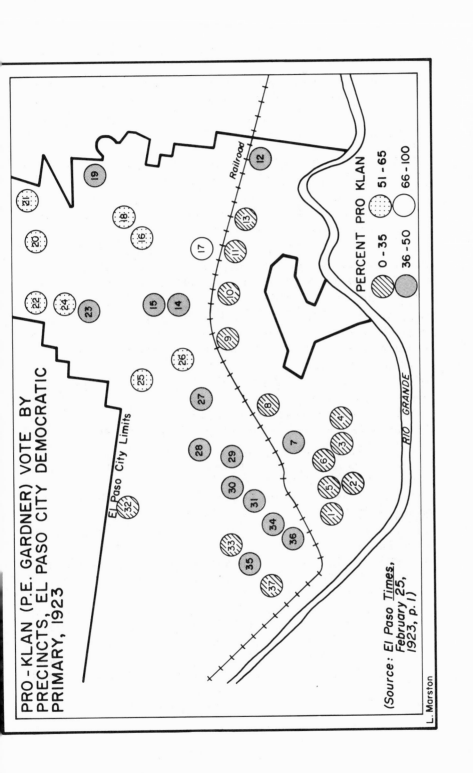

PRO-KLAN (P.E. GARDNER) VOTE BY PRECINCTS, EL PASO CITY DEMOCRATIC PRIMARY, 1923

El Paso City Limits

Railroad

RIO GRANDE

PERCENT PRO KLAN

0-35   51-65

36-50   66-100

(Source: *El Paso Times*, February 25, 1923, p.1)

L. Marston

perate ploy, but the election of even one of these men would have kept
the schools under Klan control. This was not to be. Borders and Miller
finished in the last two places in the field of six, all four anti-Klan candidates being elected. Pro-KKK strength had been confined to eleven
precincts north of the tracks.[114]

Only three days after the school board contest, the city general election was to be held, and there was fear that the Klan might again attempt a last minute campaign.[115] The election had aroused little interest because local Republicans had already endorsed the Dudley ticket
during the fight against the Klan.[116] The nearly 4,000 votes that James
Borders had received in the school trustee polling appeared to be
enough to defeat Dudley if the anti-Klan partisans did not get out the
vote.[117] On election eve a number of men attended a mysterious "moon-
light meeting" at George Oliver's fuel yard, but evidently no plans for a
Klan write-in were made. Balloting the next day produced 6,004 votes
for Dudley, while P. E. Gardner, George Oliver, and Bob Oliver received twenty-nine, fifteen, and two votes respectively.[118]

Having experienced a rapid series of political setbacks, Frontier Klan
No. 100 was forced in ensuing months to assume the role of a disgruntled clique of naysayers. Through the medium of its own four-page
newspaper, the *Frontier Klansman*, the Klan continually railed against
the new city administration, dubbing Mayor Dudley, "Dick the
Dud."[119] The municipal government responded in kind, turning down
requests by the Klan to allow out-of-town KKK speakers the use of
public parks.[120]

This animosity contributed to a minor international incident. On
August 31, 1923, the city sponsored a mass meeting at Liberty Hall to
celebrate the United States' recent recognition of the Obregón government. The hall was decorated with American and Mexican flags.[121]
During the evening following the recognition fete, Frontier Klan No.
100 gathered at the same location to hear a visiting Klan speaker.[122]
With the aid of a deputy sheriff, Klansmen took down the Mexican
flags, tearing one in the process. When word of the torn flag reached
the city council, it promptly voted a condemnation of the incident.[123]
The Mexican consul general was informed of the council's action, and
he relayed news of the flag-ripping to Mexico City and to the Mexican
embassy in Washington, D. C.[124] The Dudley administration played
the incident for all it was worth, but local Klansmen remained defiant.
The *Frontier Klansman* dismissed all the commotion as "clap trap" and

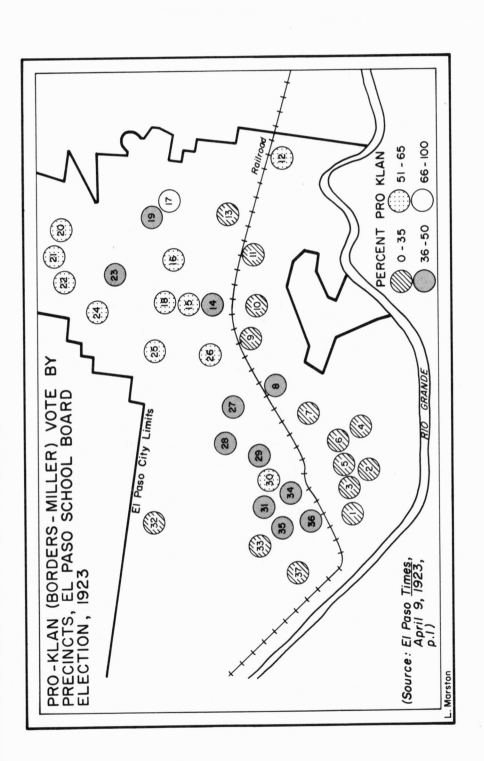

PRO-KLAN (BORDERS-MILLER) VOTE BY PRECINCTS, EL PASO SCHOOL BOARD ELECTION, 1923

PERCENT PRO KLAN

0 - 35
36 - 50
51 - 65
66 - 100

Railroad

El Paso City Limits

RIO GRANDE

(Source: El Paso Times, April 9, 1923, p.1)

L. Marston

an attempt to "play for the Anti-American vote" in the "Mexican colony of El Paso."[125]

In November 1923 Frontier Klan No. 100 made a last-ditch effort to recoup its political fortunes. That month, a proposed $1,260,000 bond issue for street improvements and new street construction was to be voted on. Because the bonds needed the approval of two-thirds of the voters, the Klan saw a good opportunity to score a victory that would embarrass anti-Klan partisans. The Invisible Empire's stand on the bond issue was reported by Horace B. Stevens at a luncheon of the El Paso Real Estate Board:

> There is the biggest kind of opposition to these bonds from the K. K. K. I received this information from members of the organization, and I am sure that unless we take some action the issue will not be carried. My understanding is that the K. K. K.'s are going to fight the issue to the very last man.[126]

Yet, despite this determination, the Klan was destined for another political defeat. The bond issue passed 3,977 to 1,405, with opponents of the measure carrying only four precincts.[127] This was, in effect, the Klan's "Last hurrah."

After the road bonds fiasco, even Klansmen realized that their organization was politically moribund. In April 1924 S. J. Isaacks, Dr. J. H. Gambrell, and Charles Ward all declined to seek re-election to the school board. Although the Klan urged its members to vote for one of the tickets that was vying for the three seats, it declined to make any public endorsement, recognizing that this would "do more harm than good." This caution went unrewarded — the electorate did not select any of the candidates favored by the Klan.[128] For the first time in more than two years, no member of the Invisible Empire would sit on the El Paso School Board.

Shorn of political clout, Frontier Klan No. 100 had to content itself with fraternal activities throughout 1923 and 1924, but a dwindling membership was a major problem in this regard. By January 1923, even before the decisive city primary, the number of active Klansmen had shrunk to 682.[129] After the defeat of P. E. Gardner, many members (especially those who had anticipated political rewards) left the organization, and by early 1924 only a little more than two hundred members regularly attended the Klan's meetings.[130] Nevertheless, the Klan remained an influence on the local scene, especially within professional

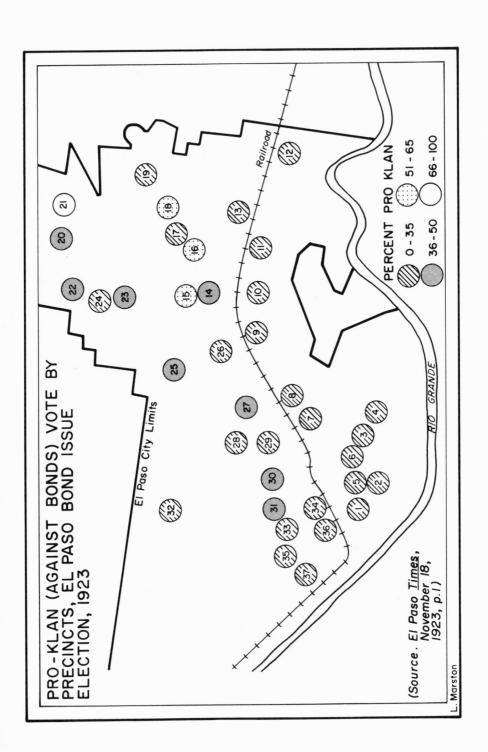

PRO-KLAN (AGAINST BONDS) VOTE BY PRECINCTS, EL PASO BOND ISSUE ELECTION, 1923

PERCENT PRO KLAN

0 - 35   51 - 65

36 - 50   66 - 100

El Paso City Limits

Railroad

RIO GRANDE

(Source: *El Paso Times*, November 18, 1923, p.1)

L. Marston

and fraternal societies. Dissension over the Klan and associated issues practically decimated the ranks of the local American Legion post. Post commander J. L. Fleischer announced in January 1923, that because of disagreements over "the Ku Klux Klan, politics, and religion," membership in the Legion's El Paso branch had declined from 1,700 to 400 in the past year.[131] The El Maida Shrine was likewise plagued by controversy; early in 1924 eleven Klansmen were prosecuted and expelled from the Shrine "for having brought about the blackballing of 31 [new] candidates."[132] There is also some indication that the KKK was exerting influence within the El Paso Bar Association. In April 1923 Ponder Carter, an attorney who was a former Klansman, claimed that Klan members of the bar were keeping him out of the organization.[133] It is interesting to note that during the year preceding Carter's complaint, S. J. Isaacks had been a member of the Bar Association's membership committee.[134]

Beyond the disruption it was causing in other organizations, the Klan was primarily occupied with its own meetings and recreational outings. Many of its functions were held at Odd Fellows Hall, with Klan rituals, political speeches, and the showing of advertising slides at "$1 a flash" among the featured activities. An informant for the *El Paso Times*, who attended several of these meetings, identified S. J. Isaacks as the Klan's Exalted Cyclops (chapter president), and Clifford L. Sirmans as both Kleagle (recruiter) and Kligrapp (secretary) of Frontier Klan No. 100.[135]

Undeterred by these exposures, the Klan continued to meet. In April 1923 it was announced that a nighttime initiation ceremony would be held on the Newman Road, a few miles beyond the northeast city limits. The public was invited to view the proceedings, it being asserted that "Two hundred Klansmen will be in robes, the other members being scattered throughout the crowd."[136] For unknown reasons the meeting did not take place on the announced date but was postponed for three days. However, the order did eventually gather at the designated site. Festivities included the burning of a double cross and the consumption of sandwiches and soft drinks.[137]

Evidently the Klansmen enjoyed their outing. In June 1923 the *Frontier Klansman* announced that a Fourth of July picnic would be held at the same location. The picnic promised to feature "Foot Races, Fat Man Races, Sack Races, Pie Eating Contests, Climbing the Greasy Pole for a Five Dollar Prize and Other Enjoyable Events."[138] By the end of the year, Frontier Klan No. 100 had purchased one hundred and sixty acres of land along the Newman Road and had announced plans to construct a large Klavern (meeting hall) and a giant fiery cross on the property.[139] The *Frontier Klansman* hoped that the acreage would become a nice park for "the white people of the community" and that the site would serve as an alternative to city parks that benefited only "Mexicans and foreigners."[140] In 1924 another Fourth of July picnic was held at "Klan Park," an event hyperbolically described as the "largest gathering of white people ever assembled in the southwest." Music was provided by the "Peerless Klan Band," and it is likely that the woman's drill team of Border Klan No. 6 performed.[141]

Despite the apparent harmlessness of these activities, enemies of Frontier Klan No. 100 kept a close watch. In early 1924 the Klan was infiltrated by N. L. Bayless, an operative of the Ben Williams Detective Agency, who managed to rise to the position of Kladd, the Klan officer responsible for taking a secret password from members as they entered meetings of the order. By virtue of his office, Bayless had access to the Klan's most intimate secrets. According to his reports (which ultimately came into the possession of Will Fryer), both Dr. J. H. Gambrell and P. E. Gardner had served as Exalted Cyclops after S. J. Isaacks was appointed to a high office in the state Klan, in 1923.[142] By May 1924, however, Isaacks had resumed his old office. It was also reported that among those attending Klan meetings during early 1924 were County Treasurer Asa R. Webb, State Representative John E. Quaid, Justice of the Peace Arthur M. Horn, J. Mack Crawford, and the Reverend William H. Joyner. On January 28 Pastor Joyner had made a speech during which he urged the two hundred and ten Klansmen in his audience to boycott El Paso's Jewish and Catholic firms. The Bayless reports further revealed that Frontier Klan No. 100 had been highly active recently in organizing new Klans in New Mexico, but that the order was currently preoccupied with financial problems.[143]

Bayless's spying ceased in mid-May 1924, when Klan members discovered his treachery and confronted him at a meeting. After Bayless confessed, he was given twenty-five dollars and told to leave town.[144] However, he remained in El Paso, and the publication of excerpts of his reports shattered what little secrecy Frontier Klan No. 100 had maintained. Nor did the spying cease. On May 14 Will Fryer announced that another informant within the KKK had given him a list of recently elected Klan officers. They were: S. J. Isaacks, Exalted Cyclops; Clifford L. Sirmans, Kligrapp; Robert E. Petty, Kludd (chaplain); Thomas A. Plumbley, Klokard (lecturer); J. M. Daniel, Klarago (inner guard); John Mershon, Klexter (outer guard); and William Lankford, Nighthawk (officer in charge of new candidates).[145]

By the late summer of 1924, Frontier Klan No. 100 had ceased to be a significant influence within either the political or social life of El Paso. During the Democratic primary held that year, several former Klansmen were nominated for local county and state offices, but only one (Bob Oliver) had remained an active member of the KKK.[146] Locally, the Klan did not figure as an issue in the campaign. Interestingly, however, in both the primary and the subsequent general election a majority of El Pasoans voted for gubernatorial candidates who were rumored to be closely linked to the KKK.[147] The apparent reason for this was the local electorate's general distaste for the eventual anti-Klan victor in both contests — Miriam "Ma" Ferguson. It is certain that these elections did not signify any overall change in heart concerning the Invisible Empire. Even a Klannish governor had seemed preferable to the restoration of Fergusonian rule.

Although reduced to a cipher in local affairs, Frontier Klan No. 100 managed to limp along for a few more years. As late as 1927 it was observed that the Klan was still meeting and still instructing members how to vote.[148] No doubt spirited speeches were made and dire warnings were pronounced; perhaps a few more crosses were burned. But all this seemed not to matter any more. By the end of 1924 the El Paso Klan had become a negligible community influence.

CONCLUSION

El Paso's rejection of the Ku Klux Klan in 1923 coincided with the rapid decline of the order elsewhere in Texas. Many of the problems of Frontier Klan No. 100 (including a disillusioned membership, increased resistance by Klan opponents, and severe financial troubles) were shared by sister chapters east to Texarkana and Beaumont. Moreover, a majority of Texas voters had decided that they did not want the Invisible Empire running their state government. This was clearly demonstrated in the 1924 Democratic primary, wherein Miriam Ferguson won the gubernatorial nomination over Felix Robertson, a candidate who openly boasted that "I am the man the Ku Klux Klan endorsed. And I am proud of it. I don't care whether it suits the Pope in Rome or not."[1] Notwithstanding continuing Klan opposition after the primary, Ferguson went on to victory in the general election; subsequently she acted to purge Klansmen from state government and from the hierarchy of the state Democratic party. The Texas legislature similarly signified its disapproval of the Klan, enacting in March 1925 a measure that prohibited the wearing of masks in public.[2]

Bereft of political influence, Texas Klansmen quickly faded into insignificance. By late 1925 Dallas Klan No. 66 was in dire financial disarray, and Sam Houston Klan No. 1 was forced to sell its meeting hall.[3] By 1927 there seems to have been only about 12,000 active Klansmen in the Lone Star State, and the following year there were apparently less than 2,500. As was noted by a prominent Texas official in 1927, the Klan was "as dead as the proverbial doornail."[4]

Although the Ku Klux Klan itself was no longer a menace, the impulses and attitudes that had spawned the organization remained viable. This was especially true in El Paso, where the crusade against "machine politics" continued. Early in 1927 a rancorous campaign for mayor transpired between former Mayor Charles Davis and R. E. Thomason, champion of the northside progressives. It is interesting to note that Thomason, a former member of the Good Government League, was strongly supported by his close friend, S. J. Isaacks.[5] Advertisements in behalf of Thomason's candidacy bore a remarkable resemblance to those previously sponsored by the Klan. For example, one blurb denounced:

> Boss Rule!
> Machine Politics!
> Illegal Voting!
> Corruption of the Ballot Box!
> Extravagant Use of Public Funds!
> Drones and Ward Heelers on the City Pay Rolls![6]

When the progressives won, they proclaimed that the days of the Ring and the wardheelers were gone forever. As Claude B. Hudspeth observed in a letter to Charles Davis, ". . .the 'Old School' of your and my thought is fast dwindling into the dim distant past."[7]

Thomason's triumph portended ill for El Paso's tradition of toleration. As we have seen, after the arrival of the railroads Anglos had accommodated to local Mexicans principally because of a desire to utilize Latin votes and Latin labor. But by 1930, local politics had evolved to a point where Hispanic votes were not so crucial, and where broad Hispanic support tended to create an Anglo backlash. Thus one of the cornerstones of the tradition of toleration had eroded, a process in which the local Klan had been significantly involved. With the advent of the Great Depression, the other cornerstone — dependence on cheap Mexican labor — was similarly undermined. With any form of employment at a premium, Anglos ruthlessly displaced Hispanic laborers who had helped sustain the prosperity of the 1920s. Public authorities pressed Mexicans — aliens and United States citizens alike — to return to the land of their fathers, and relief agencies commonly discriminated against them.[8] By 1936 discrimination was so intense that the El Paso city registrar and the city-county health officer announced that Mexicans would henceforth be classified as "colored" in official records. Though this policy was quickly rescinded, it aptly demonstrated the level to which ethnic aversions had surged.[9] The Klan was indeed dead, but its legacy was much alive.[10]

What, then, can be said about El Paso's brief experience with the Ku Klux Klan? This study has been directed toward answering four major questions and has arrived at the following conclusions.

1. How and why did the Ku Klux Klan become an influential factor in El Paso during the early 1920s?

That the Ku Klux Klan drew a following in El Paso is not surprising. For, in spite of an unusual heritage of social and racial toleration, ethnic polarity had always been a prime trait of the locality since the arrival of the railroads in the 1880s. Ethnic awareness was then intensified by the tension created by the Mexican Revolution, and by the World War I homefront commitment to "100 percent Americanism." Additionally, the war accentuated officially condoned, extralegal vigilantism. It is notable also that the revolution and the world war came in a period when thousands of additional Anglos arrived at the Pass. Many were from the racially intolerant South, and they arrived at a time of unusual tensions. Understandably they did not adjust easily to the older traditions.

When the Ku Klux Klan arrived in 1921 and espoused a program of white supremacy, Americanism, Protestant solidarity, social morality, clean government, and law enforcement, many of the newcomers were receptive. In addition, the Klan was a social novelty that particularly appealed to natives of the deep South. Within a matter of months Frontier Klan No. 100 recruited hundreds of local citizens. The organization quickly became politicized, partly because of a politically ambitious leadership, and partly because of encouragement from the national Klan hierarchy. Once it had entered the political arena, the local Klan maintained a low profile and attempted to capitalize on the electorate's general discontent with the local political and business establishments. These efforts were assisted by important changes in voting laws: El Paso's Mexican vote had been greatly reduced, and many Anglo women had recently been enfranchised. Due to these changes, and also because the Klan avoided becoming an issue in itself, the organization succeeded in placing a number of its members and sympathizers in local political offices in 1922. At the same time, a Klan presence was manifest in a number of local fraternal, religious, and social organizations, often with acrimonious results.

2. To what extent did the Klan succeed or fail in achieving its goals in El Paso?

Frontier Klan No. 100 was firmly committed to the prohibition of alcohol, better law enforcement, improved social morality, and honest elections. These goals were a reflection of the local order's membership, which was composed mainly of middle-class, southern Protestants. The Klan served basically as a medium of civic action for these disgruntled residents, who resented the dominance of a local establishment which they believed to be immoral and corrupt. As one local Klansman explained, the El Paso Klan had been formed primarily because:

> There was and is still only one way to beat the organized and illegal Mexican vote of the powers behind the present city administration [Mayor Davis was in office] — that was and is by a combination of clean and decent American voters in such form and with such power as to bring the fear of the election laws into the hearts of the men who capitalize another's faith to their own political ends. . . . The real and vital reason for [the Klan's existence] lies in the political necessity for it.[11]

Yet the frustration that sustained the local Klan never degenerated into the physical violence engaged in by Klans elsewhere. This was in large part due to the nature of the local Anglo society, which was heavily middle-class. Throughout its entire existence, Frontier Klan No. 100 was generally law-abiding and was composed of respectable citizens. The order was encouraged in this stance by local authorities, who made it clear from the outset that they would not tolerate nightriding or similar illegal behavior.

The lasting achievements of the Klan in El Paso were slight. Throughout the 1920s the level of crime and vice was extraordinary. Tourists continued to avail themselves of sinful pleasures in Juárez, and prohibition enforcement remained a near impossibility. The activities of the Good Government League may have resulted in slightly more honest elections, but this was achieved only through means which were in themselves highly suspect. The Klan's one-year dominance of the school board failed to bring substantial reforms, although the organization paved the way for an independently funded education system. Most glaringly, the KKK failed to attain firm or lasting influence within either the local political or business establishments. This failure relegated the order to the role of a disgruntled clique of naysayers.

3. Why did the El Paso community ultimately reject the Ku Klux Klan?

Once they were clearly presented with a choice between a pro-Klan or anti-Klan city government, El Pasoans strongly endorsed the latter. This was primarily due to a perception that a Klan-run municipal government would disrupt the community's social and business relations, and that ultimately such an administration would accomplish more harm than good. The voters' decision against the Klan was facilitated by the fact that the anti-Klan partisans united behind a truly progressive candidate who was not identified with the old order. If the 1923 city Democratic primary had pitted Charles Davis against P. E. Gardner, the Invisible Empire might have emerged victorious, with disastrous consequences for El Paso.

4. How was El Paso's experience with the Ku Klux Klan different or similar to the experiences of other Texas communities?

El Paso's experience with the Ku Klux Klan demonstrated the limits of the KKK's appeal in Texas. On first reflection, the Pass seemed to offer every opportunity for the successful establishment of a powerful Klan. Nowhere else in the state (or possibly even within the United States) were the "perils" of foreign immigration, Roman Catholicism, lawlessness, and moral deterioration more apparent. Yet El Paso rejected the Klan more promptly than any other large, urban Texas community. Moreover, the Klan never managed to gain substantial footing among the city's more exclusive social and economic groups; it was always essentially a fringe group, forced by circumstances to assume a low profile. This contrasts with the experiences of communities such as Dallas and Houston, where ruling elites were heavily infiltrated by the Invisible Empire for a time. Additionally, Frontier Klan No. 100 was generally peaceful and law-abiding; it never descended to the violence that characterized numerous East Texas Klans.

The El Paso Klan was basically untypical of Texas Klans because it was forced to accommodate to unusual conditions in an unusual community. Despite extraordinary social strains at the Pass after 1910, the majority of citizens eventually came to the conclusion that the Klan was bad for them. Ironically, it was precisely *because* the Pass was heavily Hispanic and Roman Catholic that residents, including a majority of Protestants, rejected the KKK. In a city that was socially and economically dependent on peaceful coexistence, moderation and common sense prevailed.

NOTES

Introduction

1. *El Paso Times*, October 1, 1922, p. 10; hereinafter cited as *Times*.
2. William J. Hooten, personal interview, December 1, 1983.
3. Charles C. Alexander, *The Ku Klux Klan in the Southwest* (Lexington, Kentucky, 1965), vii. The state of Klan scholarship has improved somewhat during the past twenty years, at least in terms of quantity. See Lenwood G. Davis and Janet L. Sims-Wood, *The Ku Klux Klan: A Bibliography* (Westport, Connecticut, 1984).
4. Robert N. Blake, "A History of the Catholic Church in El Paso" (M.A. thesis, Texas Western College, 1948), p. 88.
5. Sister M. Lilliana Owens, *The Life of Bishop Anthony J. Schuler, S.J., D.D.* (El Paso, 1953), p. 429.
6. Edward F. Sherman, "The Ku Klux Klan and El Paso Politics Following World War I" (History seminar paper, Texas Western College, 1958), p. 22.
7. *Password*, XIV (Fall 1969), p. 90.
8. C. L. Sonnichsen, *Pass of the North*, Volume II (El Paso, 1980), p. 11.
9. Leon C. Metz, *City at the Pass: An Illustrated History of El Paso* (Woodland Hills, California, 1980), p. 73.

Chapter I

1. William E. Connelley, *Doniphan's Expedition and the Conquest of New Mexico and California* (Topeka, 1907), pp. 369-370, 385 (quotes). This volume is primarily a reprint of John T. Hughes, *Doniphan's Expedition* (Cincinnati, 1847) and Hughes' private diary while serving as a soldier under Colonel Doniphan.
2. *Ibid.*, pp. 87-88 (quote on p. 88), 370-378, 589. For other firsthand accounts of the Battle of Brazito, see "Journal of Marcellus Ball Edwards, 1846-1847," in Ralph P. Bieber, Ed., *Marching with the Army of the West* (Glendale, California, 1936), pp. 228-237, and George R. Gibson, *Journal of a Soldier Under Kearny and Doniphan, 1846-1847* (Glendale, California, 1935), pp. 300-309. Interesting observations concerning the battle can be found in George Ruhlen, "Brazito — The Only Battle in the Southwest Between American and Foreign Troops," *Password*, II (February 1957), pp. 4-13, and George Ruhlen, "The Battle of Brazito — Where Was It Fought?," *Password*, II (May 1957), pp. 53-60.
3. Frank Louis Halla, "El Paso, Texas, and Juárez, Mexico: A Study of a Bi-Ethnic Community, 1846-1881" (Ph.D. dissertation, University of Texas, 1978), pp. 30-31, 46; W. H. Timmons, Ed., *Four Centuries at the Pass: A New History of El Paso on Its 400th Birthday* (El Paso, 1981), p. 35.
4. A. Wislizemus, *A Memoir of a Tour Through Northern Mexico Connected with Colonel Doniphan's Expedition, 1846-1847*, Senate Misc. Doc. No. 26, 30th Cong., 1st sess., 1848, p. 42.
5. Connelley, *Doniphan's Expedition*, pp. 88-95 (first and second quotes on pp. 90 and 93 respectively), pp. 384-387 (third quote on p. 387).

6. Ibid., 92 (quote), pp. 387, 397; Bieber, "Journal of Marcellus Ball Edwards," p. 244.

7. Timmons, *Four Centuries*, p. 45.

8. C. L. Greenwood, "Opening Routes to El Paso, 1849," *Southwestern Historical Quarterly*, XLVIII (October 1944), p. 271.

9. C. L. Sonnichsen, *Pass of the North: Four Centuries on the Rio Grande* (El Paso, 1968), pp. 127, 140-143; hereinafter cited as *Pass of the North*, I.

10. Kenneth F. Neighbours, "The Taylor-Neighbors Struggle over the Upper Rio Grande Region of Texas in 1850," *Southwestern Historical Quarterly*, LXI (April 1958), p. 445 (quote); J. Morgan Broaddus, *The Legal Heritage of El Paso* (El Paso, 1963), pp. 28-35.

11. W. W. Mills, *Forty Years at El Paso, 1858-1898* (n.p., 1901), p. 16; Broaddus, *Legal Heritage*, p. 57.

12. Broaddus, *Legal Heritage*, p. 33; Nancy Lee Hammons, "A History of El Paso County, Texas to 1900" (M.A. thesis, The Texas College of Mines and Metallurgy, El Paso, 1942), p. 80.

13. Sonnichsen, *Pass of the North*, I, pp. 105-106; Broaddus, *Legal Heritage*, p. 22 (quote).

14. Sonnichsen, *Pass of the North*, I, pp. 122-123.

15. Albert D. Richardson, *Beyond the Mississippi: From the Great River to the Great Ocean* (Hartford, 1867), p. 238.

16. Oscar J. Martínez, *Border Boom Town: Ciudad Juárez Since 1848* (Austin, 1978), p. 12; Broaddus, *Legal Heritage*, p. 62.

17. Mills, *Forty Years*, p. 27.

18. Broaddus, *Legal Heritage*, pp. 50-51, 54, 56-59; J. J. Bowden, "The Magoffin Salt War," *Password*, VII (Summer 1962), pp. 95-121.

19. Arnoldo De León, "White Racial Attitudes Toward Mexicanos In Texas, 1821-1900" (Ph.D. dissertation, Texas Christian University, 1974), pp. 30-35, 142. It was noted by Frederick Law Olmsted in the 1850s that "wherever slavery in Texas has been carried . . . into the neighborhood of Mexicans, it has been found necessary to treat them as outlaws. Guaranteed, by the treaty of Guadalupe-Hidalgo, equal rights with all other citizens of the United States and of Texas, the whole native population of county after county has been driven, by the formal proceedings of substantial planters, from its homes, and forbidden, on pain of no less punishment than instant death, to return to the vicinity of the plantations." See Frederick Law Olmsted, *A Journey Through Texas* (New York, 1857), p. 456.

20. Sonnichsen, *Pass of the North*, I, p. 168.

21. Broaddus, *Legal Heritage*, p. 67; Owen P. White, *Out of the Desert: The Historical Romance of El Paso* (El Paso, 1923), p. 184.

22. Sonnichsen, *Pass of the North*, I, pp. 106, 122-123, 151; Broaddus, *Legal Heritage*, pp. 41, 51-54, 70.

23. *The War of the Rebellion: A Compilation of the Official Records of the Union and Confederate Armies*, Series I, Vol. IV (Washington, 1897), p. 133; hereinafter all volumes in this series will be cited as *War of the Rebellion*.

24. Ibid., pp. 89, 90 (first quote); Series I, Vol. L, Part I, p. 1012 (second quote), p. 1013.

25. Sonnichsen, *Pass of the North*, I, p. 158; Broaddus, *Legal Heritage*, p. 73.

26. *War of the Rebellion*, Series I, Vol. IX, p. 567.

27. Sonnichsen, *Pass of the North*, I, pp. 159-161.

28. De León, "White Racial Attitudes," pp. 134-143, 154-155.

29. Mills, *Forty Years*, pp. 20-21.

30. Martínez, *Ciudad Juárez*, pp. 10-11; Broaddus, *Legal Heritage*, p 91.

31. Broaddus, *Legal Heritage*, pp. 95-96; Sonnichsen, *Pass of the North*, I, p. 168. For the purposes of this study, it should be noted that, despite the turmoil, there was not a branch of the Reconstruction Ku Klux Klan in El Paso.

32. Mills, *Forty Years*, pp. 79, 88, 94; Halla, "Bi-Ethnic Community," p. 201. For more on Mills, see Rex W. Strickland, "W. W. Mills — El Paso Politician," *Password*, VII (Summer 1962), pp. 83-94.

33. Sonnichsen, *Pass of the North*, I, pp. 177, 185-186.

34. Broaddus, *Legal Heritage*, pp. 107-109, 124, 129; Mills, *Forty Years*, p. 143.

35. De León, "White Racial Attitudes," pp. 211-215.

36. Sonnichsen, *Pass of the North*, I, pp. 189-190.

37. Ibid., pp. 195-210; Broaddus, *Legal Heritage*, pp. 126-127; Mills, *Forty Years*, pp. 143-144.

38. U.S., Congress, House, *El Paso Troubles*, H. Doc. 93, 45th Cong., 2d sess., 1878, p. 14.

39. Ibid., 17.

40. Ibid., 3 (quote); Sonnichsen, *Pass of the North*, I, p. 196.

41. Sonnichsen, *Pass of the North*, I, pp. 203-204; C. L. Sonnichsen, *The El Paso Salt War, 1877* (El Paso, 1961), p. 3.

42. U.S., Congress, House, *El Paso Troubles*, H. Doc. 84, 45th Cong., 2d sess., 1878, p. 4; *El Paso Troubles*, H. Doc. 93, pp. 15 (quote), 34, 54, 57; Sonnichsen, *Pass of the North*, I, p. 209.

43. *El Paso Troubles*, H. Doc. 84, p. 4; *El Paso Troubles*, H. Doc. 93, pp. 38-39, 50; Mills, *Forty Years*, p. 151.

44. Sonnichsen, *Pass of the North*, I, pp. 210, 213; Mills, *Forty Years*, p. 152 (quote).

45. Martínez, *Ciudad Juárez*, p. 159; Sonnichsen, *Pass of the North*, I, p. 211; U.S. Department of Commerce, Bureau of the Census, *Special Census of El Paso, Texas, 1916*, pp. 1-4. Indeed, the population of the El Paso area was always small prior to 1883, numbering approximately 200 in 1850, 428 in 1860, 764 in 1870, and 736 in 1880. However, the total population of the surrounding Pass communities was more significant. For example, in 1881 the population of the Juárez municipality was 20,000. See Martínez, *Ciudad Juárez*, pp. 158-160.

46. For the building and impact of the railroads in El Paso, see Mildred L. Jordan, "Railroads in the El Paso Area" (M.A. thesis, Texas Western College, 1957), and Clyde Wise, Jr., "The Effects of the Railroad Upon El Paso," *Password*, V (July 1960), pp. 91-100.

47. White, *Out of the Desert*, pp. 158-169; Sonnichsen, *Pass of the North*, I, pp. 225, 232.

48. Mario T. García, *Desert Immigrants: The Mexicans of El Paso 1880-1920* (New Haven, 1981), pp. 3-4, 9-11, 13-14, 18; Sonnichsen, *Pass of the North*, I, p. 249.

49. Martínez, *Ciudad Juárez*, p. 6.

50. Ibid., p. 24; Hammons, "El Paso County," p. 135.

51. García, *Desert Immigrants, passim.*

52. Ibid., pp. 20-21; Martínez, *Ciudad Juárez*, p. 6.

53. Broaddus, *Legal Heritage*, pp. 141-149; Sonnichsen, *Pass of the North*, I, pp. 346-347; White, *Out of the Desert*, p. 185.

54. Broaddus, *Legal Heritage*, p. 153.

55. García, *Desert Immigrants*, pp. 158, 162-164. Also see Jack C. Vowell, Jr., "Politics at El Paso: 1850-1920" (M.A. thesis, Texas Western College, 1952).

56. García, *Desert Immigrants*, pp. 6-7, 72-74, 160.

57. Hammons, "El Paso County," pp. 169-174.

58. García, *Desert Immigrants*, p. 155.

59. Sonnichsen, *Pass of the North*, I, pp. 372-375.

60. Richardson, *Beyond the Mississippi*, p. 238.

61. Broaddus, *Legal Heritage*, p. 164.

62. White, *Out of the Desert*, pp. 173-174.

63. Sonnichsen, *Pass of the North*, I, pp. 217, 283-287.

64. Ibid., pp. 216, 277-278.

65. Ibid., pp. 348, 353; White, *Out of the Desert*, pp. 217-219.

66. Martínez, *Ciudad Juárez*, pp. 30-31.

67. *Times*, June 3, 1917, p. 10.

68. *New York Times*, October 22, 1877, p. 2.

Chapter II

1. *El Paso Herald*, January 13, 1916, p. 2; hereinafter cited as *Herald*.

2. Ibid., January 11, 1916, p. 1; *Times*, January 12, 1916, p. 1; January 17, 1916, p. 10; *New York Times*, January 12, 1916, p. 1; January 13, 1916, pp. 1, 2; Zach Lamar Cobb to Robert Lansing, January 11, 1916, in U.S. Department of State, Records of the Department of State Relating to the Internal Affairs of Mexico, 1910-1929, Microcopy No. 274, 812.00/17081; hereinafter cited as Internal Affairs.

3. *Herald*, January 13, 1916, p. 3 (first quote), p. 5 (fourth quote); January 14, 1916, p. 1; *Times*, January 14, 1916, p. 6 (second and third quotes).

4. *Herald*, January 14, 1916, p. 1; *Times*, January 14, 1916, p. 1; *New York Times*, January 14, 1916, pp. 1, 2.

5. *Herald*, January 14, 1916, p. 1; *Times*, January 14, 1916, pp. 1, 2; Hortencia Villegas Transcript, ACC 235, Institute of Oral History, The University of Texas at El Paso, February 17, 1976, pp. 13-15. Institute of Oral History will hereinafter be cited as IOH.

6. Richard Medina Estrada, "Border Revolution: The Mexican Revolution in the Ciudad Juárez-El Paso Area, 1906-1915" (M.A. thesis, The University of Texas at El Paso, 1975), pp. 29-53, 141; García, *Desert Immigrants*, pp. 173-177; I. V. Bush, *Gringo Doctor* (Caldwell, Idaho, 1939), p. 163.

7. See Bush's *Gringo Doctor* for the story of one El Pasoan drawn to the Madero cause.

8. Timothy G. Turner, *Bullets, Bottles, and Gardenias* (Dallas, 1935), p. 70; Mardee de Wetter, "Revolutionary El Paso, 1910-1917" (M.A. thesis, Texas College of Mines and Metallurgy, 1946), pp. 53, 62-63; *Times*, February 3, 1911, p. 1; May 25, 1911, p. 1; May 29, 1911, p. 1.

9. *Congressional Record*, 62d Cong., 1st sess., XLVII, Part 1, p. 118.

10. *Times*, February 3, 1911, p. 1; February 9, 1911, p. 1 (first quote); April 23, 1911, p. 1 (second quote); Bush, *Gringo Doctor*, pp. 174-175.

11. *Times*, February 3, 1911, p. 1 (quote); Turner, *Bullets*, pp. 61-62; de Wetter, "Revolutionary El Paso," p. 56; Bush, *Gringo Doctor*, p. 205.

12. *Times*, May 12, 1911, p. 1; clipping from *Times*, May 11, 1922, in file "Mexico-Juárez Revolution" in Southwest Vertical File, El Paso Public Library (quote); Bush, *Gringo Doctor*, p. 205.

13. *Times*, February 9, 1911, p. 6 (quote); May 31, 1911, p. 2.

14. Ibid., May 31, 1911, p. 2 (first quote); *Plan de San Luis Potosí* quoted from *Papers Relating to the Foreign Relations of the United States, 1911*, p. 352 (second quote); hereinafter cited as Foreign Relations, 1911.

15. *Times*, May 13, 1911, p. 6.

16. Henry Lane Wilson to Philander C. Knox, November 10, 1910, *Foreign Relations, 1911*, p. 354; also see p. 353 of the same source.

17. Luther Ellsworth to Knox, April 29, 1911, Internal Affairs, 812.00/1614.

18. Marion Letcher to Knox, February 5, 1912, in *Papers Relating to the Foreign Relations of the United States, 1912*, p. 717; hereinafter cited as *Foreign Relations, 1912*.

19. de Wetter, "Revolutionary El Paso," pp. 69-76.

20. *Herald*, February 26, 1912, p. 1.

21. Henry L. Stimson to Knox, February 7, 1912, in *Foreign Relations, 1912*, p. 718; *Times*, February 24, 1912, p. 1.

22. Thomas D. Edwards to Knox, February 15, 1912, Internal Affairs, 812.00/2802.

23. *Herald*, February 24, 1912, p. 1 (second quote); February 26, 1912, p. 1 (first quote).

24. Edwards to Knox, August 20, 1912, *Foreign Relations, 1912*, p. 825.

25. For an in-depth discussion of Texas prejudice towards Mexicans, see De León, "White Racial Attitudes."

26. *Herald*, February 24, 1912, p. 6 (first quote); Owen P. White, *Them Was the Days: From El Paso to Prohibition* (New York, 1925), pp. 202-203 (second quote).

27. *Times*, September 7, 1912, p. 7.

28. *Herald*, February 19, 1913, p. 6.

29. *Times*, February 20, 1913, p. 6.

30. *Herald*, February 21, 1913, p. 6.

31. Venustiano Carranza to Woodrow Wilson, February 26, 1913, *Papers Relating to the Foreign Relations of the United States, 1913*, p. 742.

32. *Herald*, November 15, 1913, p. 1 (second quote); *Times*, November 16, 1913, pp. 6 (first quote), 10.

33. *Times*, November 19, 1913, p. 6.

34. Arthur S. Link, *Wilson: The New Freedom* (Princeton, 1956), pp. 347-416; Robert E. Quirk, *An Affair of Honor: Woodrow Wilson and the Occupation of Veracruz* (New York, 1967), pp. 2-3.

35. G. C. Carothers to William Jennings Bryan, April 23, 1914, *Papers Relating to the Foreign Relations of the United States, 1914*, p. 485; hereinafter cited as *Foreign Relations, 1914*.

36. *Times*, April 21, 1914, p. 1.

37. García, *Desert Immigrants*, p. 186.

38. *Times*, April 20, 1914, p. 6 (first quote); Zach L. Cobb to Bryan, April 23, 1914, Internal Affairs, 812.00/11656 (second quote); Cobb to Bryan, April 24, 1914, Internal Affairs, 812.00/11672 (third quote).

39. Thomas D. Edwards to Bryan, April 24, 1914, Internal Affairs, 812.00/11685.

40. *Times*, April 24, 1914, p. 1; *Herald*, April 25-26, 1914, Section A, p. 5 (quote); Carothers to Bryan, April 23, 1914, *Foreign Relations, 1914*, p. 485.

41. *Times*, July 18, 1914, p. 6.

42. Charles C. Cumberland, *Mexican Revolution: The Constitutionalist Years* (Austin, 1972), pp. 151-211; Robert E. Quirk, *The Mexican Revolution, 1914-1915* (Bloomington, Indiana, 1960), pp. 87-149.

43. Garna Loy Christian, "Sword and Plowshare; The Symbiotic Development of Fort Bliss and El Paso, Texas, 1849-1918" (Ph.D. dissertation, Texas Tech University, 1977), p. 357.

44. *Times*, May 13, 1915, p. 1. Also see "Weekly Report of General Conditions Along the Mexican Border," May 8, 1915, Internal Affairs, 812.00/15029, p. 4.

45. "Weekly Report of General Conditions Along the Mexican Border," June 12, 1915, Internal Affairs, 812.00/15278, pp. 8 (second quote), 10 (first quote).

46. Cobb to Robert Lansing, June 27, 1915, *Papers Relating to the Foreign Affairs of the United States, 1915*, pp. 828-829; *Herald*, June 28, 1915, pp. 1, 2.

47. *Times*, August 26, 1915, p. 1 (first quote); August 30, 1915, p. 6 (second quote).

48. Ibid., August 31, 1915, p. 1; September 1, 1915, p. 1; September 2, 1915, p. 1.

49. Charles C. Cumberland, "Border Raids in the Lower Rio Grande Valley — 1915," *Southwestern Historical Quarterly*, LVII (January 1954), pp. 285-311.

50. *Times*, August 12, 1915, p. 1.

51. William H. Hager, "The Plan of San Diego: Unrest on the Texas Border in 1915," *Arizona and the West*, V (Winter 1963), p. 329; U.S., Congress, Senate, *Investigation of Mexican Affairs*, S. Doc. 285, 66th Cong., 2d sess., 1920, pp. 1205-1207. El Pasoans were aware of the details of this plan, which was the product of a small cell of Mexican radicals. See *Times*, August 12, 1915, p. 1.

52. Hager, "Plan of San Diego," p. 336.

53. Cumberland, "Border Raids," pp. 292, 300-301, 310 (quotes).

54. *Times*, September 9, 1915, p. 6.

55. Cobb to Lansing, December 21, 1915, Internal Affairs, 812.00/16983 (first quote); Carothers to Lansing, December 21, 1915, Internal Affairs, 812.00/16984 (second quote); Carothers to Lansing, December 22, 1915, Internal Affairs, 812.00/16992.

56. Clarence C. Clendenon, *Blood on the Border: The United States Army and the Mexican Irregulars* (Toronto, 1969), pp. 176-200.

57. *Herald*, January 14, 1916, p. 1.

58. Ibid., p. 6; *Times*, January 15, 1916, p. 6.

59. *New York Times*, January 14, 1916, p. 1 (second quote); "Minutes of a Specially Called Meeting of the Board of Directors of the El Paso Chamber of Commerce, January 14, 1916" (first quote). All Chamber of Commerce records cited in this study are located on microfilm at the Offices of the El Paso Chamber of Commerce.

60. *Times*, January 15, 1916, p. 1.

61. "Weekly Report of General Conditions Along the Mexican Border," January 22, 1916, Internal Affairs, 812.00/17194, pp. 2-3.

62. Cobb to Lansing, March 9, 1916, Internal Affairs, 812.00/17377.

63. *Herald*, March 10, 1916, p. 6 (quote). Certain oral history inteviews maintain that there was large scale violence in El Paso after the Columbus raid, but the lack of corroboration by other sources indicates that the interviewees may have confused the reaction after the raid with the earlier Santa Ysabel rioting. See Mario Acevedo Transcript, ACC

153B, IOH, May 1, 1975, p. 25; S. L. A. Marshall Transcript, ACC 181, IOH, July 5, 1975, p. 16.

64. For one of the best diplomatic histories of the expedition, see "The Columbus Raid and the Punitive Expedition" in Arthur S. Link, *Wilson: Confusion and Crises* (Princeton, 1964), pp. 195-221.

65. *Herald*, March 13, 1916, p. 6; March 18-19, 1916, p. 4; Cobb to Lansing, March 15, 1916, Internal Affairs, 812.00/17478.

66. *Herald*, March 14, 1916, p. 6.

67. Cobb to Lansing, March 17, 1916, Internal Affairs, 812.00/17503.

68. Edwards to Lansing, March 15, 1916, Internal Affairs, 812.00/17490.

69. Cobb to Lansing, March 16, 1916, Internal Affairs, 812.00/17493.

70. *New York Times*, March 16, 1916, p. 1; Edwards to Lansing, March 23, 1916, Internal Affairs, 812.00/17601; Edwards to Lansing, April 14, 1916, Internal Affairs, 812.00/17852.

71. Carothers to Lansing, March 22, 1916, Internal Affairs, 812.00/17583.

72. "Weekly Report on General Conditions Along the Mexican Border," April 8, 1916, Internal Affairs, 812.00/17908, p. 7.

73. Link, *Confusions and Crises*, pp. 282-283.

74. Cobb to Lansing, April 13, 1916, Internal Affairs, 812.00/17834.

75. *Herald*, April 13, 1916, p. 6.

76. Link, *Confusions and Crises*, pp. 281-297.

77. *New York Times*, June 19, 1916, p. 1.

78. Christian, "Sword and Plowshare," p. 387.

79. *Times*, May 16, 1916, p. 1; *Herald*, June 8, 1916, p. 9.

80. *Herald*, June 19, 1916, p. 5.

81. Ibid., June 17-18, 1916, p. 6.

82. Cobb to Lansing, June 21, 1916, Internal Affairs, 812.00/18524.

83. *Herald*, June 17-18, 1916, p. 5; Martínez, *Ciudad Juárez*, p. 40; Cobb to Lansing, June 27, 1916, Internal Affairs, 812.00/18588½ (quote).

84. Cobb to Lansing, June 25, 1916, Internal Affairs, 812.00/18562.

85. Carothers to Lansing, June 25, 1916, Internal Affairs, 812.00/18564.

86. Cobb to Lansing, June 29, 1916, Internal Affairs 812.00/18612.

87. *Herald*, June 21, 1916, p. 4.

88. Ibid., June 22, 1916, p. 1; "Weekly Report of General Conditions Along the Mexican Border," for June 24, 1916, and July 1, 1916, in Internal Affairs, 812.00/18653 and 812.00/18709 respectively.

89. Link, *Confusions and Crises*, pp. 314-318; Arthur S. Link, *Wilson: Campaigns for Progressivism and Peace, 1916-1917* (Princeton, 1965), pp. 328-339.

90. *Times*, March 2, 1918, pp. 1, 5.

91. Ibid., April 12, 1918, p. 6.

92. Cumberland, *Mexican Revolution*, pp. 397-398.

93. *Herald*, June 16, 1919, p. 1.

94. Printed copy of a speech by Claude B. Hudspeth given before Congress on June 19, 1919. Located in file "Mexico-Revolution," Southwest Vertical File, El Paso Public Library.

95. S. L. A. Marshall Transcript, ACC 181, IOH, July 5, 1975, p. 29; hereinafter cited as Marshall Transcript.

96. *Herald*, June 17-18, 1916, p. 6. Longtime city residents that I interviewed confirmed that, by 1920, the Anglo and Mexican communities were practically segregated from each other. Mr. and Mrs. Bill Isaacks recalled that Anglo residents in northeast El Paso rarely saw any Mexicans in their neighborhood, "not even jitney drivers." William Hooten recalled that Mexicans were "very separated" and "rarely crossed Overland Street." William J. Hooten, personal interview, December 1, 1983; Mr. and Mrs. Bill Isaacks, personal interview, November 28, 1983.

97. Marshall Transcript, p. 20.

98. *Times*, February 3, 1917, p. 2.

Chapter III

1. *Times*, June 15, 1916, pp. 1, 2, 3; *Herald*, June 14, 1916, pp. 1, 2.

2. *Times*, March 10, 1917, p. 12.

3. Ibid., March 29, 1917, p. 1.

4. Ibid., March 2, 1917, p. 6 (first quote); March 12, 1917, p. 6 (second quote).

5. Ibid., March 27, 1917, pp. 1, 2; April 6, 1917, pp. 1, 2.

6. *Herald*, April 5, 1917, p. 1.

7. "Minutes of the Regular Meeting of the Board of Directors of the El Paso Chamber of Commerce, April 10, 1917."

8. *Times*, Special Night Edition, May 14, 1917, p. 12 (quote); "Minutes of a Called Meeting of the Board of Directors of the El Paso Chamber of Commerce, April 7, 1917."

9. *Times*, Special Night Edition, May 1, 1917, pp. 1, 2.

10. *Times*, May 12, 1917, p. 3.

11. "Minutes of a Specially Called Meeting of the Board of Directors of the El Paso Chamber of Commerce, April 20, 1917."

12. *Times*, April 26, 1917, p. 5; Richard K. McMasters, *Musket, Saber, and Missile: A History of Fort Bliss* (El Paso, 1963), p. 44.

13. *Times*, April 10, 1917, p. 3.

14. *Herald*, August 17, 1917, p. 6.

15. *Times*, June 6, 1917, p. 2.

16. Mary Elizabeth Bush, "El Paso County, Texas, In the First World War" (M.A. thesis, University of Texas, 1950), pp. 86-87. According to Bush, there is a good possibility that the dismissed instructor was a German spy.

17. *Times*, March 31, 1917, p. 5.

18. Ibid., June 3, 1917, p. 6.

19. Ibid., June 6, 1917, p. 1; June 7, 1917, p. 3; *Herald*, August 10, 1917, p. 2 (quote).

20. *Herald*, August 16, 1917, p. 5 (first quote); August 17, 1917, p. 6 (second quote).

21. *Times*, November 3, 1917, p. 7 (first quote); November 27, 1917, p. 5 (second and third quotes).

22. Ibid., First Edition, November 8, 1917, p. 10; November 11, 1917, p. 2 (quote).

23. Ibid., First Edition, November 8, 1917, p. 10 (first quote); November 20, 1917, p. 10 (second quote).

24. See Christian, "Sword and Plowshare," for an excellent account of El Paso's ties to the military prior to 1918. See White, *Out of the Desert*, pp. 263-264, for an interesting evaluation of the profits that accrued in El Paso due to the local troop buildup in 1916.

25. *Times*, Special Night Edition, June 2, 1917, p. 1; June 3, 1917, p. 10.

26. Ibid., June 3, 1917, p. 1. Secretary Baker had long been hearing complaints about vice in El Paso. See *Congressional Record*, 65th Cong., 1st sess., LV, Part 5, p. 4390, and C. H. Cramer, *Newton D. Baker, A Biography* (Cleveland, 1961), p. 100.

27. *Times*, June 3, 1917, p. 10; "Minutes of a Specially Called Meeting of the Board of Directors of the El Paso Chamber of Commerce, June 1, 1917" (quote). In 1968 El Pasoan Chester Chope recalled the red-light zone: "It was located at 9th and Mesa. With two exceptions, the place consisted of one-story buildings of light colored brick. In good weather, the girls stood in the doorways and beckoned to prospective customers." Chester Chope Transcript, ACC 27, IOH, July 26, 1968, p. 32; hereinafter cited as Chope Transcript. For more on prostitution in El Paso, see H. Gordon Frost, *The Gentleman's Club: The Story of Prostitution in El Paso* (El Paso, 1983).

28. *Times*, June 7, 1917, pp. 2, 4; June 8, 1917, p. 3.

29. Ibid., June 4, 1917, p. 10.

30. *Times*, June 15, 1917, p. 1; *Herald*, July 16, 1917, p. 3.

31. *Herald*, July 3, 1917, p. 2; July 7-8, 1917, p. 4.

32. *Times*, Second Edition, November 8, 1917, p. 10; Special Night Edition, December 7, 1917, p. 3 (quote).

33. *Herald*, September 18, 1917, p. 9.

34. *Times*, June 21, 1917, p. 9; December 7, 1917, p. 2.

35. Ibid., December 24, 1917, p. 2; December 27, 1917, p. 1.

36. Ibid., December 29, 1917, p. 6 (first quote); *Herald*, May 4, 1918, p. 3 (second quote).

37. *Times*, December 27, 1917, p. 1 (third quote); *Herald*, December 27, 1917, p. 8 (first and second quotes).

38. "Minutes of a Regular Meeting of the El Paso City Council, December 27, 1917," Book I-2, pp. 762-763; *Times*, December 27, 1917, p. 2; December 28, 1917, p. 5; December 29, 1917, p. 5; December 30, 1917, pp. 3, 20. All City Council minutes cited in this study are located in the office of the El Paso City Clerk.

39. *Times*, January 6, 1918, p. 1; January 7, 1918, p. 1.

40. Ibid., January 9, 1918, p. 1; "Minutes of a Regular Meeting of the El Paso County Commissioners' Court, January 8, 1918," Vol. XI, pp. 70-85. All Commissioners' Court records cited in this study are located in the office of the El Paso County Clerk.

41. *Times*, January 8, 1918, p. 2.

42. Ibid., January 9, 1918, p. 6.

43. *Herald*, January 29, 1918, p. 6.

44. Ibid., January 21, 1918, p. 12; January 22, 1918, p. 6; January 23, 1918, p. 3; *Times*, January 21, 1918, p. 1 (quote).

45. *Times*, January 16, 1918, p. 1; January 19, 1918, p. 3; *Herald*, January 19-20, 1918, p. 8. See both the *Times* and the *Herald* during January 15-30, 1918, for many examples of political advertising during the prohibition campaign.

46. *Herald*, January 23, 1918, p. 3.

47. Ibid., January 18, 1918, p. 14.

48. Ibid., January 21, 1918, p. 12; January 22, 1918, p. 12 (quote); January 24, 1918, p. 3; *Times*, January 24, 1918, p. 2.

49. "Minutes of a Regular Meeting of the Board of Directors of the El Paso Chamber of Commerce, January 22, 1918."

50. "Minutes of a Called Meeting of the Board of Directors of the El Paso Chamber of

Commerce, August 18, 1917;" "Minutes of a Specially Called Meeting of the Board of Directors of the El Paso Chamber of Commerce, November 6, 1917."

51. *Times*, Second Night Edition, January 20, 1918, p. 16.

52. Ibid., January 31, 1918, p. 1.

53. *Herald*, January 26-27, 1918, pp. 1, 27.

54. Ibid., January 15, 1918, p. 5; January 18, 1918, p. 14 (quote).

55. *Times*, January 28, 1918, p. 3.

56. El Paso County Voting Records for 1918. Located in the office of the Department of Elections in the El Paso City-County Building. Slightly different tallies are given in the *Times*, January 31, 1918, p. 1.

57. *Times*, March 3, 1918, pp. 1 (quotes), 2.

58. Ibid., March 6, 1918, p. 1; March 8, 1918, p. 4; March 10, 1918, p. 1 (quote); "Summary of Proceedings of Mass Meeting, March 5, 1918," in El Paso Chamber of Commerce records.

59. *Times*, September 26, 1918, p. 2.

60. Ibid., May 28, 1918, p. 5 (first quote); June 10, 1918, p. 3 (second quote).

61. "Minutes of a Meeting of the Highland Park Community Council of Defense, September 5, 1918;" "Minutes of a Meeting of the Smelter Community Council of Defense, September 2, 1918," (quotes). All minutes of the various community defense councils can be found in *Minutes and Records of the El Paso County Council of Defense* (n.d., n.p.), located in the El Paso Public Library.

62. *Times*, March 12, 1918, p. 1; March 22, 1918, p. 1; April 16, 1918, p. 5; May 27, 1918, p. 2; Texas, *General and Special Laws of the State of Texas Passed by the Fourth Called Session of the Thirty-fifth Legislature*, pp. 27-29, 36-40.

63. Bush, "El Paso in the First World War," pp. 92-94; Christian, "Sword and Plowshare," pp. 509-510.

64. *The Texas War Saver*, October 1918, located in File No. 512 of the El Paso Public Library archives. See this file for an extensive collection of newspaper clippings concerning El Paso servicemen during World War I. Also see El Paso County of Defense, *El Paso in the World War* (n.d., n.p.), located in the El Paso Public Library.

65. *Times*, March 8, 1918, p. 3.

66. Located in File No. 512 of the El Paso Public Library archives.

67. *Kiwanis News*, Special Edition, August 23, 1918, located in File No. 512 of the El Paso Public Library archives. "Minutes of a Meeting of the Alamo Community Council of Defense, August 16, 1918;" "Minutes of a Meeting of the Alamo Community Council of Defense, August 29, 1918."

68. "Minutes of a Meeting of the Morehead Community Council of Defense, September 19, 1918."

69. *Herald*, January 16, 1918, p. 3 (third quote); January 24, 1918, p. 2 (first and second quotes). El Paso school children were also active in drives to sell war bonds and stamps, and in soliciting Red Cross donations. See Ruth Cummings, "History of Alamo School" (History seminar paper, Texas Western College, 1951), p. 39; Alice J. Nelson, "An Historical Sketch of Alta Vista School" (History seminar paper, Texas Western College, 1954), pp. 14-15.

70. *Times*, February 16, 1918, p. 5.

71. Ibid., March 5, 1918, p. 6.

72. *Herald*, July 29, 1918, p. 2.

73. *Times*, November 7, 1918, p. 2; "Minutes of a Meeting of the Morehead Community Council of Defense, September 5, 1918."

74. "Minutes of a Meeting of the El Paso County Council of Defense, November 9, 1918."

75. *Times*, November 12, 1918, p. 1.

76. Ibid., November 11, 1918, p. 5. As was the case in almost every part of the nation, *The Birth of a Nation* was extremely popular in El Paso. See Chris P. Fox Transcript, ACC 19A, IOH, September 12, 1972, p. 64; hereinafter cited as Fox Transcript, ACC 19A.

Chapter IV

1. William G. Shepherd, "How I Put Over the Klan," *Colliers*, LXXXII (July 14, 1928), p. 34. This article is based on an extended personal interview with William Joseph Simmons and is an invaluable primary source for any study of the Klan of the 1920s.

2. Ibid., p. 32; U.S., Congress, House, Committee on Rules, *Hearings on the Ku Klux Klan*, 67th Cong., 1st sess., 1921, pp. 67-68 (quotes); hereinafter cited as *Klan Hearings*.

3. Shepherd, "How I Put Over the Klan," pp. 6, 32. For works which examine both the original Klan and the Klan of the 20th century, see David M. Chalmers, *Hooded Americanism: The First Century of the Ku Klux Klan, 1865-1965* (Garden City, New York, 1965; reprint edition, Chicago, 1968), and William P. Randel, *The Ku Klux Klan: A Century of Infamy* (Philadelphia, 1965).

4. Shepherd, "How I Put Over the Klan," p. 32; *Klan Hearings*, pp. 68-69.

5. Alexander, *Klan in the Southwest*, p. 18; *New York Times*, September 26, 1916, p. 10 (quote).

6. Shepherd, "How I Put Over the Klan," p. 35.

7. *Klan Hearings*, p. 69.

8. William G. Shepherd, "Ku Klux Koin," *Colliers*, LXXXII (July 21, 1928). p. 9 (first quote); *New York Times*, September 1, 1918, IV, p. 5; *Times*, May 6, 1918, p. 6 (second quote).

9. Shepherd, "Ku Klux Koin," pp. 38-39; Robert L. Duffus, "Salesmen of Hate: The Ku Klux Klan," *World's Work*, XLVI (May 1923), pp. 33-36.

10. Chalmers, *Hooded Americanism*, pp. 39-40; Charles C. Alexander, *Crusade for Conformity: The Ku Klux Klan in Texas, 1920-1930* (Houston, 1962), pp. 4-5.

11. Alexander, *Klan in the Southwest*, pp. 29-33.

12. *Times*, May 23, 1921, p. 10.

13. Chalmers, *Hooded Americanism*, pp. 41-43; Alexander, *Crusade for Conformity*, p. 11.

14. *El Paso City Directory, 1921*, p. 186.

15. U.S., Department of Commerce, Bureau of the Census, *Fourteenth Census of the United States, 1920: Population*, III, pp. 81, 710, 1015, 1016, 1024. I have based my population estimate on the fact that at least ninety percent (and probably more) of El Paso's foreign born residents were from Mexico. It is reasonable to assume that equal percentages of Mexicans could be found in the city's "native white of foreign parentage" and "native white of mixed parentage" populations. This would result in a total Mexican population of 43,684, a figure equivalent to 56.3 percent of El Paso's total official population in 1920. The only other sizable American communities with higher percentages of Mexicans were Laredo, Texas, and Nogales, Arizona, neither of which was comparable to El Paso in terms of population. Laredo's total population in 1920 was 22,710 and that of

Nogales was 5,199. See Martínez, *Ciudad Juárez*, p. 160, for the problems of estimating El Paso's Mexican population.

16. For example, while the 1920 census found 29,000 residents of Mexican descent living in Los Angeles, California, a census taken the following year by *La Prensa de Los Angeles* discovered 86,000 Mexicans in the city. See Ricardo Romo, "The Urbanization of Southwestern Chicanos in the Early Twentieth Century," *New Scholar*, VI (1977), p. 194.

17. *Herald*, January 20, 1914, p. 4.

18. U.S., Department of Commerce, Bureau of the Census, *Special Census of El Paso, Texas, 1916*, pp. 3, 4.

19. García, *Desert Immigrants*, pp. 127-154. For an exact explanation of which parts of El Paso composed the Chihuahuita barrio, see Enrique Acevedo Transcript, ACC 130, IOH, May 17, 1974, p. 3.

20. *Times*, July 29, 1910, p. 5.

21. *Herald*, June 16, 1914, p. 4.

22. Ibid., May 25, 1914, p. 4.

23. *Times*, April 6, 1917, p. 11; "Minutes of a Regular Meeting of the El Paso City Council, April 5, 1917," Book H-2, pp. 1305-1310.

24. García, *Desert Immigrants*, pp. 142-143; El Paso City Plan Commission, *City Plan for El Paso, 1925*, p. 14, located in El Paso, Texas, Collection, ACC 812, The University of Texas at El Paso archives; hereinafter cited as UTEP archives. The city plan commission in 1925 found Chihuahuita to be "an eyesore, unhealthful and a disgrace to the city. . . ." For more on the health problems in south El Paso during this period, see E. W. Rheinheimer Transcript, ACC 427, IOH, February 4, 1977, pp. 1-4.

25. *Fourteenth Census, 1920; Population*, III, p. 1015.

26. Mark Reisler, "Always the Laborer, Never the Citizen: Anglo Perceptions of the Mexican Immigrant during the 1920s," *Pacific Historical Review*, XLV (May 1976), p. 236.

27. *Times*, February 22, 1917, p. 6.

28. Ibid., May 1, 1917, p. 11; "The Literacy Test a Bar to Typhus," *The Survey*, XXVIII (April 21, 1917), p. 71.

29. *Times*, February 3, 1917, p. 1 (first quote); Bulldog Edition, May 10, 1917, p. 6 (second quote).

30. Lawrence A. Cardoso, "Labor Emigration to the Southwest, 1916 to 1920; Mexican Attitudes and Policy," *Southwestern Historical Quarterly*, LXXIX (April 1976), p. 403; V. Blain Gwin, "The New Mexican Immigration," *The Survey*, XL (August 3, 1918), p. 491.

31. *Times*, January 5, 1921, p. 1.

32. U.S., *Statutes at Large*, XLII, Part 1, p. 5; XLIII, Part 1, p. 155.

33. Martínez, *Ciudad Juárez*, pp. 73-74.

34. Ibid., p. 160.

35. *Klan Hearings*, pp. 96, 127.

36. Alexander, *Klan in the Southwest*, vii.

37. When considering race relations in El Paso during the 1920s, the only "minority" group of any real significance were Mexicans. In 1920 blacks constituted only 1.7 percent of El Paso's population, by far the lowest percentage in any large Texas city. As one local resident later recalled, blacks had "no effect on the community whatsoever." Nevertheless, such blacks as there were in the city had been fully segregated by 1920 and were dealt with strictly if they appeared the least bit unruly. *Fourteenth Census, 1920: Population*, III,

p. 1015; Marshall Transcript, p. 34 (quote); Marilyn T. Bryan, "The Economic, Political and Social Status of the Negro in El Paso," *Password*, XIII (Fall 1968), p. 81. Another racial minority that had once been sizable in El Paso, the Chinese, was also of little or no significance in the city by 1920. Victim of a shortage of women and the advent of modern steam laundries, the local Chinese colony had essentially evaporated by the end of World War I. See Nancy Ellen Farrar, "The History of the Chinese in El Paso, Texas: A Case Study of an Urban Immigrant Group in the American West" (M.A. thesis, The University of Texas at El Paso, 1970), pp. 88-89.

38. Texas, *House Journal*, 36th Legis., 1st and 2d called session, p. 445; Jeanne Bozzell McCarty, *The Struggle for Sobriety, Protestants and Prohibition in Texas: 1919-1935* (El Paso, 1980), pp. 6-7.

39. *Times*, August 3, 1921, p. 5.

40. Ibid., February 22, 1921, p. 30.

41. U.S., Congress, Senate, *Supplemental Estimate for the Customs Service*, Sen. Doc. p. 196, 66th Cong., 2d sess., p. 2.

42. *Times*, January 8, 1921, p. 11 (first quote); February 22, 1921, p. 30 (second quote).

43. Ibid., March 3, 1921, p. 4 (first quote); March 4, 1921, p. 4 (second quote).

44. Ibid., March 3, 1921, p. 1.

45. *Herald*, March 22, 1921, pp. 1, 2.

46. *Times*, May 1, 1921, p. 1; *Herald*, May 2, 1921, p. 3.

47. *Times*, January 25, 1921, p. 12; March 5, 1921, p. 7; July 25, 1921, p. 7. Despite the increase in arrests, it was a relatively easy matter to procure illegal liquor in El Paso. William J. Hooten recalled that he could walk to the window of his office, hold up two fingers, and within minutes receive two bottles of liquor from a Mexican bootlegger at the alley exit to the office building. Hooten interview, December 1, 1983. For similar observations, see E. W. Rheinheimer Transcript, ACC 124, IOH, April 3, 1974, pp. 27-28.

48. Texas, *House Journal*, 37th Legis., regular session, p. 316.

49. *Times*, March 7, 1921, p. 9.

50. Ibid., February 22, 1921, p. 30.

51. Ibid., June 24, 1921, p. 3; January 5, 1922, p. 2. Also see Chope Transcript, p. 2.

52. *Times*, May 7, 1921, p. 7; January 1, 1922, p. 4.

53. *Herald*, March 28, 1921, p. 2.

54. *Times*, September 10, 1921, p. 8.

55. Ibid., August 28, 1921, p. 4.

56. *Herald*, February 26-27, 1921, p. 12.

57. *Times*, May 3, 1921, p. 12.

58. Ibid., January 7, 1921, p. 2.

59. Ibid., p. 5.

60. Ibid., March 1, 1921, p. 12.

61. Ibid., January 4, 1921, p. 2; January 11, 1921, p. 12; January 26, 1921, p. 1.

62. Ibid., March 21, 1921, p. 2; July 11, 1921, p. 7.

63. Ibid., August 17, 1921, p. 2; August 28, 1921, p. 4 (quote).

64. *Herald*, June 14, 1921, p. 1; James H. Daross, "A History of the El Paso Police Department — Part II" (History seminar paper, Texas Western College, 1953), p. 18.

65. *Times*, June 20, 1921, p. 10.

66. Texas, *House Journal*, 36th Legis., 1st and 2d called sessions, p. 443; *Times*, May 25, 1919, p. 1.

67. *Times*, September 12, 1921, p. 7.

68. Ibid., June 6, 1921, p. 9.

69. Ibid., May 9, 1921, p. 5 (quote); May 12, 1921, p. 4.

70. Ibid., June 6, 1921, p. 9 (second quote); June 13, 1921, p. 2 (first quote).

71. For the impact of United States prohibition on Cuidad Juárez, see Martínez, *Ciudad Juárez*, pp. 57-77, and Edward Lonnie Langston, "The Impact of Prohibition on the Mexican-United States Border: The El Paso-Ciudad Juárez Case" (Ph.D. dissertation, Texas Tech University, 1974).

72. Langston, "The Impact of Prohibition," p. 90; *Times*, January 24, 1921, p. 10; June 29, 1921, Section 2, p. 4.

73. Martínez, *Ciudad Juárez*, p. 57 (quote); Chope Transcript, p. 13.

74. *Times*, February 2, 1921, p. 4. William Hooten informed me that the red-light district was indeed vile, consisting primarily of sordid hutches occupied by extremely young girls, some accompanied by infants or young children. Hooten interview, December 1, 1983.

75. *Times*, September 10, 1921, p. 8.

76. For the erratic fortunes of the gambling industry in Juárez, see Chapter V, "The Heyday of the Gambling Palaces," in Langston, "The Impact of Prohibition," pp. 130-179.

77. *Times*, February 7, 1921, p. 10.

78. Ibid., January 24, 1921, p. 10.

79. Ibid., January 3, 1921, p. 9.

80. Ibid., March 8, 1921, p. 1; Langston, "The Impact of Prohibition," p. 68.

81. *Times*, November 27, 1921, p. 24. These cards were free for El Paso residents. See *Times*, August 25, 1921, p. 12.

82. Ibid., June 27, 1921, p. 10.

83. *Herald*, September 26, 1921, p. 10.

84. *Times*, January 2, 1922, p. 10.

85. Marshall Transcript, pp. 82-83.

86. *Times*, January 1, 1921, p. 9.

87. Ibid., January 1, 1922, p. 3.

88. Ibid., January 19, 1921, p. 5.

89. Ibid., January 3, 1921, p. 9 (first quote); January 24, 1921, p. 10 (second quote); February 21, 1921, p. 10.

90. Ibid., January 5, 1922, p. 8. Evidently Knickerbocker's stance met with the approval of local Methodists. During his tenure as pastor (1916-1922), the membership of Trinity Methodist Church increased from 1,026 to 1,986. See Margaret Norwood, "History of Trinity Methodist Church" (History seminar paper, Texas Western College, 1950), p. 44.

91. *Times*, January 19, 1921, p. 4.

92. U.S., Department of Commerce, Bureau of the Census, *Thirteenth Census of the United States, 1910: Population*, III, p. 852; *Fourteenth Census, 1920: Population*, III, p. 1015; *Times*, June 29, 1921, Section 3, p. 10.

93. Martínez, *Ciudad Juárez*, p. 161; *Times*, June 29, 1921, Section 5, p. 10. The *El Paso City Directory, 1921* lists the population of El Paso and its suburbs, excluding Fort Bliss, at 91,137 (p. 186).

94. *Fourteenth Census, 1920: Manufacturing*, IX, p. 1470.

95. *Times*, June 29, 1921, Section 3, p. 11; Section 5, p. 11; Section 6, pp. 6, 7.

96. *Herald*, July 10, 1919, p. 2; June 7, 1920, p. 7.

97. *Times*, February 22, 1921, p. 11; September 29, 1921, p. 4.

98. *El Paso City Directory, 1921*, pp. 872-873; *Times*, June 29, 1921, Section 3, p. 6.

99. *Times*, February 22, 1921, p. 29.

100. Ibid., June 29, 1921, Section 3, p. 6.

101. Ibid., August 16, 1921, p. 12 (first quote); *Herald*, August 3, 1921, p. 12 (second quote).

102. *Herald*, November 4, 1921, p. 15.

103. *Times*, January 23, 1921, p. 5.

104. Langston, "The Impact of Prohibition," p. 137; *Times*, January 27, 1921, p. 4; August 23, 1921, p. 12; November 27, 1921, p. 14; *Herald*, July 23-24, 1921, p. 6.

105. *Times*, March 20, 1921, p. 20.

106. Frederick Lewis Allen, *Only Yesterday: An Informal History of the 1920s* (New York, 1931; reprint edition, 1964), p. 73.

107. *Times*, September 21, 1921, p. 12. Ciudad Juárez was particularly attractive to young people because of the dearth of exciting nightlife in El Paso. Longtime city resident Chris P. Fox recalled that "In the '20s, groups of us would go down there [to Juárez] on Saturday night to eat; and we had a drink or two, dance around. . . . I always got along very well in Juárez. I had lots of enjoyable acquaintances and experiences." Chris P. Fox Transcript, ACC 214, IOH, January 22, 1976, p. 18 (quote); Hooten interview, December 1, 1983; Isaacks interview, November 28, 1983.

108. *Times*, March 28, 1921, p. 10.

109. Ibid., January 4, 1922, p. 3.

110. Ibid., February 21, 1921, p. 10.

111. Marshall Transcript, pp. 59-60. Other El Pasoans who grew up during this period also later recalled that the youth of the city were generally well behaved. See Chris P. Fox Transcript, ACC 19A, IOH, July 25, 1972, p. 11, and Florence Cathcart Melby Transcript, ACC 121, IOH, March 26, 1974, p. 2.

112. *Times*, August 22, 1920, p. 13.

113. Ibid., August 30, 1920, p. 2.

114. Ibid., September 6, 1920, p. 10.

115. Ibid., March 2, 1921, p. 5.

116. Ibid., June 6, 1921, p. 10.

117. Ibid., June 14, 1921, p. 12.

118. Ibid., October 4, 1921, p. 2.

119. Ibid., September 15, 1921, p. 7.

120. Ibid., July 21, 1921, p. 7.

121. Ibid., September 17, 1921, p. 2; *Herald*, September 16, 1921, p. 1 (quote).

122. *Times*, June 20, 1921, p. 4; August 7, 1921, p. 8 (quotes); John J. Middagh, *Frontier Newspaper: The El Paso Times* (El Paso, 1958), pp. 193-195. Black was highly admired by his fellow journalists. Chester Chope, who worked as a reporter for the *Times*, later recalled that Black was "a quiet, easygoing gentleman . . . but he was fearless in the operation of his paper." Former *Herald* reporter S. L. A. Marshall claimed that Black was "probably the most articulate and the best writing editor that this city had ever known — an extraordinary person in every respect." Chope Transcript, p. 5; Marshall Transcript, p. 52.

123. *Herald*, July 26, 1921, p. 6.

124. *Times*, September 10, 1921, p. 3.
125. Ibid., September 25, 1921, p. 1.
126. White, *Out of the Desert*, pp. 306, 310; Lucille Soltner, "Early El Paso Newspapers" (M.A. thesis, Texas College of Mines and Metallurgy, 1945), pp. 68-82.
127. *Herald*, July 20, 1921, p. 10.
128. Ibid.
129. Ibid., September 3-4, 1921, p. 28.
130. Ibid., September 15, 1921, p. 1.
131. *Times*, September 27, 1921, p. 12.
132. Ibid., September 25, 1921, p. 1. The alderman who joined the Klan was William T. Griffith. Mr. and Mrs. William E. Griffith, telephone conversation, February 18, 1985.
133. Ibid., October 3, 1921, p. 10.
134. "Minutes of a Regular Meeting of the El Paso City Council, September 15, 1921," Book M-2, p. 65 (quote); *Times*, September 16, 1921, p. 1; September 23, 1921, p. 12; *Herald*, September 15, 1921, p. 1.
135. "Minutes of a Regular Meeting of the El Paso City Council, September 29, 1921," Book M-2, pp. 88-89; *Times*, September 29, 1921, p. 12; September 30, 1921, p. 12. The council recognized the need for immediate action, Section 4 of the ordinance stating: "The fact that there now exists no adequate ordinance requiring parades or processions within the City of El Paso to be held upon the consent of any authority creates a great public emergency so that the charter rule requiring the reading of this ordinance in open meeting of the City Council at two regular meetings be suspended, which is done by unanimous vote of all the Aldermen present and with the consent of the mayor pro tem." The speedy enactment of the ordinance greatly relieved Catholics living in the city's southside. See *Revista Católica*, XLVII (October 2, 1921), p. 1. All copies of *Revista Católica* cited in this study are located in ACC 774, UTEP archives.
136. *Times*, September 25, 1921, p. 1; October 2, 1921, p. 1 (quote).
137. Ibid., September 16, 1921, p. 4.
138. Ibid., September 26, 1921, p. 4 (first quote); October 3, 1921, p. 10 (second quote).
139. Ibid., November 8, 1921, pp. 1, 2; *Herald*, November 7, 1921, p. 1; Middagh, *Frontier Newspaper*, p. 198; William J. Hooten, *Fifty-Two Years a Newsman* (El Paso, 1974), p. 10.
140. *Herald*, November 9, 1921, p. 11.
141. Ibid., July 27, 1921, p. 1; *Times*, July 28, 1921, p. 3.
142. *Herald*, August 15, 1921, p. 5.
143. *Times*, October 2, 1921, p. 1.
144. Ibid., October 3, 1921, p. 10.
145. Ibid., October 15, 1921, p. 3. Rabbi Zielonka was a remarkable local figure whose life is deserving of further study. For more information, see Evelyn R. Rosen, "Martin Zielonka, Rabbi and Civic Leader in El Paso, and His Interest in the College of the City of El Paso" (History seminar paper, Texas Western College, 1958).
146. *Times*, September 25, 1921, p. 1.
147. I have based this assertion on the fact that the Klan recently had been very active in trying to recruit Las Cruces, New Mexico, Masons into the KKK. In late October 1921 Francis G. Lester of Mesilla Park, Las Cruces, grand master of Masons in New Mexico, stated: "Definite evidence has come to my attention of solicitation among Masons and officers of Masonic lodges in this grand jurisdiction for membership in the organization

known as the Ku Klux Klan. . . ." No doubt similar efforts were being made in El Paso, where the chief recruiter (Kleagle) was a leading Shriner. When Grand Master Andrew L. Randell visited the city in July 1921, he felt it necessary to "forcibly, earnestly, and ably [remind] the brethren of their duties as citizens, and [warn] them against following after false gods, especially cautioning them to avoid standing sponsor for, or in any manner aiding and abetting, the Ku Klux Klan." Despite these warnings, the Klan found a strong following among local Masons. *Las Cruces Citizen*, October 22, 1921, p. 1 (first quote); *Times*, October 19, 1921, p. 7; November 11, 1921, p. 5; *Herald*, November 10, 1921, p. 9; John W. Denny, "One Hundred Years of Freemasonry In El Paso, 1854-1954" (M.A. thesis, Texas Western College, 1954), pp. 150-151 (second quote); Marshall Transcript, p. 70; Hooten interview, December 1, 1983.

148. *Times*, October 1, 1921, p. 8.

149. Ibid., October 5, 1921, p. 5; October 11, 1921, p. 2 (quote).

150. See *Klan Hearings*.

151. *Times*, September 21, 1921, p. 7.

152. *Herald*, November 1, 1921, p. 3.

153. Ibid., November 12-13, 1921, p. 5.

154. *Times*, September 21, 1921, p. 4.

155. Ibid., December 19, 1921, p. 7.

156. Ibid., November 4, 1921, p. 7; *Herald*, November 3, 1921, pp. 1, 2.

157. *Times*, November 5, 1921, p. 6 (first quote); November 7, 1921, p. 4 (second quote).

158. *Herald*, November 5-6, 1921, p. 1.

159. Ibid., November 9, 1921, p. 11.

160. *Times*, November 11, 1921, p. 5; November 17, 1921, p. 8; November 20, 1921, p. 10 (quote); *Herald*, November 16, 1921, p. 5. The Associated Charities was the central relief agancy for El Paso, similar to today's United Way. See Helen Rainey "A History of Organized Welfare in El Paso, 1892-1948" (M.A. thesis, Texas Western College, 1949), pp. 40-62.

161. *Herald*, November 21, 1921, p. 12.

162. *Times*, November 24, 1921, p. 4 (quote); November 25, 1921, p. 10.

163. *Herald*, November 17, 1921, p. 16 (quotes); *Times*, November 17, 1921, p. 3.

164. *Herald*, November 18, 1921, p. 6; *Times*, November 18, 1921, p. 3.

165. *Herald*, November 19-20, 1921, p. 32 (first quote); *Times*, December 5, 1921, p. 3 (second quote).

166. *Herald*, November 21, 1921, p. 12.

167. Ibid., November 17, 1921, p. 16.

168. *Times*, December 30, 1921, p. 1; December 31, 1921, p. 4 (quote); *El Paso Labor Advocate*, December 30, 1921, p. 1. All copies of the *El Paso Labor Advocate* cited in this study are in the private possession of Mr. Marvin Shady.

169. *Times*, February 10, 1922, p. 3.

170. Ibid., January 12, 1922, p. 8.

171. Ibid., December 12, 1921, p. 10. The group spearheading the drive was the El Paso City Federation of Women's Clubs.

172. Ibid., February 22, 1922, p. 10. Edwards' duties entailed an "extensive course of reading, and whenever he finds a book that is real naughty he is to place thereon his official stamp of disapproval." As mentioned, the procedure was primarily intended to protect juveniles.

Chapter V

1. Kenneth T. Jackson, *The Ku Klux Klan in the City, 1915-1930* (New York, 1967), pp. 12-13; Charles C. Alexander, "Secrecy Bids for Power: The Ku Klux Klan in Texas Politics in the 1920s," *Mid-America*, XLVI (January 1964), p. 7.

2. Alexander, *Klan in the Southwest*, p. 79; Randel, *A Century of Infamy*, p. 195.

3. Jackson, *Klan in the City*, p. 14; William G. Shepherd, "The Fiery Double-Cross," *Colliers*, LXXXII (July 28, 1928), pp. 8-9, 47.

4. Alexander, "Secrecy Bids for Power," p. 8 (quote); Randel, *A Century of Infamy*, pp. 196-197.

5. "The Reign of the Tar-Bucket," *Literary Digest*, LXX (August 27, 1921), p. 12; Albert De Silver, "The Ku Klux Klan — 'The Soul of Chivalry'," *The Nation*, CXIII (September 14, 1921), pp. 285-286.

6. George B. Tindall, *The Emergence of the New South, 1913-1945* (Baton Rouge, 1967), pp. 192-193; Chalmers, *Hooded Americanism*, p. 42.

7. Alexander, "Secrecy Bids for Power," p. 9.

8. Marshall Transcript, p. 73.

9. García, *Desert Immigrants*, pp. 169-170; de Wetter, "Revolutionary El Paso," p. 156. For more on Mayor Kelly, see Mary Jean Martin, "C. E. Kelly, Mayor of El Paso, 1910-1915" (History seminar paper, Texas Western College, 1956). A short discussion of the 1915 election can be found in Vowell, "Politics at El Paso," pp. 139-141.

10. García, *Desert Immigrants*, p. 170; *Times*, March 2, 1921, p. 5 (quote). An adequate history of El Paso politics during this period has yet to appear. Nevertheless, there is no doubt that a new political machine had been formed by 1920. Hooten interview, December 1, 1983.

11. *Times*, January 30, 1917, p. 1.

12. Ibid., July 10, 1921, p. 8 (quote); Texas, *General Laws of the State of Texas Passed by the 37th Legislature at the Regular Session, 1921*, pp. 275-276; *West's Texas Statutes*, I (Saint Paul, 1974), p. 33.

13. *Herald*, March 29, 1922, p. 2. It should be recognized that the paying of the poll tax did not automatically qualify a resident as a voter. There were a number of residency requirements, and after 1921, one had to be a citizen. The poll tax, however, was considered a revenue measure and was assessed against *all* property owners, regardless of whether they were otherwise qualified to vote. Naturally, this tended to create confusion in El Paso, particularly among resident aliens who had previously been allowed to vote.

14. The exact number of Anglos in El Paso in 1910 and 1920 cannot be precisely determined, because Hispanics were included under the Bureau of the Census' designation "white." A fairly accurate estimate could probably be culled from the 1910 manuscript census schedules; hopefully such effort will be made some day. In 1916 a special census did classify residents into more precise racial categories, finding 27,356 whites (Anglos) and 32,724 Mexicans in the city. See *Thirteenth Census, 1910: Population*, III, p. 852; *Special Census of El Paso, Texas, 1916*, p. 4; *Fourteenth Census, 1920: Population*, III, p. 1015.

15. For the large number of southerners among El Paso's Anglo population in 1900 and 1910, see the manuscript censuses for those years. Church memberships in 1921 similarly reflect the transplantation of Southern culture to the Pass. Of the city's total of approximately 3,230 Methodist church members, 2,400 belonged to the Methodist Episcopal Church, South. All four of El Paso's white Baptist churches were affiliates of the Southern Baptist Convention, with a total membership of 2,520. Local Anglo Presbyterians,

however, showed a preference for the northern branch of their church; northern Presbyterians outnumbered southern Presbyterians 1,133 to 473. See *Times*, June 29, 1921, Section 4, p. 5.

16. Contemporary observer Frank Tannenbaum argued that the Klan held a special attraction for southerners because it expressed "a deep-rooted social habit — a habit of ready violence in defense of a threatened social status," and also because the original Klan was particularly idealized in the South. The latter reason is probably of more importance in explaining why the order found a following in El Paso; many city residents were indeed fascinated by the romance and mystery that initially surrounded the KKK. Frank Tannenbaum, "The Ku Klux Klan: Its Social Origin in the South," *Century Magazine*, CV (April 1923, pp. 873-874; Hooten interview, December 1, 1983.

17. García, *Desert Immigrants*, p. 89.

18. One of the best treatments of the progressive aspirations of middle-class southerners during the 1920s can be found in Tindall, *New South*, pp. 219-284.

19. A. Elizabeth Taylor, "The Woman Suffrage Movement in Texas," *Journal of Southern History*, XVII (May 1951), p. 215. Women had previously (1918) been given the right to vote in primary elections. Texas, *General and Special Laws of the State of Texas Passed by the Fourth Called Session of the Thirty-Fifth Legislature, 1918*, pp. 61-64.

20. Anne Firor Scott, "After Suffrage: Southern Women in the Twenties," *Journal of Southern History*, XXX (August 1964), p. 298.

21. *Times*, January 15, 1921, p. 4 (quote); February 1, 1921, p. 12; February 10, 1921, p. 12.

22. *Herald*, July 7, 1911, p. 7. Mr. and Mrs. Bill Isaacks both recalled that many white women in El Paso were averse to close contact with Mexicans circa 1920. Isaacks interview, November 28, 1983.

23. *Times*, February 4, 1914, p. 12.

24. Ibid., February 7, 1914, p. 6. In *Desert Immigrants* (p. 41), Mario García has attributed these remarks to a certain J. C. Jarvis. However, it is probably more significant that they were made by *Mrs.* J. C. Jarvis.

25. *Times*, February 10, 1914, p. 4.

26. Ibid., September 7, 1921, p. 8.

27. Ibid., September 4, 1921, p. 5.

28. Ibid., July 3, 1921, p. 19.

29. Ibid., July 31, 1921, p. 7.

30. Ibid., May 20, 1921, p. 8.

31. Ibid., February 10, 1921, p. 12; February 1, 1922, p. 2; March 30, 1922, p. 8. The total number of El Paso women paying poll taxes or being issued exemptions due to advanced age was 6,645. These women were predominantly Anglo; only 830 of them were Mexicans. See *Times*, November 5, 1922, p. 20.

32. White, *Out of the Desert*, pp. 162-163.

33. *Times*, June 29, 1921, Section 4, p. 5.

34. Ibid., February 22, 1921, p. 23.

35. Ibid., November 15, 1921, p. 14.

36. Ibid., November 29, 1921, p. 5.

37. Ibid., September 15, 1921, p. 3.

38. *Herald*, January 28-29, 1922, p. 19.

39. *Times*, February 22, 1921, p. 23. For other instances of Protestant church growth during this period see Bertha Lee Bailey, "History of Asbury Methodist Church in El Paso,

Texas" (History seminar paper, Texas Western College, 1952), p. 40; Margaret Norwood "History of Trinity Methodist Church" (History seminar paper, Texas Western College, 1950), p. 44; Julie Ann Guthrie, "History of the Orchard Park Methodist Episcopal Church" (History seminar paper, Texas Western College, 1951), p. 14; Leanora Mosier, "History of the Manhattan Presbyterian Church" (M.A. thesis, Texas Western College, 1956), p. 3; Ruth Cummings, "History of the Fort Boulevard Methodist Episcopal Church" (History seminar paper, Texas Western College, 1952), pp. 1-7; Elouise La Londe, "History of the First Methodist Church" (History seminar paper, Texas Western College, 1953), p. 22; *Journal of the Thirty-Second Session of the New Mexico Annual Conference of the Methodist Episcopal Church, South, 1921*, p. 30; *Journal of the Thirty-Fourth Session of the New Mexico Annual Conference of the Methodist Episcopal Church, South, 1923*, p. 53; "Statistician's Report for the Annual Conference and the General Minutes, English District, New Mexico Conference of the Methodist Episcopal Church, 1921" in *Minutes of the New Mexico Conference of the Methodist Episcopal Church, Seventh Annual Session, 1921; Minutes of the New Mexico Conference of the Methodist Episcopal Church, Eighth Annual Session, 1922*, p. 63. All materials utilized in this study that pertain to the proceedings of the New Mexico conferences of both the Methodist Episcopal Church and the Methodist Episcopal Church, South, were located in the El Paso Methodist Church archives, 1526 Montana Ave. The archives have recently been moved to Santa Fe, New Mexico.

40. *Herald*, January 28-29, 1922, p. 19; Mosier, "Manhattan Presbyterian Church," p. 3; Cummings, "Fort Boulevard Methodist Episcopal Church," pp. 1-7; Guthrie, "Orchard Park Methodist Episcopal Church," p. 19.

41. *Times*, February 6, 1921, p. 6. Church groups themselves were convinced that they had an important role to play during these distressing times. In October 1921 the Board of Temperance and Social Service reported to the New Mexico Annual Conference of the Methodist Episcopal Church, South, that "Your committee notes the confused condition of the country commercially, politically, and religiously. We believe the gospel of Jesus Christ the only remedy for the ills of mankind. We recommend the fearless and prayerful preaching of this gospel as the most forceful expression of our Methodism." All of El Paso's M.E., South, ministers were members of this conference. *Journal of the Thirty-Second Session of the New Mexico Annual Conference of the Methodist Episcopal Church, South, 1921*, p. 59.

42. *Times*, October 17, 1921, p. 3.

43. Ibid., January 5, 1922, p. 8.

44. Ibid., February 14, 1921, p. 10; March 21, 1921, p. 10; La Londe, "First Methodist Church," p. 22, op. 22.

45. An adequate treatment of the clash of Protestantism and Catholicism in El Paso has not yet appeared. This is a fascinating subject worthy of future attention. For a radical yet perceptive discussion of the intrusion of Protestantism into the Southwest, see E. C. Orozco, *Republican Protestantism in Aztlán: The Encounter Between Mexicanism and Anglo-Saxon Secular Humanism in the United States Southwest* (Glendale, California, 1980).

46. Blake, "Catholic Church in El Paso," pp. 88-90; *Diocesan Review: Pro-Cathedral Record* (El Paso, 1917), pp. 17-21; *Diocese of El Paso: Texas Centennial Celebration* (El Paso, 1936); James P. Maloney, "Saint Patrick's Church, El Paso, Texas: Early Beginnings and Dedication" (History seminar paper, Texas Western College, 1952), pp. 18, 28-40; Mary B. Rasavage, "A History of St. Joseph's Parish" (History seminar paper, Texas Western College, 1953), p. 11. El Paso's Catholic population was overwhelmingly Mex-

ican. In 1914, when the Diocese of El Paso was first organized, there were only 2,000 Anglo Catholics in the entire diocese. By 1922, of the 45,000 Catholics in the city, 3,000 to 4,000 were Anglos. See *The Southwest Catholic Register*, VII (May 14, 1965), p. 9; *Herald*, August 26-27, 1922, Section 3, p. 3; September 14, 1922, p. 5. With the exception of daily newspapers, seminar papers, and master's theses, all materials utilized in this study that pertain to the Catholic Church in El Paso are located in the Catholic Diocese of El Paso Museum and Historical Archives, 118 N. Campbell Street.

47. *Times*, June 20, 1921, pp. 1, 2.

48. Ibid., November 4, 1921, p. 2.

49. Ibid., January 3, 1921, p. 9.

50. Ibid., May 2, 1921, p. 9.

51. Ibid., February 20, 1922, p. 10.

52. *Herald*, March 18-19, 1922, p. 6. A comprehensive treatment of Protestant activities in South El Paso is needed. Information related to this topic can be found in May Wilson Barton, "Methodism At Work Among the Spanish-Speaking People of El Paso, Texas" (M.A. thesis, Texas Western College, 1950); Fred Savage, "Baptist Missions Among Foreign Language Groups in El Paso" (History seminar paper, Texas Western College, 1954), pp. 5-12; Delfino Torres, "Brief History of Divine Saviour Presbyterian Church and Its Work Among Spanish-Speaking People" (History seminar paper, Texas Western College, 1958), pp. 8-9; García, *Desert Immigrants*, pp. 220-222.

53. *Times*, December 4, 1921, p. 10; December 9, 1921, p. 8 (quote); Msgr. Henry D. Buchanan Tape, ACC 3, IOH, February 13, 1968; hereinafter cited as Buchanan Tape.

54. *Times*, December 4, 1921, p. 10. The rules agreed to by Father Benedet and Pastor Vargas can be found in *Revista Católica*, XLVII (December 4, 1921), p. 837.

55. *Times*, December 10, 1921, p. 8; December 13, 1921, p. 3.

56. Ibid., December 13, 1921, p. 3; Buchanan Tape. Apparently the commissioners' inquiry was done informally; there is no official record of a meeting of the commissioners' court on the day prior to the debate.

57. *Times*, December 13, 1921, p. 3; Buchanan Tape. The southside Catholic press estimated the crowd attending the debate at 12,000. The failure of Vargas to appear was a source of delight for Catholics for several weeks. See *El Suplemento*, XLVII (January 1, 1922), p. 884, and *El Propagandista Católico*, XLVII (February 5, 1922), p. 86; both located in ACC 774, UTEP archives.

58. *Herald*, January 9, 1922, p. 2; *Times*, March 23, 1922, p. 9; Savage, "Baptist Missions," p. 11. According to Savage, Daniel was arrested on a complaint by a "Roman Catholic leader."

59. *Herald*, January 9, 1922, p. 2.

60. Ibid., January 10, 1922, p. 12.

61. Ibid.

62. Ibid., January 11, 1922, p. 7. The tolerance movement was a spontaneous, popular effort that was not initiated by any particular sect or organization.

63. *Times*, March 18, 1922, p. 4.

64. Ibid., p. 8. I have not been able to ascertain which body printed *La Verdad*. Fred Force, "The Spanish Baptist Publishing House" (History seminar paper, Texas Western College, 1956), p. 13, lists several Baptist publications printed in El Paso, but not *La Verdad*.

65. *Herald*, March 17, 1922, p. 1.

66. Ibid., March 22, 1922, p. 16; *Times*, March 23, 1922, p. 9.

67. *Times*, March 20, 1922, p. 4.

68. *Herald*, January 28-29, 1922, p. 1; March 25-26, 1922, p. 6; *Times*, January 29, 1922, p. 24; *El Paso Labor Advocate*, February 3, 1922, p. 1.

69. Buchanan Tape; *Times*, February 17, 1923, p. 5; *Herald*, May 14, 1924, p. 1; Sherman, "Klan and El Paso Politics," p. 13.

70. *Herald*, March 30, 1922, p. 2.

71. Ibid., February 11, 1915, p. 4.

72. *Times*, May 20, 1921, p. 3. For example, in the district served by Beall School, only 1,427 of the district's 3,177 scholastic age children attended school. See Robert Leyva, "An Historical Sketch of Zavala School" (History seminar paper, Texas Western College, 1951), p. 1.

73. *Times*, September 7, 1921, p. 16; September 8, 1921, p. 7; January 24, 1922, p. 9; García, *Desert Immigrants*, p. 124; Leyva, "Zavala School," p. 1; Edna S. Foley, "A History of Beall School, El Paso, Texas" (History seminar paper, Texas Western College, n.d.), p. 13.

74. *Times*, January 22, 1922, p. 6.

75. *Herald*, February 9, 1922, p. 4. Complaints were also made before the school board. See letters from patrons of Manhattan and Morehead Schools in "Minutes of a Special Meeting of the El Paso School Board, March 2, 1922," in El Paso School Board Records, Vol. 10. All school board records cited in this study are located in the office of the Superintendent of the El Paso Independent School District.

76 .*Times*, February 18, 1922, p. 8.

77. Ibid., March 19, 1922, p. 5.

78. Ibid., March 21, 1921, p. 10.

79. Ibid., July 20, 1921, p. 5; July 21, 1921, p. 12 (quote); "Minutes of a Regular Meeting of the El Paso School Board, July 19, 1921," in El Paso School Board Records, Vol. 10; hereinafter cited as EPSBR.

80. In addition to fears of Catholics who worked for the public schools, there were reservations concerning Catholic parochial schools. In June 1921, Myra C. Winkler, county superintendent of schools, complained that the use of Spanish in private schools was hindering the "Americanization" of El Paso school children. Perhaps such concern was related to the fact that parochial school enrollments were increasing and several new Catholic schools had opened or would open soon. Among the Catholic schools opening during this period were Guardian Angel School (1919), St. Patrick's Elementary School (1924), a new St. Joseph's School (1923), and Loretto Academy (1922).

The official minutes of regional church conferences demonstrate that El Paso Protestants were not alone in their fears. In 1921 the New Mexico Annual Conference of the Methodist Episcopal Church, South, (the conference that included El Paso) passed a resolution to "respectfully memorialize the Congress to take steps to introduce an amendment to the Constitution of the United States of America, making it unlawful to appropriate either national or state funds for sectarian purposes." Another resolution passed at the same conference protested appropriations by the New Mexico state government that benefitted "sectarian schools and hospitals; namely, the schools and hospitals under the Roman Catholic Church. . . ." *Times*, June 19, 1921, p. 10; (first quote); September 12, 1921, p. 10; Adelina T. Gwin, "A History of the Sisters of Loretto in El Paso" (History seminar paper, Texas Western College, 1950), pp. 17-22; *Journal of the Thirty-Second Session of the New Mexico Annual Conference of the Methodist Episcopal Church, South, 1921*, pp. 61-62 (second quote), 62 (third quote).

81. *Herald*, February 17, 1922, p. 10.

82. *Times*, June 17, 1921, p. 12.

83. Ibid., June 23, 1921, p. 12; *Herald*, July 5, 1921, p. 9.

84. *Herald*, July 13, 1921, p. 10.

85. *Times*, February 10, 1922, p. 3. The inspectors were representatives of the War Department and were assigned to examine conditions within the Eighth Army Corps area. Their charges probably had considerable merit. William J. Hooten informed me that widespread prostitution continued in El Paso until the 1930s. Hooten interview, December 1, 1983.

86. *Times*, February 11, 1922, p. 8.

87. *Herald*, February 27, 1922, p. 4.

88. Ibid., March 6, 1922, p. 12. For the purposes of this study, it should be noted that Oliver was a trustee of Asbury Methodist Church. Bailey, "History of Asbury Methodist," p. 9.

89. *Times*, March 7, 1922, p. 3 (third and fourth quotes); *Herald*, March 7, 1922, p. 3 (first quote); March 8, 1922, p. 13 (second quote).

90. *Times*, March 10, 1922, p. 4.

91. Buchanan Tape.

92. *Times*, March 10, 1922, p. 12; March 14, 1922, p. 4. March 26, 1922, p. 24. For the life and career of Burges, see J. F. Hulse, *Texas Lawyer: The Life of William H. Burges* (El Paso, 1982).

93. *Times*, March 12, 1922, p. 5; *Herald*, March 10, 1922, p. 10. Joe Dunne was one of the most colorful local figures of this period, a short, stout, red-headed Irishman who was known as the "Mayor of East El Paso" due to his ability to deliver the Mexican vote. See Marshall Transcript, pp. 24-25; Judge George Rodríguez, Sr., Transcript, ACC 177, IOH, July 29, 1975, pp. 5-6.

94. *Times*, March 14, 1922, p. 5; *Herald*, March 14, 1922, p. 14 (quote).

95. *Herald*, March 15, 1922, p. 5.

96. Ibid., March 17, 1922, p. 4; March 20, 1922, p. 3. *Times*, March 19, 1922, p. 6 (quote).

97. *Herald*, March 30, 1922, p. 4.

98. *Times*, March 21, 1922, p. 3.

99. "Minutes of a Regular Meeting of the El Paso School Board, March 21, 1922," in EPSBR, Vol. 10; *Herald*, March 22, 1922, p. 4; *Times*, March 22, 1922, p. 9; *El Paso Labor Advocate*, March 24, 1922, pp. 1, 2.

100. *Herald*, March 21, 1922, p. 14.

101. Ibid., March 23, 1922, p. 14.

102. Ibid., March 29, 1922, p. 2.

103. *Times*, March 26, 1922, p. 11; *Herald*, March 25-26, 1922, p. 6; Middagh, *Frontier Newspaper*, p. 191.

104. *El Paso Labor Advocate*, March 10, 1922, p. 1; March 24, 1922, p. 1; March 31, 1922, pp. 1, 4; *Herald*, March 13, 1922, p. 12; March 14, 1922, p. 14; March 24, 1922, p. 4; Charles E. Hershberger, "The El Paso Labor Advocate and Its Editors From 1909 to 1939: A Study of Labor Journalism In the Southwest" (M.A. thesis, Texas Western College, 1962), pp. 151, 177-178. Labor's backing of the W-I-G ticket did not signify wholehearted approval of the Ku Klux Klan. The stance of the *Labor Advocate* was very similar to that taken by the *Herald*. Shortly after the local KKK had been organized, Editor William Moran wrote: "The people of this land in the main are God-fearing and

law-abiding, and such virtues as we are credited with have been arrived at through open acts, and not secret ministrations, and for that reason the Ku Klux is not going to be successful in its intentions and has only been the breeder of crime up to now, for the only thing it has been successful in so far is the gathering of considerable pelf, divided among a few grafters, as was plainly brought out by the Congressional investigations, and as we have stated before, gentlemen of the Ku Klux Klan your intentions may be good but your methods are wrong and a wrong method never bore a good result." There also seemed to be second thoughts about the Good Government League, Moran promising labor's support for the organization "just so long as it remains in the fullest sense a good government league." *El Paso Labor Advocate*, November 11, 1921, p. 4 (first quote); March 17, 1922, p. 4 (second quote).

105. *Herald*, March 23, 1922, p. 14 (first quote); *Times*, March 29, 1922, p. 2 (second quote).

106. *Times*, March 30, 1922, p. 8; March 31, 1922, p. 2 (third quote); April 1, 1922, p. 3 (second quote).

107. Ibid., March 30, 1922, p. 8.

108. *Herald*, March 31, 1922, p. 2.

109. *Times*, April 1, 1922, p. 3.

110. *Herald*, March 24, 1922, p. 4.

111. Ibid., March 24, 1922, p. 19.

112. *Times*, March 30, 1922, p. 8.

113. *Herald*, March 27, 1922, p. 2.

114. Ibid., March 28, 1922, p. 14.

115. *Times*, March 31, 1922, p. 3.

116. *Herald*, March 31, 1922, p. 2.

117. *Times*, April 1, 1922, p. 1; *Herald*, April 1-2, 1922, p. 2.

118. *Herald*, April 1-2, 1922, p. 1.

119. *Times*, April 2, 1922, pp. 1, 2 (quote); *Herald*, April 1-2, 1922, p. 1.

120. *Herald*, April 3, 1922, p. 2.

121. Ibid., p. 1.

Chapter VI

1. *Herald*, February 14, 1922, p. 15.

2. *Times*, January 9, 1922, p. 12; January 16, 1922, p. 8; *Herald*, January 9, 1922, p. 2; January 14-15, 1922, p. 7.

3. *Herald*, January 23, 1922, p. 4.

4. Ibid., February 6, 1922, p. 12 (first quote); March 11-12, 1922, p. 7 (second quote); Norwood, "Trinity Methodist Church," p. 37.

5. *Times*, March 10, 1922, p. 3 (second quote); *Herald*, March 9, 1922, p. 1 (first and third quotes).

6. *Herald*, March 11-12, 1922, p. 24.

7. *Times*, March 11, 1922, p. 2 (quote); *Herald*, March 11-12, 1922, p. 24. It probably had not been an easy matter for the Klansmen to drive up Scenic Drive. The road had recently been completed and only had a crushed rock and gravel surface. Mr. and Mrs. Bill Isaacks informed me that driving over the scenic route remained quite dangerous until the road was paved during the 1930s. Isaacks interview, November 28, 1983; Clinton P. Hartman, "A Study of Scenic Drive" (History seminar paper, Texas Western College,

1951), pp. 19-20, 22. For a photograph of Scenic Drive in the early 1920s, see City Plan Commission, *City Plan for El Paso, 1925* (El Paso, 1925), p. 25, in ACC 812, UTEP archives.

8. *Herald*, March 16, 1922, p. 14. The displays emanated from a location above Scenic Drive, but it is not clear whether they were on the eastern or western side of Mount Franklin. I suspect that they were directly above the drive's parking lot, in which case they would have been visible throughout almost all of the city.

9. *Herald*, March 9, 1922, p. 2 (second quote); March 13, 1922, p. 12 (first quote).

10. *Times*, March 14, 1922, p. 5; Buchanan Tape. According to Father Buchanan, many of those involved in the preparations to forceably stop any Klan parade were members of the Knights of Columbus. In the course of researching this paper, I have unsuccessfully sought permission to examine the records of the local K of C. Hopefully, some future researcher with access to these records can adequately appraise the role of local Catholic organizations in fighting the Klan. For more on the K of C in El Paso, see Cleofas Calleros, *Seventieth Anniversary of Columbianism in Texas* (El Paso, 1972), located in the Catholic Diocese of El Paso Museum and Historical Archives.

11. *Times*, March 16, 1922, p. 5; March 17, 1922, p. 14; *Herald*, March 15, 1922, p. 8 (quote).

12. Buchanan Tape.

13. *Times*, March 18, 1922, p. 4.

14. *Herald*, March 23, 1922, p. 6.

15. Ibid., April 12, 1922, p. 14.

16. Ibid.

17. *Times*, April 13, 1922, p. 2 (quote); *Herald*, April 13, 1922, p. 5.

18. *Herald*, April 18, 1922, p. 3.

19. Ibid., May 12, 1922, p. 16.

20. *Times*, May 17, 1922, p. 8 (second quote); *Herald*, May 17, 1922, p. 14 (first quote); "Minutes of a Regular Meeting of the El Paso School Board, May 16, 1922," in EPSBR, Vol. 11.

21. *Herald*, June 12, 1922, pp. 1, 2. The veterans later wrote a letter to the Klan that stated: "Be assured that we are with you heart and hand in all your noble order stands for."*Herald*, June 13, 1922, p. 2.

22. *Herald*, April 24, 1922, p. 14; *Times*, April 25, 1922, p. 2 (quote). The Klan's concern probably was related to the recent organization of the United Citizens League, a predominantly Catholic group whose stated aim was "to meet a possible need of opposition to the Ku Klux Klan and work for religious tolerance in El Paso." The league, however, never managed to play an important role in local affairs. *Herald*, April 6, 1922, p. 14 (quote); *Times*, April 6, 1922, p. 3.

23. *Times*, April 23, 1922, p. 9.

24. *Herald*, July 19, 1922, p. 5.

25. *Times*, August 7, 1922, p. 10.

26. *Herald*, May 31, 1922, p. 6. Cleofas Calleros, Knights of Columbus member and a city resident in 1922, later estimated that the local Klan managed to recruit a total of 3,500 El Pasoans. Sherman, "Klan and El Paso Politics," p. 21.

27. Marshall Transcript, pp. 69-71.

28. *Times*, June 2, 1922, p. 8 (second quote); *Herald*, June 2, 1922, p. 3 (first quote); July 6, 1922, p. 5. For more on the colorful Sam Dreben, see Chope Transcript, pp. 24-25, and Marshall Transcript, pp. 41-43.

29. *Times*, May 19, 1922, p. 14.

30. "Minutes of a Special Meeting of the El Paso School Board, April 4, 1922," in EPSBR, Vol. 11; *Times*, April 7, 1922, p. 2; May 17, 1922, p. 16; *Herald*, April 7, 1922, p. 5; Mabel Keeney, "An Historical Sketch of the Morehead School" (History seminar paper, Texas Western College, 1949), pp. 17-18; Maude Maddox, "History of Crockett School" (History seminar paper, Texas Western College, 1951), p. 7. Southside schools did not fare as well in regard to improvements. Franklin School was promised an auditorium, but it never materialized. However, the heating and plumbing systems in that school were improved, and a new playground was purchased for Aoy School. Nevertheless, practically nothing was done to relieve the extremely overcrowded conditions in schools that were heavily Hispanic beyond pressing ahead with the previously approved construction of Zavala School. Elma Galentine Ramírez, "A Brief History of Franklin School" (History seminar paper, Texas Western College, 1950), p. 33; Bertha Archer Schaer, "An Historical Sketch of Aoy School" (History seminar paper, Texas Western College, n.d.), pp. 23-24; Leyva, "Zavala School," p. 1.

31. "Minutes of a Special Meeting of the El Paso School Board, May 8, 1922," in EPSBR, Vol. 11; Sherman, "Klan and El Paso Politics," p. 14.

32. "Minutes of a Special Meeting of the El Paso School Board, May 8, 1922," in EPSBR, Vol. 11. The resolution adopted by the school board stated: "RESOLVED that the new schools under construction and to be constructed, as well as the schools already built that are not named for some El Pasoan or Texan, or for some place cherished in the memory of Texas people, be named for some Texas hero, statesman, or jurist." The new names were as follows: Austin School for the new school at Elm and Grant; Crockett School for Manhattan Heights School; Bowie School for the new school at Cotton and 7th; Burleson School for the new school in the Hadlock Addition; Fannin School for Highland Park School; and Rusk School for Grandview School. El Paso High School was renamed Sam Houston High School. In 1923 the high school reacquired its old name, and the school at Elm and Grant took on the name, Houston School. In 1930, El Paso's second high school was named Austin High School. For more information, see George E. W. Love, "History of Houston School" (History seminar paper, Texas Western College, 1952), pp. 5, 7; Maddox, "Crockett School," p. 5; Alfredo P. Escalante, "A History of Bowie High School" (M.A. thesis, Texas Western College, 1959), p. 2; Dorothy A. Rigdon, "History of El Paso High School to 1943" (M.A. thesis, Texas Western College, 1958), pp. 45-46.

Isaacks's desire to rename the schools almost certainly stemmed from his pride in being descended from one of the original Anglo pioneers in Texas. See Maud Isaacks to Mrs. H. N. Phillips, March 18, 1965, in Maud Isaacks Collection, ACC 725, UTEP archives.

33. "Minutes of a Regular Meeting of the El Paso School Board, May 16, 1922," in EPSBR, Vol. 11; *Herald*, May 18, 1922, p. 11; May 19, 1922, p. 10; Rigdon, "El Paso High School," pp. 45-46.

34. "Minutes of a Regular Meeting of the El Paso School Board, May 16, 1922," in EPSBR, Vol 11; *Times*, May 17, 1922, p. 8. Mrs. William R. Brown abstained from voting on the measure. It should be noted that this was a highly unusual function for a school board to be performing.

35. *Times*, May 18, 1922, p. 4.

36. Ibid., May 27, 1922, p. 2 (first quote); *Herald*, May 27-28, 1922, p. 10 (second quote); "Minutes of a Special Meeting of the El Paso School Board, May 26, 1922," in EPSBR, Vol 11. Also dismissed were Demetria Stanfield of Lincoln Park School and E. T.

Walker of Manhattan School. See "List of Superintendent's Comments on Principals, with Recommendations," in EPSBR, Vol. 11.

37. *Times*, May 27, 1922, p. 2.

38. *Herald*, May 29, 1922, p. 11.

39. *Times*, May 29, 1922, p. 5 (quotes); *Herald*, May 29, 1922, p. 2. One action that local Catholics took to counter anti-Catholicism in the city was to purchase a printing plant and subsequently publish *Our View*, a pro-Catholic periodical whose first issue appeared in October, 1922. Owens, *Life of Bishop Schuler*, pp. 429-430.

40. *Times*, May 31, 1922, p. 8. For more on Maria Gallagher, see Cummings, "History of Alamo School," p. 46.

41. *Times*, May 30, 1922, p. 3; June 11, 1922, p. 4 (quote).

42. Ibid., May 28, 1922, p. 24.

43. "Minutes of a Special Meeting of the El Paso School Board, June 5, 1922," in EPSBR, Vol. 11; *Times*, June 6, 1922, p. 8.

44. *Times*, June 21, 1922, p. 12.

45. Ibid., May 20, 1922, p. 4.

46. Ibid., April 5, 1922, p. 9; April 6, 1922, p. 3; *Herald*, April 4, 1922, p. 14; April 6, 1922, p. 14. It appears that Fierro, as was the case with other suspects, voluntarily appeared before the League, fearful that trouble would result if he did not.

47. *Times*, April 9, 1922, p. 21.

48. Ibid., April 11, 1922, p. 4.

49. Ibid., p. 12. County Attorney Will H. Pelphrey was the complainant in three of the cases. See Grand Jurors' Time Book, 1922-1923, pp. 29-31, located in ACC 765, UTEP archives.

50. *Times*, April 12, 1922, p. 8.

51. Ibid., April 20, 1922, p. 5.

52. Ibid., April 21, 1922, p. 3.

53. Ibid., April 26, 1922, p. 5.

54. Ibid., May 27, 1922, p. 8; May 31, 1922, p. 8.

55. True bills were found against Manuel Velásquez, Estanislas García, G. V. Valenzuela, Enselio Mejía, Paula Navarro, Francisco Fierro, Fernando Gonzales, Salvador Guerrero, Cirilio Zubia, and Eufracia Zubia. Grand Jurors' Time Book, 1922-1923, pp. 29-31, located in ACC 765, UTEP archives. Also see *Times*, May 13, 1922, p. 8; *Herald*, May 13-14, 1922, p. 3.

56. *Times*, June 2, 1922, p. 14; *Herald*, June 2, 1922, p. 5.

57. *Herald*, June 7, 1922, p. 1.

58. Ibid., June 5, 1922, p. 11.

59. Ibid., June 7, 1922, p. 1.

60. *Times*, April 12, 1922, p. 5.

61. Ibid.

62. *Herald*, June 13, 1922, p. 12.

63. *Times*, May 30, 1922, p. 3 (quote); *Herald*, May 30, 1922, p. 12. Perhaps it was because the organization anticipated a large increase in the number of arrests for illegal voting that the GGL decided at this time to no longer offer rewards for information leading to the conviction of illegal voters. Rewards were later offered, however, for information that proved that election judges had acted illegally. *Herald*, July 8-9, 1922, p. 14.

64. *Times*, June 20, 1922, p. 12.

65. Ibid., June 13, 1922, p. 10. Oliver's proposed activities caused some concern among local politicians. Alderman William T. Griffith believed that Oliver had acquired damaging information concerning both himself and Alderman R. C. Semple. In the event Oliver attempted to use this information, Griffith was prepared to reveal that Oliver had been involved in illegal activities related to the awarding of federal fuel contracts. William T. Griffith to Joseph U. Sweeney, June 30, 1922, in J. U. Sweeney Collection, ACC 730, UTEP archives.

66. Alexander, *Klan in the Southwest*, pp. 122-123.

67. *Herald*, July 19, 1922, p. 2; July 27, 1922, p. 2.

68. Ibid., July 8-9, 1922, p. 3. In fact, Mayfield had joined Capitol City Klan No. 81, in Austin. Alexander, *Crusade for Conformity*, p. 44.

69. U.S., Congress, Senate, "Senator from Texas," *Hearings before a Subcommittee of the Committee on Privileges and Elections*, 68th Cong., 1st sess., p. 51; *Times*, October 22, 1922, p. 1.

70. *Herald*, April 21, 1922, p. 4.

71. Ibid., April 19, 1922, p. 12; *Times*, May 15, 1924, p. 7.

72. *Times*, May 10, 1922, p. 11 (second quote); *Herald*, May 10, 1922, p. 2 (first and third quotes).

73. *Times*, June 30, 1922, p. 8; *Herald*, May 25, 1922, p. 12; June 14, 1922, p. 4; June 20, 1922, p. 11; July 14, 1922, p. 10.

74. *Herald*, July 6, 1922, p. 2 (first quote); July 14, 1922, p. 10 (second quote).

75. Ibid., July 20, 1922, p. 9.

76. Ibid., July 17, 1922, p. 12.

77. Ibid., July 14, 1922, p. 10. It is probably not insignificant that Pastor Elfring's congregation was currently meeting in the Scottish Rite Masonic Temple. Alice J. Nelson, "The Congregational Church in El Paso" (History seminar paper, Texas Western College, 1955), pp. 16-17.

78. *Herald*, July 12, 1922, p. 14 (first quote); July 13, 1922, p. 16 (second quote).

79. *Herald*, July 14, 1922, p. 10.

80. Ibid., July 17, 1922, p. 12. Other candidates were listed on the flyer, but they were not involved in contested races.

81. *El Paso Labor Advocate*, July 21, 1922, p. 3; *Times*, June 28, 1922, p. 12. *Labor Advocate* editor William Moran accurately observed that labor had a "ringside seat" in the primary. *El Paso Labor Advocate*, July 21, 1922, p. 4.

82. *Herald*, June 30, 1922, p. 10.

83. Ibid., May 8, 1922, p. 11.

84. *Times*, June 20, 1922, p. 12; *Herald*, July 3, 1922, p. 6 (quote).

85. *Herald*, July 4, 1922, p. 3.

86. Ibid., July 5, 1922, p. 13.

87. Ibid., July 11, 1922, p. 7.

88. *Times*, October 31, 1922, p. 3.

89. *Herald*, July 22-23, 1922, p. 1. Unfortunately, the *Herald* is the only source available for researching this election. All July 1922 editions of the *Times* are missing from both the El Paso Public Library and the UTEP Library.

90. *Herald*, July 21, 1922, p. 5.

91. Ibid., July 22-23, 1922, pp. 1 (quote), 2; July 25, 1922, p. 12. Indeed, from this period on, Seth Orndorff appears to have been a pro-Klan partisan.

92. Ibid., July 24, 1922, p. 1. The anti-establishment victors were: Will Pelphrey, county attorney; Frank Scotten, Jr., county tax assessor; Asa R. Webb, county treasurer; Arthur M. Horn, justice of the peace; Charles King, county commissioner; Erastus F. Higgins, justice of the 8th Court of Civil Appeals; and Lillian Huggett, county school superintendent.

93. Ibid., July 24, 1922, pp. 1, 3 (quote).

94. Ibid., July 25, 1922, p. 12 (quotes); July 26, 1922, p. 1.

95. Ibid., July 25, 1922, p. 1.

96. Ibid., July 28, 1922, p. 12. The lieutenant governor was Lynch Davidson, not to be confused with T. W. Davidson, who succeeded him in office.

97. Times, August 4, 1922, p. 12; August 5, 1922, p. 14; August 11, 1922, p. 5; August 12, 1922, p. 2; August 13, 1922, p. 1; Herald, August 10, 1922, p. 12; August 11, 1922, pp. 1, 2; August 12-13, 1922, pp. 1, 3, 12; August 14, 1922, p. 12.

98. Herald, August 11, 1922, pp. 1, 2.

99. Times, August 4, 1922, p. 3; August 26, 1922, p. 12.

100. Ibid., August 27, 1922, p. 1; Herald, August 28, 1922, pp. 1, 2.

101. Times, September 10, 1922, p. 5.

102. Ibid., September 26, 1921, p. 4.

103. Herald, May 29, 1922, p. 2.

104. Hooten interview, December 1, 1983.

Chapter VII

1. Times, August 17, 1922, p. 3 (quote); August 18, 1922, p. 12; August 25, 1922, p. 3; September 4, 1922, p. 3; Herald, September 4, 1922, p. 9; El Paso Post, August 21, 1922, p. 1; hereinafter cited as Post. Bob Jones is perhaps best remembered as being the founder of Bob Jones University, in Greenville, South Carolina.

2. Times, September 7, 1922, p. 2.

3. Ibid.

4. Post, September 18, 1922, p. 1.

5. Times, September 13, 1922, p. 10.

6. Herald, September 22, 1922, pp. 1, 14. I do not know if Stevens was a Klansman; however, I find it curious that the collection of his personal financial papers does not contain any records for 1921 and 1922, yet contains extensive records for both earlier and later years. See Horace B. Stevens Collection, ACC 761, UTEP archives.

7. Times, September 25, 1922, p. 10; Herald, September 22, 1922, p. 14 (quote).

8. Times, October 1, 1922, p. 2; October 3, 1922, p. 8. Each member of the Chamber was alloted a certain number of votes according to the dues paid by the member. There were eight categories of ballots, ranging from category A (eight votes for a member paying over $960 in annual dues) to category H (one vote for a member paying $24 in annual dues). Eighty percent of the votes in favor of maintaining the current closing time were cast by members in categories H, G, and F. Thus it can be seen that even though the vote was close, a large majority of businesses balloted in favor of the status quo.

9. Times, September 15, 1922, p. 3; Post, September 22, 1922, p. 3. The Juárez Chamber of Commerce bluntly warned that it would agitate for a free trade zone and strict enforcement of customs laws concerning goods coming into Mexico if the bridge was closed at an earlier hour. See Times, September 22, 1922, p. 12.

Yet another reason for local businessmen to oppose an early bridge closing was that plans were currently being laid for the construction of a new international bridge, a costly project that would only be profitable if there was a steady stream of tourists. See J. B. White to Alba H. Warren, January 5, 1922, in Harlan H. Hugg Collection, ACC 541, UTEP archives.

10. *Times*, October 5, 1922, p. 6.

11. Ibid., September 21, 1922, p. 3 (quote); *Herald*, September 20, 1922, p. 4.

12. *Times*, September 21, 1922, p. 3; *Herald*, September 21, 1922, p. 7.

13. *Post*, September 21, 1922, p. 1.

14. *Times*, October 3, 1922, p. 2. The old Odd Fellows Hall was located at 503 N. Santa Fe Street.

15. Ibid., September 30, 1922, p. 2.

16. Ibid., October 2, 1922, p. 10.

17. *Herald*, October 2, 1922, p. 1.

18. *Times*, October 2, 1922, p. 10.

19. Ibid., October 3, 1922, p. 2; *Herald*, October 3, 1922, p. 4.

20. *Times*, October 3, 1922, p. 2.

21. *Herald*, October 3, 1922, p. 4.

22. *Times*, October 4, 1922, p. 12. The oath was a fake and it was vehemently denounced by the Knights of Columbus. See *Times*, October 4, 1922, p. 2; *Herald*, October 4, 1922, p. 4.

23. *Herald*, October 9, 1922, p. 12.

24. For more on Fryer, see Ralph W. Scoggins, "Past and Present Life of William H. Fryer, Attorney" (History seminar paper, Texas Western College, 1958). A more comprehensive treatment of Fryer's colorful career is needed.

25. Scoggins, "Life of William Fryer," pp. 8-9.

26. Isaacks interview, November 28, 1983. Bill Isaacks is the son of S. J. Isaacks.

27. Isaacks interview (quote); J. F. Hulse, November 29, 1983, personal interview. Bill Isaacks recalled that his father was very strict, an absolute teetotaler, and a staunch member of the First Christian Church. Longtime city resident J. F. Hulse remembered Fryer as being a colorful character with "strong likes and dislikes."

28. *Herald*, July 31, 1922, p. 12.

29. *Times*, August 1, 1922, p. 12.

30. Ibid., September 9, 1922, p. 8.

31. One of the reporters assigned to keep an eye on the Klan was Chester Chope, who later recalled, "[One] time I was sent to write down the names of the men who entered the Odd Fellows Lodge building, where a Klan meeting was being held. I also checked the car licenses to gain a list of the members of the Klan." Information was also supplied by a spy the *Times* had managed to place within the Klan for a short period, Hal Kelly. Ironically, Kelly had been sponsored into the Klan by Klansmen who worked for the *Herald*. Later, Kelly was rewarded for his spying with the city editorship of the *Times*. Chope Transcript, p. 6; Hooten interview, December 1, 1983; Hooten, *Fifty-Two Years a Newsman*, pp. 9-10.

32. *Times*, September 27, 1922, p. 2. It is probable that the city editor was investigating George Oliver's activities at the bridge.

33. Ibid.

34. *Herald*, September 16-17, 1922, p. 12.

35. *Times*, September 16, 1922, p. 3; *Herald*, September 16-17, 1922, p. 12; September 27, 1922, p. 2.

36. *Times*, September 28, 1922, p. 2.

37. *Herald*, September 27, 1922, p. 1.

38. On September 26 Assistant District Atorney Charles Vowell noted that the police investigation had primarily resulted from "the fact that information as to the goings on of the police and other city departments was getting out and could only get out thru members of the departments being connected with the Ku Klux Klan or the Invisible Empire." *Post*, September 27, 1922, p. 1.

39. *Times*, September 27, 1922, pp. 1, 2. Sirmans failed to bring the complete membership list of the local Klan, claiming that the file was too heavy to carry. He did, however, produce the pertinent records in regard to the policemen who were under investigation. The legal basis for the subpoenaing of the Klan records was that the District Attorney's office was currently investigating charges that involved "making false affidavits in writing."

40. The policemen who had joined the Klan were Andrew J. Davis, K. M. Linker, Emmett Hargett, T. M. Brown, Jesse A. Tyler, Rufus M. Williams, James B. Gibson, William W. Anderson, F. B. Overland, Charles Wood, Lawrence T. Robey, W. Clifton Elliott, Stanley Good, and Lynn McClintock. Linker, Gibson, Brown, and Davis had been members within the past six months. Williams, Wood, Elliott, and McClintock were charter members. *Times*, September 27, 1922, pp. 1, 2; September 28, 1922, p. 1.

The one paper that has been done on the El Paso Police Department during this period, James H. Daross, "A History of the El Paso Police Department — Part II" (History seminar paper, Texas Western College, 1953), makes no mention of the Klan's successful recruiting among the local police force.

41. *Times*, September 28, 1922, p. 2.

42. Ibid., September 28, 1922, pp. 1, 2; October 1, 1922, p. 11; October 3, 1922, p. 9; *Herald*, September 30-October 1, 1922, p. 2; October 2, 1922, p. 1; October 5, 1922, p. 7. Obviously, Samuel L. Townsend had overestimated how much time had elapsed since he had joined the original Klan.

43. *Herald*, September 29, 1922, pp. 1, 2.

44. Ibid., October 7-8, 1922, p. 27; incorrectly dated as October 6-7 on microfilm copy.

45. Ibid., September 30-October 1, 1922, p. 23.

46. *Times*, September 28, 1922, p. 2; *Herald*, September 27, 1922, p. 1 (quote); September 28, 1922, p. 2.

47. Times, October 29, 1922, pp. 1, 2.

48. Ibid., p. 1; *Herald*, October 30, 1922, pp. 1, 2.

49. *Times*, October 30, 1922, pp. 1, 2.

50. Ibid., October 31, 1922, p. 3.

51. *Herald*, October 31, 1922, p. 2.

52. Ibid., October 30, 1922, p. 2.

53. *Times*, October 31, 1922, p. 1 (quote); *Herald*, October 31, 1922, pp. 1, 2.

54. *Times*, October 31, 1922, p. 3; *Herald*, October 30, 1922, p. 2 (quote).

55. *Times*, October 31, 1922, p. 3; *Herald*, October 31, 1922, p. 3 (quote).

56. *Times*, November 3, 1922, p. 5. Not surprisingly, when Clarence Harper was asked in 1968 to reminisce about El Paso politics in the 1920s, he said, "I don't like to talk about that." Clarence Harper Transcript, ACC 38, IOH, July 17, 1968, p. 7.

57. *Times*, August 1, 1922, p. 12 (second quote); February 16, 1923, p. 4; *Herald*, March 17, 1922, p. 2 (first quote).

58. *Herald*, March 27, 1922, p. 13.

59. *Times*, August 8, 1922, p. 8.

60. I certainly do not mean to imply that the problems resulting from prohibition had ceased. For the continuing loss in human life resulting from the 18th amendment, see Lee A. Riggs (compiler) *A Short History of the District of El Paso* (El Paso, 1938), p. 7, in Joe K. Parrish Collection, ACC 710, UTEP archives.

61. *Times*, September 20, 1922, pp. 1, 5; *Herald*, September 20, 1922, p. 16; *Post*, September 20, 1922, p. 1 (quote); "Minutes of a Regular Meeting of the El Paso School Board, September 19, 1922," in EPSBR, Vol. 11.

62. *Herald*, July 19, 1922, p. 14 (quote); September 20, 1922, p. 16; "Minutes of a Regular Meeting of the El Paso School Board, July 18, 1922," in EPSBR, Vol. 11; "Minutes of a Regular Meeting of the El Paso School Board, September 19, 1922," in EPSBR, Vol. 11.

63. Hooten interview, December 1, 1983.

64. *Post*, October 30, 1922, p. 2 (quote).

65. *Herald*, October 9, 1922, p. 12; October 23, 1922, p. 14; Sherman, "Klan and El Paso Politics," p. 9.

66. *Herald*, October 9, 1922, p. 12.

67. *Times*, December 13, 1922, p. 9; April 15, 1923, p. 28 (quote). It was officially recognized by the New Mexico Conference of the Methodist Episcopal Church that "Dr. Van Valkenburgh found one of the most trying situations ever confronting a Methodist preacher when he took charge at El Paso. . . ." He had first arrived in El Paso in 1918. *Minutes of the New Mexico Conference of the Methodist Episcopal Church, Eighth Annual Session, 1922*, p. 25 (quote); La Londe, "First Methodist Church," p. 22.

68. *Times*, October 13, 1922, p. 5. Poe evidently made a genuine and wholehearted conversion to religious tolerance, he being one of the main forces behind the ecumenical Easter sunrise services which were first implemented in 1922 for the purpose of easing religious tensions in El Paso. Benna Lee Ehrenstein, "History of the Easter Sunrise Services, 1922-1955" (History seminar paper, Texas Western College, 1955), pp. 1-5.

69. *Times*, October 26, 1922, p. 4.

70. *Herald*, October 11, 1922, pp. 1, 2. The results of the symposium outraged the *Revista Católica*, which denounced the pro-Klan pastors in an article entitled "¡Que Verguenza! [How Shameful!]." *Revista Católica*, XLVIII (November 12, 1922), pp. 733-734.

71. *Times*, November 8, 1922, pp. 1, 3.

72. *Herald*, August 9, 1922, p. 14; August 25, 1922, p. 16; *Post*, December 16, 1922, p. 1.

73. *Times*, October 30, 1922, p. 2.

74. *Herald*, October 30, 1922, p. 2. El Paso's Hispanic population was also generally aware that Gardner was a Klansman. Mauricio Cordero Transcript, ACC 142, IOH, February 15, 1974, p. 43.

75. *Herald*, December 16-17, 1922, p. 14; *Post*, December 16, 1922, p. 1; *Journal of the Thirty-Fourth Session of the New Mexico Annual Conference of the Methodist Episcopal Church, South, 1923*, p. 37; Norwood, "Trinity Methodist Church," p. 45.

76. *Times*, February 2, 1923, p. 4; February 14, 1923, p. 16; *Herald*, January 11, 1923, p. 1; *Post*, January 15, 1923, p. 1.

77. *Times*, November 12, 1922, p. 8; *Herald*, November 11-12, 1922, p. 1.

78. *Times*, December 19, 1922, p. 8; December 31, 1922, p. 7.

79. *Post*, December 19, 1922, pp. 1, 4.

80. Davis' lingering political ambitions were demonstrated by the fact that he again ran for mayor in 1927.

81. *Post*, November 11, 1922, p. 1. Indeed, there was a rumor circulating that Dudley had made a bid for Klan support by offering to put two Klansmen on his ticket. Hooten interview, December 1, 1983.

82. *Times*, December 10, 1922, p. 9.

83. Ibid., January 12, 1923, p. 8; *Herald*, January 11, 1923, p. 1; *Post*, January 11, 1923, p. 1 (quote).

84. *Post*, February 12, 1923, p. 4.

85. *Times*, January 7, 1923, pp. 1, 5.

86. Alexander, *Klan in the Southwest*, pp. 73-75.

87. The murders placed local Klansmen on the defensive. Asa R. Webb informed the press that "I know the men in the El Paso Klan are of too high a calibre to ever stoop to such an outrage. We are constantly warning against this in our meetings. . . . We are working here to assist in law enforcement. That's why we got into politics." *Post*, December 29, 1922, p. 1.

88. *Times*, February 9, 1923, p. 5; February 13, 1923, p. 8; February 18, 1923, p. 24; *Herald*, February 9, 1923, p. 4 (quote); February 12, 1923, p. 14.

89. *Times*, February 9, 1923, p. 5.

90. Ibid., January 7, 1923, p. 20.

91. *Post*, December 19, 1922, pp. 1, 4.

92. *Times*, February 10, 1923, p. 8.

93. Ibid., January 14, 1923, p. 28; February 17, 1923, p. 5; *Herald*, February 14, 1923, p. 15; *Post*, February 20, 1923, pp. 1, 2.

94. *El Paso Labor Advocate*, February 2, 1923, p. 1; February 9, 1923, p. 1. This support did not extend to making a formal endorsement. However, William J. Moran made his sentiments evident, citing Dudley's "record of legislative work, approved by labor's representatives. Mr. Gardner has not such a record, nor [has he] sought opportunity previously to establish such." *El Paso Labor Advocate*, February 16, 1923, p. 4.

95. *Times*, February 10, 1923, p. 8; February 14, 1923, p. 5.

96. *Herald*, February 13, 1923, p. 4.

97. *Times*, February 22, 1923, pp. 1, 2, 3; Sherman, "Klan and El Paso Politics," p. 9.

98. *Times*, February 13, 1923, p. 5.

99. Ibid., February 2, 1923, p. 8.

100. Ibid., February 22, 1923, p. 1; *Herald*, February 21, 1923, p. 1; "Minutes of a Regular Meeting of the El Paso City Council, February 23, 1923," Book O-2, p. 107 (quote).

101. *Times*, February 24, 1923, p. 3; *Herald*, February 22, 1923, p. 5; February 23, 1923, p. 4; *Post*, February 24, 1923, p. 1.

102. *Herald*, February 24, 1923, p. 14; *Post*, February 24, 1923, p. 1 (De Groff quote). For more on Mrs. De Groff, see Helen Orndorff, "A History of Hotel Cortez" (History seminar paper, Texas Western College, 1956), pp. 54-56.

103. *Herald*, February 24, 1923, p. 14.

104. *Times*, February 24, 1923, p. 3 (quote); *Post*, February 24, 1923, p. 1.

105. *Times*, February 11, 1923, p. 2.

106. Ibid., February 23, 1923, p. 6 (first quote); February 25, 1923, p. 1; *Herald*, February 24, 1923, p. 1 (second quote).

107. *Times*, February 23, 1923, p. 14; *Herald*, February 3, 1923, p. 1; February 27, 1923, p. 16.

108. *Herald*, February 26, 1923, p. 4.

109. *Times*, February 25, 1923, p. 28. The neighboring community of Las Cruces, New Mexico, also seemed relieved by the outcome of the election, the *Las Cruces Citizen* congratulating El Paso on the "Magnificent victory obtained at the polls Saturday last when the Ku Klux Klan . . . was ignominiously defeated. . . . There shouldn't be any room in this country for such organizations." Not surprisingly, the Catholic press was elated as well, viewing the polling as a strong rebuke to El Paso's pro-KKK pastors. *Las Cruces Citizen*, March 3, 1923, p. 2 (quote); *Revista Católica*, XLIX (March 11, 1923), p. 145.

110. *Times*, March 1, 1923, p. 3.

111. Ibid., March 27, 1923, p. 12. The anti-Klan ticket consisted of Mrs. John A. Wright, Mrs. Milton A. Warner, J. H. McBroom, and Wyeth Doak.

112. Ibid., April 4, 1923, p. 4 (first quote); April 5, 1923, p. 4 (second quote).

113. Ibid., April 6, 1923, pp. 1, 2; *Herald*, April 6, 1923, p. 7. For more on Dr. Miller, see M. J. Handgraaf, "A Brief History of the Masonic Hospital in El Paso" (History seminar paper, Texas Western College, 1958), Appendix 7.

114. *Times*, April 8, 1923, pp. 1, 4. After being installed in office, the new trustees took firm control of school board affairs. J. H. McBroom was elected president, and the Klansmen on the board were not allowed to form a majority on any of the board's committees. One interesting action that the anti-Klan trustees took was to restore El Paso High School's original name. In later months they also worked to reduce the size of school bond issues. "Minutes of a Special Meeting of the El Paso School Board, April 10, 1923," in EPSBR, Vol. 12; Rigdon, "El Paso High School," pp. 45-46; Leyva, "Zavala School," p. 3.

115. *Times*, April 9, 1923, p. 1; *Herald*, April 5, 1923, p. 4; *Post*, April 9, 1923, p. 1.

116. *Times*, March 7, 1923, p. 1.

117. Ibid., April 9, 1923, p. 1; April 10, 1923, pp. 1, 2.

118. Ibid., April 10, 1923, pp. 1, 2; April 11, 1923, p. 1.

119. Apparently the *Frontier Klansman* had first appeared during late 1922 or early 1923. On January 5, 1923, Rabbi Martin Zielonka responded to anti-Semitic comments in the "El Paso Ku Klux propaganda organ." Among other things, the Klan paper had stated: "If you are a Jew, attend to your own business, refreshing your mind that you had little to do with the making of this civilization or any other as to that matter and that you are enjoying the labor of others. No mongrel America, just America!" Such overt anti-Semitism was a sudden development; by and large, Frontier Klan No. 100 was almost exclusively concerned with the "peril" posed by Catholicism. Such Jews as there were in El Paso were among the city's most prominent residents and had thoroughly assimilated themselves into local Anglo society; thus they were not convenient targets for the Klan's bigoted attacks. *Times*, January 6, 1923, p. 3.

120. *Times*, July 7, 1923, p. 12; *Herald*, August 29, 1923, p. 10. In addition, the Dudley administration kept a close eye on the Klan's activities, the mayor's secretary being assigned the duty of clipping all newspaper articles that pertained to the local KKK. The clippings are in a set of scrapbooks in the Richard M. Dudley papers, Southwest Collection, El Paso Public Library.

121. *Times*, September 1, 1923, p. 1.

122. Ibid., September 7, 1923, p. 3. As was evidenced by this gathering, the county commissioners (including Klansman Bob Oliver) did not share the city administration's qualms about allowing Klan speakers the use of public facilities. Permission of the commissioners was needed for use of Liberty Hall. Exactly when permission was given, however, is not clear, there being no record of such action in local records.

123. *Times*, September 7, 1923, p. 3.

124. Ibid., September 12, 1923, p. 8.

125. *Frontier Klansman*, September 14, 1923, p. 1. All Klan papers cited in this study are located in the Richard M. Dudley papers, Southwest Collection, El Paso Public Library.

126. *Times*, November 14, 1923, p. 8.

127. Ibid., November 18, 1923, p. 1.

128. Ibid., April 5, 1924, p. 1 (quote); April 6, 1924, p. 1.

129. *Herald*, January 11, 1923, p. 1.

130. *Times*, May 15, 1924, p. 7.

131. Ibid., January 27, 1923, p. 3.

132. *Herald*, May 14, 1924, p. 1. The blackballing was reportedly in reprisal for the defeat of Dr. J. H. Gambrell's recent bid to be the potentate of the Shrine. There is no doubt that the Shrine was deeply shaken by controversy over the Klan. William J. Hooten, who served as potentate during the 1930s, told me that the Klan "nearly wrecked the Shrine." Hooten interview, December 1, 1983.

133. *Herald*, April 30, 1923, p. 14. In addition, Carter had been removed as deacon of Government Hills Baptist Church due to his anti-KKK stance. See *Herald*, November 3, 1922, p. 5.

134. Broaddus, *Legal Heritage*, pp. 185-186.

135. *Times*, February 14, 1923, p. 16; February 16, 1923, p. 8. It appears that by early 1923 the Klan had generally ceased an active role in attempting to regulate community morals. One exception occurred in April 1923, when Clifford Sirmans swore out a search warrant that resulted in the arrest of nineteen gamblers who were operating above the Gem saloon. Sirmans accompanied sheriff's deputies when they raided the gambling den; and he later vowed, "We are going to keep after the gamblers until they get clear out of El Paso." However, there is no further evidence of Klan activity against gambling. *Post*, April 12, 1923, p. 1; Alexander, *Crusade for Conformity*, p. 17.

136. *Post*, April 21, 1923, p. 1.

137. *Times*, April 24, 1923, p. 12.

138. *Frontier Klansman*, June 29, 1923, p. 4.

139. Ibid., October 19, 1923, p. 2.

140. Clipping from *Frontier Klansman*, March 14, 1924.

141. Clipping from *Klan Kourier*, July 11, 1924. This paper appears to have been the successor to the *Frontier Klansman*. According to the *Kourier*, Border Klan No. 6 was based in El Paso, but this is the only reference I have found concerning it.

142. *Times*, May 15, 1924, pp. 1, 7; *Herald*, May 14, 1924, p. 1. Judge Isaacks served as one of the nine "hydras" of the Realm of Texas.

143. *Times*, May 15, 1924, p. 7; *Herald*, May 14, 1924, pp. 1, 4. Frontier Klan No. 100 appears to have been closely connected, in particular, with New Mexico Klans in Hatch and Deming. See *Times*, February 14, 1923, p. 16; *Herald*, May 14, 1924, p. 1.

144. *Times*, May 15, 1924, p. 1; *Herald*, May 14, 1924, pp. 1, 4.

145. *Times*, May 15, 1924, p. 7.

146. *Herald,* May 14, 1924, p. 4.

147. *Times,* July 28, 1924, p. 10; November 6, 1924, p. 3. Although it drew little attention at the time, it was during the 1924 primary that Dr. Lawrence A. Nixon, a black El Paso physician, was denied the right to vote. Nixon subsequently sued for his franchise and began laying the legal groundwork that eventually resulted in the end of the "white primary." As far as I have been able to determine, Frontier Klan No. 100 was not directly involved in any aspect of the Nixon episode. See Conrey Bryson, *Dr. Lawrence A. Nixon and the White Primary* (El Paso, 1974).

148. Charles Davis, Jr., to Claude B. Hudspeth, February 14, 1927, in Claude B. Hudspeth Collection, ACC 738, UTEP archives.

Conclusion

1. Alexander, *Crusade for Conformity,* p. 60.

2. Ibid., pp. 71-72; *General Laws of the State of Texas Passed by the Thirty-Ninth Legislature,* pp. 213-214.

3. Alexander, *Crusade for Conformity,* pp. 69, 75.

4. Ibid., p. 77; Arnold S. Rice, *The Ku Klux Klan in American Politics* (Washington, D.C., 1962), p. 73 (quote).

5. Isaacks interview, November 28, 1983. Isaacks also strongly supported Thomason in the latter's congressional race in 1932. See S. J. Isaacks to R. E. Thomason, June 1, 1932, R. E. Thomason Collection, ACC 744, UTEP archives.

6. Undated newspaper clipping from R. E. Thomason Collection, ACC 744, UTEP archives.

7. Hudspeth to Davis, February 6, 1926, Claude B. Hudspeth Collection, ACC 738, UTEP archives.

8. Hooten interview, December 1, 1983; Martínez, *Ciudad Juárez,* pp. 80-82.

9. Mario T. García, "Mexican Americans and the Politics of Citizenship: The Case of El Paso, 1936," *New Mexico Historical Review,* LIX (April 1984), pp. 187-204.

10. This was best demonstrated by the fact that in 1938, S. J. Isaacks was elected as state representative from El Paso. He remained in office until 1954.

11. *Post,* January 12, 1923, pp. 1, 3.

INDEX

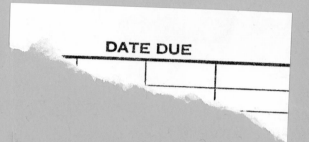

DATE DUE